Researching Higher Education

SRHE and Open University Press Imprint
General Editor: Heather Eggins

Current titles include:

Catherine Bargh *et al.*: *University Leadership*
Ronald Barnett: *Beyond all Reason*
Ronald Barnett: *The Limits of Competence*
Ronald Barnett: *Higher Education*
Ronald Barnett: *Realizing the University in an age of supercomplexity*
Tony Becher and Paul R. Trowler: *Academic Tribes and Territories (2nd edn)*
Neville Bennett *et al.*: *Skills Development in Higher Education and Employment*
John Biggs: *Teaching for Quality Learning at University (2nd edn)*
Richard Blackwell & Paul Blackmore (eds): *Towards Strategic Staff Development in Higher Education*
David Boud *et al.* (eds): *Using Experience for Learning*
David Boud and Nicky Solomon (eds): *Work-based Learning*
Tom Bourner *et al.* (eds): *New Directions in Professional Higher Education*
Anne Brockbank and Ian McGill: *Facilitating Reflective Learning in Higher Education*
Ann Brooks and Alison Mackinnon (eds): *Gender and the Restructured University*
James Cornford & Neil Pollock: *Putting the University Online*
John Cowan: *On Becoming an Innovative University Teacher*
Gerard Delanty: *Challenging Knowledge*
Chris Duke: *Managing the Learning University*
Heather Eggins & Ranald Macdonald (eds): *The Scholarship of Academic Development*
Gillian Evans: *Academics and the Real World*
Andrew Hannan and Harold Silver: *Innovating in Higher Education*
David Istance, Hans Schuetze and Tom Schuller (eds): *International Perspectives on Lifelong Learning*
Norman Jackson and Helen Lund (eds): *Benchmarking for Higher Education*
Merle Jacob and Tomas Hellström (eds): *The Future of Knowledge Production in the Academy*
Peter Knight: *Being a Teacher in Higher Education*
Peter Knight and Paul Trowler: *Departmental Leadership in Higher Education*
Peter Knight and Mantz Yorke: *Assessment, Learning and Employability*
Mary Lea and Barry Stierer (eds): *Student Writing in Higher Education*
Ian McNay (ed.): *Higher Education and its Communities*
Louise Morley: *Quality and Power in Higher Education*
Moira Peelo and Terry Wareham (eds): *Failing Students in Higher Education*
Craig Prichard: *Making Managers in Universities and Colleges*
John Richardson: *Researching Student Learning*
Stephen Rowland: *The Enquiring University Teacher*
Maggi Savin-Baden: *Problem-based Learning in Higher Education*
Maggi Savin-Baden: *Facilitating Problem-based Learning*
Michael L. Shattock: *Managing Successful Universities*
Maria Slowey and David Watson: *Higher Education and the Lifecourse*
Colin Symes and John McIntyre (eds): *Working Knowledge*
Richard Taylor, Jean Barr and Tom Steele: *For a Radical Higher Education*
Malcolm Tight: *Researching Higher Education*
Paul R. Trowler (ed.): *Higher Education Policy and Institutional Change*
Melanie Walker (ed.): *Reconstructing Professionalism in University Teaching*
Gareth Williams (ed): *The Enterprising University*
Diana Woodward and Karen Ross: *Managing Equal Opportunities in Higher Education*

Researching
Higher Education

Malcolm Tight

Society for Research into Higher Education
& Open University Press

Published by SRHE and
Open University Press
McGraw-Hill Education
McGraw-Hill House
Shoppenhangers Road
Maidenhead
Berkshire
England
SL6 2QL

email: enquiries@openup.co.uk
world wide web:www.openup.co.uk

First Published 2003

A catalogue record of this book is available from the British Library

ISBN 0 335 21117 8 (pb)   0 335 21118 6 (hb)

Library of Congress Cataloging-in-Publication Data
CIP data applied for

Typeset by RefineCatch Limited, Bungay, Suffolk

Printed in the UK by Bell & Bain Ltd, Glasgow

for Christina, as ever

Contents

Case studies and tables are separately listed after the main contents pages.

List of case studies and tables

Case studies

Full versions of most of these case studies are reprinted in another book – Tight, M. (ed.) (2003a) *The RoutledgeFalmer Reader in Higher Education* (London: RoutledgeFalmer) – which may, therefore, be usefully used in conjunction with this one.

Tables

Part I

Recently published research on higher education

This part of the book, the first of three, contains three chapters.

The first chapter offers a framework for thinking about contemporary higher education research. Three schema are suggested for analysing this research: in terms of the themes or issues being researched, the methods or methodologies being used in conducting the research, and the level at which the research is focused. A guide is also provided to the organization and use of the remainder of the book.

In the next two chapters, I use the framework outlined in Chapter 1 to analyse recently published research on higher education in the form of specialist academic journal articles (Chapter 2) and books (Chapter 3). The analysis of journal articles relates to those that were published in academic journals specializing in higher education during the year 2000. The analysis of books relates to those that were in print during that year. Two further key constraints were placed on these analyses to keep them focused and manageable. First, the analysis was restricted to publications in the English language. Second, it was limited to materials published outside of North America.

I would argue that academic journal articles and books are the key publications for understanding the nature and variety of contemporary higher education research. However, they are clearly not the only possible sources that could have been examined (Blaxter et al. 1998a). Other sources would include:

- documents produced by governments and their agencies;
- guides designed for students and their advisers;
- accounts appearing in newspapers and magazines (Tight 2000a; Yorke 2003);
- internally published documents produced by institutions and academics;

- reports produced by consultants and research centres; and
- conference papers and presentations.

I have chosen not to analyse these sources here not merely to keep my task manageable, but for two other reasons as well. Thus, on the one hand, as in the case of newspaper reports and many policy documents, the research base is either less obvious or less developed. And, on the other hand, as in the case of conference papers, internal and research reports, this material represents an earlier draft of what will commonly later be worked up and published as an academic journal article or book.

The overview of contemporary higher education research that is provided in the three chapters contained in this first part of the book is then supplemented by:

- a detailed exploration, with case study examples, of themes in, and approaches to, researching higher education (in Part II); and
- an examination, with practical suggestions, of the process of researching higher education (in Part III).

I

Introduction

The changing context for higher education research

[T]here has been surprisingly little research and analysis concerning higher education until the very recent period.

(Altbach 1997: 4)

Whatever it is – a discipline, a field of study, or just an opportunity for researchers in whatever discipline to earn some reputation and income – research on higher education in Western Europe is still in search of confirmation of its role and status. As such it is a strongly externally and events-driven undertaking.

(Frackmann 1997: 108)

As these two opening quotations – from leading researchers in North America and Europe respectively – indicate, higher education is perceived as a relatively under-researched field, even though dozens of books and hundreds of articles are now published each year on this topic. But this apparent outpouring of research, description and comment is a very recent phenomenon. At the same time, and in part because of this, the field of higher education research may appear as relatively disorganized and little understood or appreciated. The purpose of this book, then, is to help to create some order in this field, by providing an overview of the current state of higher education and a guide to how it is (and may be) researched.

There are a number of related reasons why higher education research is assuming greater importance at the present time, and why, therefore, the appearance of this book should be timely. The underlying reason is undoubtedly that higher education itself is assuming greater importance. In developed countries, the last few decades have witnessed a move from a reliance on elite systems of higher education, involving only a small minority of the population, to mass systems (Scott 1995), in which the assumption is becoming that most people will participate and on more than one occasion. Behind this trend lies, of course, the rise of the so-called 'knowledge society', technological developments, globalization and increasing international competition. All of these trends are seen by governments throughout the world as necessitating increasing investment, by all concerned, in education, training and learning throughout life.

Higher education is now, therefore, 'big business', as well as being increasingly connected to other businesses in the public and private sectors, and throughout society as a whole (Barnett 2000). Not surprisingly, then, both the major funders of higher education (and particularly national governments and their agencies) and the managers of higher education institutions are concerned to ensure that they are expending their funds and using their resources in the most effective ways. This requires research. Linked to the massification of the higher education experience, and the increasing resources being devoted to it, is an understandable concern to check up on the quality or standard of the higher education product, particularly in relation to the outputs of teaching and research. This also necessitates research.

The recent moves towards making appropriate training for academic staff mandatory are another linked trend. This impacts on potential, new and probationary staff in terms of both research training (when they are research students, with the possession of a research degree being increasingly required for new academic appointments) and teacher training (as novice academics). It also increasingly effects established staff in terms of continuing professional development for their varied roles. The provision of such training not only requires research in itself, but also commonly requires academic staff in all departments, particularly those on probationary appointments, to undertake small-scale, or 'quick and dirty' (Ashcroft 1996) research projects on higher education themselves.

Hence, we may expect the amount and scope of higher education research, and the number of outlets for its publication, to continue to increase for the foreseeable future. So the need – for those involved in or concerned about higher education – to understand what is going on in higher education research, and to be able to participate in researching higher education, is strong and will also continue to grow. Hopefully, therefore, the demand for a book like this should also be strong and growing.

In the remainder of this chapter, I will discuss three alternative, but complementary, ways of analysing higher education research. In so doing, I aim to provide a framework for understanding higher education research, one that will be applied in the remainder of the book:

- first, I will provide an overview of the themes or issues currently being researched in higher education;
- second, I will offer a similar overview of the methods and methodologies currently being employed to research higher education; and
- third, I will discuss the different levels, from a focus on the individual to an international concern, at which higher education research may be conducted.

The final two sections of the chapter will then outline the organization of the book and discuss how it might be used.

Themes and issues in higher education research

A number of attempts have been made in recent years to organize or classify higher education research in terms of themes or issues. I will consider three of these here, before going on to propose my own categorization.

First, we may consider the views of Teichler, clearly a leading, perhaps the leading, contemporary European authority and writer in this area, and someone who has offered one of the fullest developed classifications of higher education research. While recognizing the lack of 'a generally accepted "map" of higher education research', he suggests four categories or 'spheres of knowledge in higher education' (Teichler 1996: 440–1):

- quantitative-structural aspects of higher education;
- knowledge and subject-related aspects of higher education;
- person-related as well as teaching and research-related aspects of higher education;
- aspects of organization and governance of higher education.

Teichler then suggests typical areas of higher education research for each of these four spheres, and relates them to the disciplinary location of those undertaking the research:

> *Typical* quantitative-structural aspects *are access, admission, elite and mass higher education, diversification, types of higher education institutions, duration of study programmes, graduation, educational and employment opportunities, job prospects, income and status, returns for educational investment, appropriate employment, mobility. Economists and sociologists tend to address these aspects most frequently.*
>
> *Major* knowledge and subject-related aspects *are disciplinarity versus interdisciplinarity, studium generale, academic versus professional emphasis, quality, skills and competences, utilisation of competences, overqualification. These areas are often addressed by experts from education as well as various subdisciplines addressing science (history, sociology, etc).*

Some person and process-related aspects *might suffice to characterise this sphere: motivation, communication, counselling and guidance, didactics, learning style, assessment and examinations. Education and psychology are the key disciplines addressing this domain, but sociology plays some role as well.*

Examples for organisation and governance-related aspects *might be planning, administration, management, power and consensus, decision-making, efficiency and effectiveness, funding, resource allocation. Law, political science, economics, public and business administration are major disciplines involved.* (Teichler 1996: 441–2)

Second, and more succinctly, Frackmann, focusing solely on higher education research in Western Europe, has suggested five 'clusters of issues' for research (Frackmann 1997: 125–6):

- role and function of higher education
- nature of knowledge and learning
- co-ordination mechanisms between society and higher education
- learning and teaching
- higher education and European integration.

While the last of these is specific to the European context, the other four appear fairly closely related to the spheres identified by Teichler.

Third, Hayden and Parry (1997), writing from an Australasian perspective, identify two main approaches to higher education research: a focus on higher education policy, and an emphasis on academic practice. While this is undoubtedly the simplest of the three categorizations, and might not appear to offer much for present purposes, it should have resonance for anyone who has looked at the range of contemporary research and writing on higher education. Even a fairly cursory overview suggests that two strategies for higher education research are dominant: the policy critique and the small-scale, evaluative case study.

My own categorization of higher education research is rather more complex than any of the three that I have just reviewed. It was produced for this book, and for a related project (Tight 2003a), and is reflected in the organization of the book. To produce it I analysed all of the articles contained in 17 specialist higher education journals, published in the English language outside of North America, during the year 2000 (the results of this analysis are discussed in detail in Chapter 2).

As part of this analysis, the themes or issues addressed by each of the articles examined were identified and coded in up to four keywords. Once all of the articles had been classified in this way, all of the keywords that had been used were then listed in alphabetical order. There were more than 100 in total. Similar and related keywords were then successively grouped together to arrive at a limited number of key themes or issues. Of course, the way in which the keywords were grouped together was particular to me, and others would doubtless do it at least somewhat differently, but I do feel that it has some logic and is functional. I also re-checked the categorization when I came to do the related analysis of books in print reported in Chapter 3.

I ended up with eight key themes or issues, as follows:

- Teaching and Learning: including student learning, different kinds of students, teaching in higher education, and the 'how to' genre.
- Course Design: including the higher education curriculum, technologies for learning, student writing, assessment and postgraduate course design.
- The Student Experience: including accessing higher education, the on-course experience, success and non-completion, the postgraduate experience, the experience of different student groups, and the transition from higher education to work.
- Quality: including course evaluation, grading and outcomes, national monitoring practices, and system standards.
- System Policy: including the policy context, national policies, comparative policy studies, historical policy studies, and funding relationships.
- Institutional Management: including higher education management practice, institutional leadership and governance, institutional development and history, institutional structure, economies of scale and institutional mergers, and relations between higher education, industry and community.
- Academic Work: including academic roles, academic development, academic careers, women academics, the changing nature of academic work, and academic work in different countries.
- Knowledge: including the nature of research, disciplinarity, forms of knowledge, and the nature of the university.

I would not claim, of course, that this is a definitive listing – how could it be? – and there are inevitably some, at least potential, overlaps between the categories identified. Others would want to identify more, less or different categories, and to include particular items under different themes. Nevertheless, I would argue that it is an indicative and, more importantly, a useful approach, as I hope this book demonstrates.

This categorization may be usefully compared with those proposed by Teichler and Frackmann. Clearly, what I am proposing is rather more disaggregated. Thus, what Teichler termed quantitative/structural aspects, and what Frackmann labelled as co-ordination mechanisms, appear in my listing as both system policy and institutional management. Quality, which was subsumed by Teichler under knowledge/subject-related aspects, appears here separately, in large part because of the amount of attention it has been given in recent years. What Frackmann calls learning and teaching, and Teichler terms person/process-related aspects, have been split up into three related headings: teaching and learning, course design, and the student experience.

The categorization developed and used here has the advantage of being empirically based. As such, it did not entirely confirm my expect-ations. Thus, my own impression, from being involved for many years in both higher education research and the editing of higher education journals, of the frequency with which different themes were being addressed was rather different from what I found when I undertook this study.

Methods and methodologies in higher education research

As part of the analysis described in the previous section, I also categorized each article, and later book, examined in terms of the main methods and methodologies used in the research. In some cases this was a fairly straightforward exercise, as the article or book in question contained a section or chapter explicitly labelled methods or methodology. In many others, however, the method or methodology used was, at best, implicit, and had to be deduced from a careful reading. Some articles, and more commonly books, made use of a number of methods or methodologies, and in these cases the dominant one needed to be identified.

After some grouping, this resulted in another eightfold categorization (so I should emphasize, at this point, that I don't think that there is anything magical or significant for me in the number eight: it is simply a convenient quantity, neither too large, nor too small). The eight key methods or methodologies identified were as follows:

- Documentary Analysis: including historical studies, literature reviews, synopses of practice and most policy analyses.
- Comparative Analysis: international studies comparing two or more national systems.
- Interviews: including face-to-face and internet-based studies, and focus groups.
- Surveys and Multivariate Analyses: including questionnaires, the analysis of large quantitative databases, and experimental studies.
- Conceptual Analysis: including more theorized and philosophical studies.

- Phenomenography: and related approaches such as phenomenology.
- Critical/Feminist Perspectives: including studies that set out to critique established positions.
- Auto/Biographical and Observational Studies: including accounts based largely on personal or individual experience.

Again, this listing might be questioned or altered, but it does bear a close resemblance to many standard overviews of social and educational research methods (e.g. Blaxter et al. 2001; Cohen et al. 2000; Punch 1998). One obvious modification, for example, would be to break down some of the categories further, and, indeed, this is done in the more detailed discussion later in the book.

Two other points are worth addressing here. First – and despite my comment on Hayden and Parry's analysis earlier – I have not separately identified 'case study' as a method or methodology, though I did try to initially, given its prominence in the research method/ology literature (e.g. Stake 1995; Yin 2003a, 2003b). The reason is that most pieces of research can be described as being, in some sense, case studies (indeed, I have used the term in this generic sense in identifying examples of research for discussion in Part II of this book). This is not, therefore, a very useful way for categorizing and differentiating between the outputs of research, whether on higher education or other aspects of society.

Second, some may question why I have chosen to separately identify what are, as will become apparent, relatively specialized or 'minority interest' methodologies such as phenomenography and critical/feminist approaches. My answer would be precisely for that reason. To me, phenomenography appears to be the *only* methodology that has been particularly, though not exclusively, developed within higher education research (Ashworth and Lucas 2000). Critical and feminist approaches to the analysis of higher education, for their part, while easy to overlook, offer some of the most challenging and, therefore, most interesting – and most methodologically developed – pieces of research currently being undertaken in this area.

This point also serves to highlight the important distinction between methods and methodologies, which may appear to have been somewhat conflated in the categorization I have produced:

> *The term* method *can be understood to relate principally to the tools of data collection: techniques such as questionnaires and interviews.* Methodology *has a more philosophical meaning, and usually refers to the approach or paradigm that underpins the research. Thus, an interview that is conducted within, say, a qualitative approach or paradigm will have a different underlying purpose and produce broadly different data from one conducted within a qualitative paradigm* (Blaxter et al. 2001: 59)

Phenomenography, critical and feminist approaches can all be termed methodologies. Most of the other terms – for example, documents, interviews, surveys – in the categorization I have produced for this book are primarily methods, though, as the quotation suggests, they may be applied from a particular methodological context. If this is an unfamiliar distinction to you, what it means in practice should become clearer as examples of research are discussed in Part II, and as the process of researching is examined in Part III.

Using these two categorizations – of themes and issues, and methods and methodologies – it was a fairly straightforward process to produce an 8×8 matrix, on which the relative frequency of published articles and books, or the location of specific outputs, could be plotted. Of course, any one item – particularly a book – may cover more than one of the themes identified, and may also make use of more than one of the methods or methodologies. It was not that difficult, however, in most cases, to identify a dominant theme and method, though in a minority of cases a given article or book might have been placed in two or perhaps more different cells.

Level of analysis in higher education research

In addition to themes and issues, and methods and methodologies, a third dimension of analysis has been taken into account in the analyses that follow, namely level. Clearly, research into higher education, and into other aspects of society, may focus at a number of levels within a hierarchy that ranges, in this case, from the individual student or academic up to the whole world. The level at which research is undertaken has important implications: for feasibility, methodology and generalizability, amongst other things. Consequently, it will be analysed and taken into account in this book, though it will not be given as much emphasis as what I believe to be the two most fundamental dimensions: themes and issues, and methods and methodologies.

Having read thus far, you may be surprised to learn that I have not identified eight but only seven hierarchical levels of analysis. I could easily have chosen eight, with the most obvious addition being a regional level between institution and nation; but there were relatively few examples of such research, so I judged it unnecessary. The seven levels identified were:

- the individual, student or academic;
- the course, or group of students and their teachers;
- the department or centre, or group of academics and students;
- the institution, university or college;

- the nation or country;
- the system, or idealized arrangement of higher education; and
- the international, involving a consideration of two or more national systems.

These seven levels are mostly self-explanatory and, I would argue, are less likely to be the subject of debate than the categorizations of themes and methods that I have put forward.

One distinction that deserves a little more discussion, however, is that between nation and system. I would categorize an article, book or research project as focusing on the national level when it is clear that the discussion is limited to one country – Australia, the Netherlands, the United Kingdom or wherever. However, some articles and books, while they will of course be informed by the authors' particular experience of working within one or more national systems of higher education, make no explicit or central reference to any one country. This is common, for example, in more philosophical, conceptual or critical writing, and also in many guides to academic practice, where the authors are, in effect, discussing an ideal system of higher education. In these cases I have used the term system, though the placing of this level between national and international in the hierarchy is essentially arbitrary and somewhat debatable.

The organization of the book

If you have glanced at the contents pages for this book, you will already have realized that the book has been organized chiefly in terms of the themes and issues, methods and methodologies, and levels of analysis discussed in the preceding three sections.

Thus the main part of the book, Part II, contains eight chapters focusing successively on research into the key themes and issues identified. In each of those chapters, three examples or case studies of published higher education research are introduced and discussed, so as to illustrate the kinds of approaches to research being adopted. The examples used have also been chosen so as to show the range of methods and methodologies in use, and the different levels at which higher education research may focus. Most of the case studies of published higher education research referred to and analysed in this book are reprinted in a *Reader in Higher Education* which I have recently edited (Tight 2003a). That book may, therefore, usefully be used in conjunction with this volume.

The two remaining chapters in this part (Part I) of the book, as already indicated, offer an in-depth analysis of higher education research publications – in the form of academic journal articles and books – published or in print in the year 2000. The year 2000 was chosen so as to provide an up-to-date analysis of the state of higher education research at the end of the twentieth century and/or the start of the twenty-first century (depending upon how you calculate your calendar).

Two key restrictions were placed on the range of higher education publications examined in Chapters 2 and 3 in order to make the task both more manageable and more focused. First, on practical grounds, the selection was limited to material published in the English language. Second, it was restricted to material published outside of North America. Higher education, and higher education research, is better established in the United States and Canada than elsewhere in the world (Altbach and Engberg 2001). Perhaps because of this, higher education researchers there also tend to be rather inward looking, rarely showing much awareness of research conducted outside of North America (Maassen 2000). It struck me as more interesting and more useful, as well as more manageable, therefore, to focus on research published outside of North America (though this does include research produced by some North Americans).

The final part of this book, Part III, builds on the overview of current research provided in Part I, and the discussion of themes and issues in Part II. It contains three chapters, offering a guide to the methods and methodologies commonly used to research higher education, the different levels at which higher education may be researched, and the process of researching higher education. This is aimed at both existing and potential researchers, and contains practical guidance on the design and management of research projects, and the dissemination and publication of their findings. It also includes useful listings of journals and societies.

Using this book

The way in which this book has been organized suggests a number of ways in which it might be used, and also indicates the different audiences who may (and I hope will) want to make use of it. For example:

- Readers who are already experienced in the conduct of higher education research might find the overview of contemporary higher education research in Part I, and the analysis of issues and approaches in Part II, of most interest.
- Readers who are particularly interested in one or more themes or issues might want to focus on just one or two chapters in Part II.
- Readers who are interested in the application of particular methods or methodologies to higher education research might want to focus on Chapter 12 and some of the examples discussed in Part II.

- Readers who are interested in undertaking higher education research, or in getting their research published or disseminated, might wish to focus on Part III.

However you use this book, and however much of it you use, I hope you enjoy it and find it useful.

2

Journals

Introduction

This chapter contains an analysis of the 406 articles published in 17 specialist academic journals, based outside North America, that focus on higher education during the year 2000.

The chapter has seven sections:

- the selection of the journals analysed is discussed and justified;
- the characteristics of the selected journals are reviewed;
- the themes and issues addressed in the articles are considered;
- the methods and methodologies used in the research concerned are examined;
- the level of analysis of the articles is analysed;
- the location, sex, institution, department and job title of the authors is discussed; and
- some conclusions are then offered.

Selection of journals for analysis

There are hundreds of journals published every year in the English language, even if – as I do here – we exclude those published in North America, which contain articles dealing with higher education. For the analysis presented in this chapter, I have chosen to concentrate solely on academic journals that focus exclusively on higher education. I have done this for three reasons:

- The articles published in academic journals are normally peer reviewed; that is, they are typically assessed prior to publication by two or more academic specialists, and then modified in the light of their comments. Such procedures tend to ensure that the articles published are of a certain minimum quality;

- such articles are also normally research-based; that is, they involve some empirical data collection and analysis and/or serious reflection related to the issues addressed;
- and, from a more practical point of view, analysing only specialist higher education journals keeps this analysis more focused.

Before going on to discuss in more detail the journals and articles selected for analysis, it is important to note, however, what has been left out. Thus, I have not examined what are commonly called professional or popular journals. These include both 'glossy' journals, such as *The New Academic* and *Perspectives: policy and practice in higher education*, which circulate widely amongst higher education managers, and newspapers, such as *The Times Higher Education Supplement*, which are read by many academics. The articles published in such journals are typically neither peer-reviewed nor research-based, as well as being much shorter than those found in academic journals (and usually without references). This is not to say that such journals, and the articles they publish, are not worthy of examination (see, for example, Tight 2000a), just that they are not so relevant in an examination of research on higher education.

I have also excluded what I judged to be less well-established journals, which might, in the course of time, become respected academic journals. I would include in this category, for example, both the *Journal of Graduate Education* and *Reflections on Higher Education*. Such journals are characterized not only by their recent establishment, but also by infrequency of publication and the lack of a commercial publisher, and are probably not as thoroughly peer-reviewed as more established academic journals. Again, however, I would stress that I do not mean to imply by this exclusion that these journals are of lesser quality or are not performing a worthwhile function.

Perhaps the most significant exclusion from the analysis which follows, however, are those academic journals – typically either general education journals or discipline-specific social science journals – which do not focus specifically on higher education, but which regularly or occasionally publish articles on higher education. There are dozens of such journals, and their cumulative coverage of higher education issues is significant. General education journals of this nature include, for example, the *British Journal of Sociology of Education*, *Comparative Education*, *Gender and Education*, *Instructional Science*, the *Journal of Education and Work*, *Learning and Instruction* and the *Oxford Review of Education*.

Examples of other discipline-specific journals that carry articles focusing on higher education include *Organisation*, *Policy Studies* and *Sociology*. They feature articles by the many researchers with an interest in higher education who are not based in education or higher education departments or centres (Clark 1984; Teichler 1996). There are also a handful of journals of an inter- or multi-disciplinary nature that publish quite a few articles on higher education, such as *Industry and Higher Education* and *Minerva*, but which do not focus exclusively upon it.

While the exclusion of this third group of journals and articles from the analysis is regrettable, it was essential to keep the study within reasonable bounds. It would have been very difficult to identify all those academic journals that carry occasional articles dealing with higher education. Conversely, I would argue that academic journals that focus on higher education contain the core of contemporary higher education research.

One other group of articles that might have been worth exploration are what might be called 'unpublished' journal articles: that is, articles existing in draft, or perhaps final, form as internal documents or conference papers. Examining such articles would have added considerably to the scale of the analysis, and there would also be some access difficulties. My main reason for excluding them, however, is that many 'unpublished' articles, where they are of sufficient quality, later become published journal articles after some revision.

These exclusions, together with the focus on English language publications from outside North America, left me, by my calculations, with 17 specialist higher education academic journals for analysis. I say 'by my calculations' because it is always possible that I have missed something, particularly perhaps something published outside Europe and Australasia, but my defence would be that whatever I may have missed is likely to be less well established and less well known internationally.

The seventeen journals selected for analysis were:

Active Learning in Higher Education (ALHE)
Assessment and Evaluation in Higher Education (AEHE)
European Journal of Education (EJE)
Higher Education (HE)
Higher Education in Europe (HEE)
Higher Education Management (HEM)
Higher Education Policy (HEP)
Higher Education Quarterly (HEQ)
Higher Education Research and Development (HERD)
Higher Education Review (HER)
International Journal for Academic Development (IJAD)
Journal of Geography in Higher Education (JGHE)
Journal of Higher Education Policy and Management (JHEPM)
Quality in Higher Education (QHE)

Studies in Higher Education (SHE)
Teaching in Higher Education (THE)
Tertiary Education and Management (TEAM).

These 17 journals published a total of 406 refereed articles during the year 2000, and these form the subject of the analysis in the remainder of this chapter. Editorials, book reviews, review articles and symposia have been excluded from consideration.

Characteristics of the selected journals

Table 2.1 summarizes the key characteristics of the 17 journals examined.

The longest established journal, HEQ, reached its 54th volume in the year 2000, having been established immediately after the end of the Second World War (Shattock 1996). On average, the journals considered had produced 20 volumes by the end of 2000. This means, of course, that quite a few were relatively new (e.g. IJAD, QHE, THE, TEAM), having been set up in the 1990s. I have also included one academic journal (ALHE) that actually started publication in 2000. While this may seem to run counter to my earlier exclusion of a number of 'less well-established' journals, I am interpreting this to refer to more than simply age. ALHE has both the characteristics of a refereed academic journal and substantial institutional backing.

The journals to be examined also differ somewhat in terms of their scale of activity. At one extreme, HE published two complete volumes and eight issues in 2000, while ALHE, IJAD and JHEPM each only managed two issues. Most of the journals publish either three or four issues a year. The number of articles published displays a similar variation, ranging from a minimum of 10, in the case of ALHE, to a maximum of 55 in the case of HEE. The mean number of articles published per journal was 23.9, or 6.5 per issue. Articles, of course, do vary in length. Those in HEE, for example, tend to be relatively shorter, so the most substantive output during the year is undoubtedly that of HE, with 46 articles published.

The 17 journals were published by only seven different publishers. Taylor & Francis, with over half (nine) of the journals, could be said to dominate this particular market. Two other publishers, Blackwells and Kluwer, each published two of the titles under consideration, so over three-quarters of the journals were published by just three publishers. The great majority of the journals, 14 in total, were published by publishers based in the United Kingdom.

As Table 2.1 shows, more than half of the journals (10) are linked with professional associations, societies or centres. Four of these are based in

Table 2.1 Characteristics of the 17 Academic Journals Analysed in the Year 2000

Title	Volume Number	No. Issues	No. Articles	Publisher	Society	Editor
ALHE	1	2	10	Paul Chapman (UK)	Institute for Learning and Teaching in Higher Education (UK)	Sally Brown (UK)
AEHE	25	6	30	Taylor and Francis (UK)		William Scott (UK)
EJE	35	4	34	Blackwells (UK)	European Institute of Education and Social Policy (France)	Jean-Pierre Jallade (France) Jose-Gines Mora (Spain)
HE	39/40	8	46	Kluwer (Netherlands)		Grant Harman (Australia) Dai Hounsell (UK) Gary Rhoades (USA) Ulrich Teichler (Germany)
HEE	25	4	55	Taylor and Francis (UK)	European Centre for Higher Education (Romania)	Leland Barrows (Romania)
HEM	12	3	24	Organization for Economic Cooperation and Development (France)	Organization for Economic Cooperation and Development (France)	Maurice Kogan (UK)
HEP	13	4	21	Pergamon (UK)	International Association of Universities (France)	Guy Neave (France)

HEQ	54	4	21	Blackwells (UK)	Society for Research into Higher Education (UK)	Gareth Williams, then Oliver Fulton (UK) Peter Wright (UK) Malcolm Tight, then Rosalind Pritchard (UK) Gareth Parry (UK)
HERD	19	3	20	Taylor and Francis (UK)	Higher Education Research and Development Society of Australasia (Australia)	Elaine Martin (Australia) Michael Prosser (Australia)
HER	33	3	12	Tyrell Burgess (UK)		John Pratt (UK)
IJAD	5	2	15	Taylor and Francis (UK)	International Consortium for Educational Development	David Baume (UK) Christopher Knapper (Canada) Patricia Weeks (Australia)
JGHE	24	3	12	Taylor and Francis (UK)		Hugh Matthews (UK) Ian Livingstone (UK)
JHEPM	22	2	14	Taylor and Francis (UK)		Helen Sjoman (Australia)
QHE	6	3	18	Taylor and Francis (UK)		Lee Harvey (UK)
SHE	25	3	21	Taylor and Francis (UK)	Society for Research into Higher Education (UK)	Mantz Yorke (UK), then Malcolm Tight (UK)
THE	5	4	33	Taylor and Francis (UK)		Len Barton (UK)
TEAM	6	4	20	Kluwer (Netherlands)	European Association for Institutional Research (Netherlands)	Roddy Begg (UK)

the United Kingdom, three in France, and one each in Australia, the Netherlands and Romania. It is clear from their titles, however, that, while four have a national focus, three are European in scope and three are international. One organization, the United Kingdom's Society for Research into Higher Education (SRHE) owns two journals (HEQ and SHE). Here, I must make clear a personal interest, as I have had an editorial role with both of these journals.

Between them, the 17 journals had 31 editors during 2000 (including the three editorial changes that took place during the year). While most (11) had only a single editor, three shared the role between two editors, one between three editors, and two (including the largest operation, HE) had four editors. The great majority (26) of the editors were men; of the women editors, three out of five were based in one country, Australia. Not surprisingly, given the publishers' and societies' locations, over half of the editors, 19, were based in the United Kingdom, with five in Australia, two in France, and one each in Canada, Germany, Romania, Spain and the United States. Even in journals based outside of North America, therefore, there can be a significant North American influence.

The titles of some of the journals suggest that they vary in their focus on higher education as an area of research. Some, such as HE, HEQ, HERD, HER and SHE, sound like they adopt a fairly generic approach, and might be open to publishing on any topic. Others appear to focus on particular aspects or approaches, such as academic development (IJAD), assessment and evaluation (AEHE), active learning (ALHE), management (HEM, TEAM), policy (HEP), management and policy (JHEPM), quality (QHE) and teaching (THE). Two (EJE, HEE) appear from their titles to have a European orientation.

Both of the last named journals, EJE and HEE, also appear from examination to publish mostly themed issues, and some others (e.g. HEQ) do so from time to time, clearly making some use of specially commissioned articles. In most cases, however, the journals appear to rely on submitted articles that have successfully gone through their review process.

EJE is also a little unusual in very occasionally publishing articles not wholly focused on higher education, but, since the overwhelming majority of its articles do, it has been included in this analysis. JGHE is also unusual, in focusing on a particular subject or discipline, namely geography. There are other journals that take a similar approach, and more are being set up, but at the moment they are not so well established or do not focus exclusively on higher education.

The analysis that follows in the remainder of this chapter will test the veracity of these initial perceptions.

Themes and issues

Table 2.2 categorizes the 406 articles under review in terms of both the themes or issues covered and the methods or methodologies applied, using the eight-fold categorizations presented in Chapter 1. If we examine first the bottom row of this table, it is clear that two of the eight themes or issues identified dominate in higher education research – at least, as it is represented in the journal articles published in 2000. Four other themes or issues might be described as popular, and the remaining two as relatively specialist interests.

The two dominant themes or issues represented are system policy and course design, accounting for nearly 100 articles each, and together making up 48 per cent of the articles under review. Analyses of system policy are typically pursued using documentary analysis (54 articles), with multivariate and comparative forms of analysis (19 and 17 articles respectively) also fairly popular. Studies of course design also make considerable use of documentary analysis (34 articles), as well as multivariate (23) and interview-based (21) analyses.

Academic work (15 per cent of articles), the student experience (11 per cent), institutional management (10 per cent) and quality (8 per cent) were also popular themes or issues for research, though not on the same scale as system policy and course design. Studies of academic work are unusual in making significant use of biographical methods (15 articles), along with interviews (17), multivariate and documentary analyses (12 articles each). Multivariate analyses dominate research into the student experience (28 articles), as do documentary analyses of institutional management (26 articles). Quality is also most commonly researched through documentary analysis (14 articles).

The themes or issues on the extreme left and right hand sides of the table, teaching/learning and knowledge, appear to be the least often researched. In each case, interviews appear to be the most popular method for research, though a range of alternative approaches is clearly in use.

There are significant differences in the extent to which the 17 journals analysed published articles on each of the eight themes or issues identified in 2000. Table 2.3 summarizes the findings.

Two main conclusions may be drawn from this table. First – but bearing in mind the caveat that the sample is for one year only – some journals appear more generic in their publication strategy than others. Thus, HE is the only one of the 18 journals to have published at least one article on each of the eight key themes or issues identified during 2000. One other journal, HEQ, had published articles on seven of the themes, and four others (HEE, JHEPM, SHE, TEAM) had published articles on six of them. This is not quite what might be expected from some of their titles, or even

Table 2.2 Journal Articles Published in 2000 Categorized by Themes and Methods

	Themes and Issues								
Method/ology	*Teaching/ Learning*	*Course Design*	*Student Experience*	*Quality*	*System Policy*	*Institutional Management*	*Academic Work*	*Knowledge*	*Total*
Biography	1	9		3	2	5	15		35
Critical		2					1	1	4
Phenomenography	2	1						1	4
Conceptual	3	7			1	1	2	1	15
Multivariate	4	23	28	7	19	9	12	2	104
Interviews	10	21	9	5	5	1	17	3	71
Comparative			3	4	17				24
Documentary	2	34	5	14	54	26	12	2	149
Totals	22	97	45	33	98	42	59	10	406

Table 2.3 Articles Published in Individual Journals in terms of Themes or Issues

Themes and Issues

Journal	Teaching/ Learning	Course Design	Student Experience	Quality	System Policy	Institutional Management	Academic Work	Knowledge	Total
ALHE	2	7			1				10
AEHE	1	21		5	2		1		30
EJE			12		21	1			34
HE	3	6	8	5	7	5	10	2	46
HEE		11	4	1	18	10	11		55
HEM				2	10	10	1	1	24
HEP		2		2	13	3	1		21
HEQ	1	2	4	1	10	2	1		21
HERD	5	8	2		2		3		20
HER			1		5	1	3	2	12
IJAD		3					12		15
JGHE	1	8					2	1	12
JHEPM		1	1	2	6	1	3		14
QHE		2	2	11			2	1	18
SHE	5	8	2			1	2	3	21
THE	4	17	4	2			6		33
TEAM		1	5	2	3	8	1		20
Totals	22	97	45	33	98	42	59	10	406

their editorial policies (where stated), but suggests that many higher education journals are open to publishing articles on most aspects of higher
education, so long as they are of the requisite quality.

Second, it seems clear that most of the 17 journals do nevertheless tend
to have specialist foci:

- In seven cases, articles on system policy dominate the journals: EJE
  (62 per cent of articles), HEP (62 per cent), HEQ (48 per cent), JHEPM
  (43 per cent), HEM (42 per cent), HER (42 per cent) and HEE (33 per
  cent).
- In six cases, articles on course design dominate: ALHE (70 per cent),
  AEHE (70 per cent), JGHE (67 per cent), THE (52 per cent), HERD
  (40 per cent) and SHE (38 per cent).
- Three journals focus on other specialist themes: IJAD on academic work
  (80 per cent of articles), QHE on quality (61 per cent) and TEAM on
  institutional management (40 per cent).
- Only one journal, HE, appears truly generic, with no theme or issue
  accounting for more than 22 per cent of the articles published in 2000.

So, while most of these journals may be open to publishing good quality
articles on most aspects of higher education, researchers working on particular themes should also be able to get a pretty clear idea, from looking
through recent issues, of the most likely journals to target.

Methods and methodologies

If we refer back to Table 2.2, it can be seen that the range of methods
or methodologies in use appears to be more constrained than the range of
themes or issues under study. Looking at the right hand column, three
method/ologies dominate – documentary analysis (37 per cent of articles), multivariate analyses (26 per cent) and interview-based studies (17
per cent) – together accounting for 80 per cent of the total sample. This is
not, however, really surprising, as literature reviews, questionnaire surveys,
interviews and their analysis are the basis of most social research. By contrast, biographical (9 per cent), comparative (6 per cent) and conceptual
(4 per cent) analyses are much less common, while critical and phenomenographical analyses (1 per cent each) are rare.

There are examples in the sample of the three most popular method/
ologies – documentary, multivariate and interview-based analyses – being
applied to researching all of the themes or issues identified. Documentary
analysis is most commonly used as a means for researching system policy
(54 articles), but also widely applied to the study of course design (34) and
institutional management (26). Multivariate analysis – which includes

both straightforward questionnaire surveys and applications of complex techniques such as cluster and factor analysis – is the most popular method for studying the student experience (28 articles), but also features widely in studies of course design (23), academic work (12) and system policy (19). Interview-based analyses are a key approach to researching course design (21 articles), academic work (17) and teaching/learning (10).

The less popular method/ologies are not so widely applied to the study of different themes or issues, and there are many blank cells in their rows of the table. Biographical analyses are common in studies of academic work (15 articles) and, to a lesser extent, course design (9). Comparative analysis appears to be mainly applied to research into system policy (17 articles), while conceptual analysis is most commonly directed towards the study of course design (7 articles).

In the case of critical and phenomenographic analysis, there are few examples in the sample. Both have been applied to the study of course design and knowledge, and there are also examples of the former being used to study academic work, and of the latter being applied to researching teaching and learning.

As in the case of themes and issues, individual journals vary in the extent to which they publish articles making use of particular method/ologies. Table 2.4 summarizes the findings. As with the analysis in the previous section, two sorts of conclusions may be drawn from this table. We need again, however, to bear in mind the limitation of the sample size: the year 2000 might have been an odd publication year for some of these journals.

First, and in contrast to the discussion of themes and issues, when we examine the methods or methodologies applied to research, there appear to be more similarities than differences between the 17 journals. Thus, only one journal, HER, did not publish at least one article primarily using the three most popular method/ologies: documentary, multivariate and interview-based analyses. No journal published articles using all of the eight key method/ologies identified, though one, HE, did manage seven of the eight, only omitting to publish an article based primarily on a critical methodology. Four other journals – HEE, HERD, SHE and THE – published examples of six of the eight method/ologies during the year in question.

Second, we may, nevertheless identify a number of groups of journals with particular method/ological foci:

- There are five journals which appear to publish mainly articles that take a documentary or multivariate approach to conducting research: HEM (92 per cent of articles in these two categories), HER (92 per cent), HEQ (86 per cent), AEHE (80 per cent) and EJE (79 per cent). We might, then, typify these journals as encouraging a quantitative and/or positivist approach.

Table 2.4 Articles Published in Individual Journals in terms of Methods or Methodologies

Journal	Methods or Methodologies								
	Documentary	Comparative	Interviews	Multivariate	Conceptual	Phenomenography	Critical	Biography	Totals
ALHE	4		3	1				2	10
AEHE	11		6	13					30
EJE	14	4	2	13	1				34
HE	11	2	11	16	2	1		3	46
HEE	26	7	4	6	2			10	55
HEM	12	1	1	10					24
HEP	10	4	4	3					21
HEQ	10	1	2	8					21
HERD	5		9	3	1	1		1	20
HER	5			6	1				12
IJAD	2		1	2			1	9	15
JGHE	1		4	5			2		12
JHEPM	7	2	1	2				2	14
QHE	7	2	3	3				3	18
SHE	4		7	6	2	1	1		21
THE	5		11	5	6	1		5	33
TEAM	15	1	2	2					20
Totals	149	24	71	104	15	4	4	35	406

- There are three journals which appear to publish mainly articles that take a documentary or interview-based approach to conducting research: ALHE (70 per cent of articles in these two categories), HERD (70 per cent) and HEP (67 per cent). To these, we might add two other journals which appear to publish mainly articles based on documentary and/or biographical analyses: IJAD (73 per cent of articles in these two categories) and HEE (65 per cent). While the focus is not so strong as for the previous group, we might typify these journals as encouraging more of a qualitative and/or interpretive approach.
- Five journals appear more open to regularly publishing both qualitative and quantitative, interpretive and positivist, analyses. These are HE (24 per cent documentary, 24 per cent interview-based, 35 per cent multi-variate), JGHE (8 per cent, 33 per cent, 42 per cent respectively), QHE (39 per cent, 17 per cent, 17 per cent), SHE (19 per cent, 33 per cent, 29 per cent) and THE (15 per cent, 33 per cent, 15 per cent). In method/ological terms, therefore, we might categorize these journals as taking a generic approach.
- This leaves two journals which appear to focus mainly on documentary analyses: TEAM (75 per cent of articles in this category) and JHEPM (50 per cent). We might typify these journals as less concerned with the collection and analysis of fresh empirical data.

As in the case of themes and issues, then, it seems fairly clear which journals researchers with particular method/ological preferences should, and do, target. The linkage between themes and issues, on the one hand, and methods and methodologies, on the other, in the foci of journals will be considered in the concluding section of this chapter.

Level of analysis

Table 2.5 categorizes the articles published in the 17 journals in 2000 in terms of their level of analysis and theme. Seven more or less hierarchical levels have been recognized, varying from a focus on the individual – in many cases the author of the article – through the course, department, institution, nation and system, to an international focus. The distinction between nation and system, as articulated in Chapter 1, is perhaps more subtle. Articles with a national level of analysis are clearly focused on the circumstances of the higher education system in a particular country; those with a system focus are couched in terms of some idealized higher education system.

Table 2.5 clearly shows that the dominant level on which higher education articles focus is the nation, which accounts for well over one-third (38

Table 2.5 Articles Published in 2000 Categorized by Themes and Level of Analysis

| | Themes and Issues | | | | | | | | |
Level of Analysis	Teaching/ Learning	Course Design	Student Experience	Quality	System Policy	Institutional Management	Academic Work	Knowledge	Total
Individual		3		1	1		2	1	8
Course	10	26	6	1	1		11	1	55
Department		10	1	2		1	3		18
Institution	3	20	12	8	5	23	14		85
National	5	22	20	15	58	12	18	5	155
System	4	14	1	1	10	3	5	3	41
International		2	5	5	23	3	6		44
Totals	22	97	45	33	98	42	59	10	406

per cent) of all the articles published in 2000. Articles focusing at the level of the institution (21 per cent) or course (14 per cent), and internationally (11 per cent) and at the level of the system (10 per cent) are also popular. By contrast, there are few articles focusing at either the departmental or the individual level. This might seem surprising, as these are – along with the course – the levels at which most academics and students are engaged, and they are also the kinds of research projects that would be most manageable. There may, however, be issues of unfamiliarity, respectability and outlets for publication involved here.

National level studies are popular for all eight of the themes identified, but most particularly for research into system policy (this cell alone accounts for 14 per cent of all the articles). International and system level studies also show a bias towards system policy, and, in the latter case, course design. Course, departmental and institutional level studies tend to focus on course design, plus, in the case of the first of these, teaching/learning, and, in the case of the last, institutional management.

Table 2.6 relates level of analysis to method/ologies. Documentary analyses focused at the national level stand out as the most popular combination, with this cell accounting for 20 per cent of all the articles analysed. National level studies applying multivariate analyses are also popular, accounting for a further 12 per cent of the articles. All comparative analyses, by definition, focus on the international level. Similarly, most conceptual studies are focused on the system level. Both biographical and interview-based studies, by contrast, tend to focus at either the course or institutional level.

Table 2.7 shows that there are both similarities and variations in the level of analysis in the articles published by different journals. Given its overall popularity, it is hardly surprising that all but one (JGHE) of the journals considered published articles focusing on the national level during the year in question; and that, by contrast, only about a third published articles focused at the individual level. The table shows, however, that there are a number of journals publishing significant proportions of articles focused at each of the other levels. Thus, at least for the year in question, the following journals also published several articles focused at these levels:

- course – ALHE, AEHE, HERD, IJAD, JGHE, SHE, THE;
- department – SHE, THE;
- institution – AEHE, HE, HEE, HEM, HERD, IJAD, QHE, SHE, THE, TEAM;
- international – EJE, HEE.

Most journals, therefore, published articles focused at a range of levels. In only three cases did one level of analysis appear to dominate. For both EJE and HER, this dominant focus was at the national level, whereas, for JGHE, it was, unusually, at the course level.

Table 2.6 Articles Published in 2000 Categorized by Method/ologies and Level of Analysis

| | Methods or Methodologies | | | | | | | | |
	Documentary	Comparative	Interviews	Multivariate	Conceptual	Phenomenography	Critical	Biography	Totals
Level of Analysis									
Individual	1		3					4	8
Course	6		20	16	1		1	11	55
Department	1		9	4		1	1	2	18
Institution	27		19	25		1	1	12	85
National	83		15	50	2	1		4	155
System	22		2	2	12	1	1	1	41
International	9	24	3	7				1	44
Totals	149	24	71	104	15	4	4	35	406

Table 2.7 Articles Published in Individual Journals in terms of Level of Analysis

	Level of Analysis							
	Individual	Course	Department	Institution	National	System	International	Totals
Journal								
ALHE		5			4	1		10
AEHE		9	3	9	7	2		30
EJE				1	22	5	6	34
HE	1	4	2	10	20	4	5	46
HEE		2		15	20	5	13	55
HEM				8	13	2	1	24
HEP	1		2	3	10		5	21
HEQ				3	15	1	2	21
HERD	1	5	1	5	3	3	2	20
HER				2	9	1		12
IJAD		5		7	1		2	15
JGHE		8	1			3		12
JHEPM			1	3	7	1	2	14
QHE	1	1	1	4	9		2	18
SHE	1	4	3	5	4	4		21
THE	3	11	4	5	3	6	1	33
TEAM		1		5	8	3	3	20
Totals	8	55	18	85	155	41	44	406

Authors' location, sex and institutional base

The 406 articles published in the 17 journals analysed during 2000 had a total of 668 authors, an average of 1.6 authors per article. In one extreme case an article had eleven authors, but the great majority had one (59 per cent of articles, 35 per cent of authors), two (25 per cent, 31 per cent) or three (10 per cent, 18 per cent). This section looks at these authors, rather than their articles, and in particular at their location, sex, institution, departmental affiliation and job title.

The 668 authors were located in a total of 48 different countries. As Table 2.8 shows, the country contributing the largest proportion of authors was the United Kingdom, which accounted for 33 per cent. It was followed by Australia (with 19 per cent of authors), the United States (9 per cent), the Netherlands (5 per cent) and Hong Kong (here considered as a separate country: 4 per cent). The relatively small contribution made by North American authors may seem surprising, given the size of the higher education systems in the United States and Canada. It may be explained, however, by the authors in these countries directing their articles primarily to North American journals. By contrast, the contribution to these journals made by Australian authors seems to be significantly greater than might be expected.

Not surprisingly, about two-thirds of the authors contributing to these English language journals are located in countries where English is the first language. That still, however, leaves one-third of authors located in non-English speaking countries, and demonstrates the importance of English as an international language, for higher education as for other subjects of research. The contribution of authors (24 per cent of the total) based in other European countries – 25 different countries in total – is particularly impressive. By contrast, but not that surprisingly, relatively few authors were based in the less developed systems in Asia, Africa and Latin America.

If we examine the detail of Table 2.8, it is possible to discern, journal by journal, a range of different geographic foci, at least for the year in question. Thus:

- four journals – ALHE, HEQ, HER and SHE – mainly published articles by authors based in the United Kingdom;
- two journals – EJE and HEE – as might be expected from their titles, mainly published articles by authors based in Europe;
- two journals – HERD and JHEPM – perhaps not surprisingly, given their editorial base, mainly published articles by authors based in Australasia;
- one journal, IJAD, mainly published articles by authors based in either the UK or Australasia;

Table 2.8 Location of Authors published in Individual Journals

Journal	Geographic Location							
	United Kingdom	Other Europe	Australasia	North America	Asia	Africa	Latin America	Totals
ALHE	13	1		1				15
AEHE	30	6	10	3	14	2		65
EJE	12	50		2				64
HE	22	16	11	20	14	3	1	86
HEE	6	37	10	9	4	3	1	70
HEM	3	13	5	5	4			31
HEP	2	16	1	7	7			33
HEQ	27	3	2					32
HERD	7		40					47
HER	12		1			1	1	15
IJAD	11		16	4	1			32
JGHE	12		2	7				21
JHEPM	1	1	14	2				18
QHE	7	7	6	3	1	4		28
SHE	30	1	6	3				40
THE	17	3	10	6	7	4		47
TEAM	6	8	2	7		1		24
Totals	218	162	136	79	52	18	3	668

Table 2.9 Sex of Authors published in Individual Journals

	Sex			
	Men	Women	Unknown	Totals
Journal				
ALHE	12	3		15
AEHE	36	23	6	65
EJE	38	16	10	64
HE	48	25	13	86
HEE	31	32	7	70
HEM	18	5	8	31
HEP	22	2	9	33
HEQ	27	5		32
HERD	20	25	2	47
HER	9	2	4	15
IJAD	15	17		32
JGHE	14	7		21
JHEPM	12	6		18
QHE	16	9	3	28
SHE	24	13	3	40
THE	20	21	6	47
TEAM	18	6		24
Totals	380	217	71	668

- one journal, JGHE, mainly published articles by authors based in either the UK or North America; and
- the remaining seven journals – AEHE, HE, HEM, HEP, QHE, THE and TEAM – could be described as more or less international in terms of their authorship.

Turning now to the sex of the authors, as Table 2.9 shows, if we exclude those authors whose sex I was unable to determine – either because they only used their initials, or because their names were unfamiliar to me – then about two-thirds of the authors were men and one-third were women. In the case of four of the journals – HEE, HERD, IJAD and THE – a slight majority of the authors were women, but in only one other case, AEHE, was there an above average number of women authors. Indeed, in three journals – HEP, HEQ and HER – the proportion of women authors was below one-fifth in the year in question.

In individual terms, 14 authors contributed two or more articles in their own right (that is contributed two single authored articles or the equivalent in terms of co-authored articles, these being divided equally amongst all named authors). Of these:

- five were based in the United Kingdom: Ron Barnett, Gill Evans, Peter Knight, Maurice Kogan and Mantz Yorke;
- five were based in Australia: Lee Andresen, Philip Candy, Peter Coaldrake, Grant Harman and Richard James;
- one each were from Germany (Ulrich Teichler), Hong Kong (James Pounder), Norway (Jens-Christian Smeby) and Spain (Javier Vidal).

Only one of these 14 authors, Gill Evans, was a woman. The most prolific single contributor, to the journals analysed in 2000, was Mantz Yorke, who managed to publish three articles in his own right and be co-author on two others. Interestingly, only one of these authors – Maurice Kogan – appeared in the list of the ten most prolific authors in an earlier analysis of four of the journals (HE, HEQ, HER and SHE) over a five-year period, 1993–1998 (Tight 1999, Table 3). Though the two analyses are not wholly comparable, this would seem to suggest both a turnover in authorship and a fluctuation, from year to year, in the output of individual authors; which is pretty much what you might expect.

In terms of institutions, 24 universities, colleges or centres contributed the equivalent of six or more authors. Of these:

- ten were located in the United Kingdom: Birmingham, Lancaster, Leeds Metropolitan, Open, Oxford Brookes, Nottingham Trent, Sheffield, Strathclyde and Ulster universities, plus the Institute of Education in London;
- eight were located in Australia: Curtin, Griffith, Macquarie, Melbourne, Monash, Queensland, Queensland Technology and Sydney universities;
- two were in the Netherlands: Maastricht and Twente universities;
- one each were in Finland (Turku University), Hong Kong (Hong Kong Polytechnic University), Norway (NIFU, the Norwegian Institute for Research in Higher Education) and Sweden (Goteborg University).

About half of these institutions appeared in the list of the 20 most prolific I produced as part of my earlier analysis (Tight 1999, Table 5), suggesting that institutional specialisms or strengths often outlast individual authors. The analysis also shows that higher education research is important on both sides of the former binary divide in the United Kingdom, and that it is very well established in the Australian system.

Information is available (that is, was published in the journals) on the departmental or other affiliations, within their institutions, of 414 (62 per cent) of the authors. This shows an almost equal division between authors based in educational departments or centres, and those located in other disciplinary departments. While it is not possible to reach precise conclusions simply from the names of departments or centres, it would seem that the former group are fairly evenly split between generic education departments, departments specializing in higher education or adult/continuing education, and academic practice or staff development centres. In the case of the latter group, while authors can be found based in most major disciplines, the majority is clearly in the social sciences, with significant numbers in business/management, geography, politics, psychology and sociology departments.

Information on authors' job titles is not so widely recorded, being available for only 233 (35 per cent) of them. Nevertheless, what information there is is suggestive. About two-thirds of these titles are what might be called conventional academic job titles – research officer, research fellow, research associate, lecturer, senior lecturer, principal lecturer, reader, associate professor, professor and so on – with professors being the most common of this bunch. The remaining third give administrative or managerial titles, varying from vice-chancellor or president, through head or director, to officer or co-ordinator.

These two sets of information confirm the spread of interest in higher education research throughout a wide range of subjects or disciplines, something already remarked upon in Chapter 1 (see Teichler 1996). It also suggests an involvement in higher education research not only from senior managers in universities, but also from the much larger and more diverse group of people charged with running different sorts of higher education programmes, initiatives and support services.

Conclusions

Table 2.10 summarizes the analysis presented in this chapter. It demonstrates that the 17 journals analysed can be characterized as occupying a variety of different niches or markets within higher education research.

Thus, each journal may be categorized in terms of its focus on:

- particular themes or issues for research, such as system policy, course design, academic work, institutional management or quality (one journal did not have a particular focus);
- quantitative, qualitative or non-empirical method/ologies for undertaking research (five journals did not have a particular focus);
- different levels of analysis, ranging from the course, through the department, institution and nation or system to an international focus;
- authors based in particular countries or regions, or internationally;
- a dominance of male authors or a more balanced contribution from both men and women.

The caveat must be repeated here, though, that the articles published during the year 2000 may not be typical, particularly for those journals with a relatively small annual output.

Table 2.10 Summary Characteristics of Individual Journals

Journal	Themes/Issues	Method/ologies	Level	Nationality	Sex
ALHE	course design	qualitative	course/nation	UK	male
AEHE	course design	quantitative	course/institution/nation	international	mixed
EJE	system policy	quantitative	nation/international	European	male
HE	mixed	mixed	institution/nation	international	male
HEE	system policy	qualitative	institution/nation/international	European	mixed
HEM	system policy	quantitative	institution/nation	international	male
HEP	system policy	qualitative	nation	international	male
HEQ	system policy	quantitative	nation	UK	male
HERD	course design	qualitative	course/institution/nation	Australasia	mixed
HER	system policy	quantitative	nation	UK	male
IJAD	academic work	qualitative	course/institution	UK/Australasia	mixed
JGHE	course design	mixed	course	UK/North American	male
JHEPM	system policy	non-empirical	nation	Australasia	male
QHE	quality	mixed	nation	international	male
SHE	course design	mixed	institution/nation	UK	male
THE	course design	mixed	course/nation	international	mixed
TEAM	institutional management	non-empirical	nation	international	male

While it would be false to claim that every variety was available amongst the journals examined for both readers and authors, it would appear that there is a considerable and probably sufficient variety. Thus at one extreme, we have a truly international journal publishing articles on all aspects of higher education that make use of a wide range of method/ologies: HE. At the other extreme, there are a number of journals that focus on particular topics, methods and levels, and have a localized authorship, such as ALHE, HEQ, HER and JHEPM. And, in between, there is a range of journals that are less tightly focused, but not, at least yet, as open in their publishing strategy as HE.

3

Books

Introduction

This chapter contains an analysis of the books in print in the year 2000 – published outside North America in the English language – that focus on higher education.

The chapter has the same format as the previous one, and is organized in seven sections:

- the selection of the books analysed is discussed and justified;
- the characteristics of the book publishers involved are reviewed;
- the themes and issues addressed by the books are considered;
- the methods and methodologies used in the research concerned are examined;
- the level of analysis of the books is analysed;
- the location, sex, institution, department and job title of the book authors or editors is discussed; and
- some conclusions are then offered.

Selection of books for analysis

There are dozens of books published every year in the English language, even if those published in North America are excluded, which deal with higher education. For the analysis presented in this chapter, I have chosen to concentrate solely on books published by mainstream publishers that focus exclusively or chiefly on higher education. I have also excluded, essentially for convenience, the output of mainstream publishers who had fewer than five books in print on higher education in the year in question.

I have adopted these restrictions for similar reasons for my focus on specialist academic journals in the previous chapter. The books published by mainstream publishers are normally peer reviewed, either at the proposal or early draft stage and/or when a complete draft has been produced. Such procedures tend to ensure that the books published are of a certain minimum quality. This is reinforced when the publisher has a series of books on higher education topics, rather than just the odd one or two.

By taking this approach, I have made my task more focused and manageable, though I have also excluded from the analysis several kinds of books that would also be worth reviewing. These include, for example:

- Self-published books and those issued by small publishers (the latter include, incidentally, many 'minor' – in the sense of not publishing much – university presses). No judgement on quality is necessarily implied by this exclusion.
- Self-help books and directories targeted at students, their families and advisors (though those targeted at staff have been included).
- Reports, policy statements and other documents produced by governments, their agencies and research centres.
- Autobiographical accounts and novels.

All of these literatures – and other literatures on higher education – would be worth further investigation (Blaxter et al. 1998a, 1998b). Examining the outputs of a selected sample of higher education research centres would, perhaps, be particularly fruitful for present purposes. That I have not done so, at least yet, is chiefly to do with keeping the project within manageable bounds. Preliminary analysis suggests, however, that a significant proportion of the work of such research centres does find its way into published books and journal articles. I am confident, therefore, that the analysis contained in this chapter and the previous one provides a more than sufficient grounding for understanding research into higher education, which is the purpose of this book.

One of the problems posed by an analysis of books in print on higher education, even with these restrictions imposed, is that – at least so far as I am aware, and I have looked – there is no single reliable source of information on what is in print. Various databases do exist, but they tend to be neither comprehensive nor readily searchable for books on higher education (which can be listed under a variety of headings).

I did have the advantage, however, not only of having been a higher education researcher for over 20 years, but also of being a journal editor, book reviews editor and book abstractor for much of that time. So I started with a considerable familiarity with the main publishers of books on higher education, and I already possessed many of those that were in print in 2000. The collection of the data for analysis made considerable use of publishers' catalogues, both in hardcopy and online, as well as library and other databases. Once identified, all books were acquired or borrowed, and then examined closely, to create the database used for the study. The actual book, rather than the catalogue, was taken as the primary data source: authors and publishers can be over-optimistic about when their books are going to be published, and details listed in catalogues may differ from those of the actual finished book.

It has to be acknowledged, though, that I will have missed some books. For example, books on the history of higher education frequently appear to be categorized by publishers solely under history, so some will have been overlooked. Mainstream publishers outside the anglophone world who publish some books in English, particularly away from the main centres of the United Kingdom, Europe and Australasia, are also likely to have been under-sampled. And, as already indicated, I have deliberately excluded mainstream publishers who produce only one or two books on higher education (though, so far as I am aware, these collectively only amount to a handful of books).

Despite these reservations, the analysis that follows should offer a reasonably comprehensive guide to contemporary books on higher education.

Characteristics of higher education book publishers

In total, 284 books on higher education were identified as being in print during 2000, produced by eight different publishers (see Table 3.1). The Open University Press was the most prolific publisher on this topic, with 111 books in print, or 39 per cent of the total. Together with three other publishers – Kogan Page, Jessica Kingsley and Taylor & Francis – they

Table 3.1 Publishers of Books in Print in the Year 2000

Publisher	Books in Print	% of Total
Open University Press	111	39
Kogan Page	63	22
Jessica Kingsley	49	17
Taylor & Francis	26	9
Ashgate	11	4
Elsevier	11	4
Cassell	7	2
Oxford University Press	6	2
Totals	284	100

dominate this particular market, with these four publishers accounting for 88 per cent of all of the books on higher education in print in 2000. Interestingly, only one of these eight publishers – Taylor & Francis – was also involved in publishing journals on higher education (see Table 2.1), suggesting that these two markets are treated separately by publishers.

Publishing is a relatively volatile business at the present time, and this affects the publication of books on higher education as much as any other area. Thus, in 2002 the Open University Press was taken over by the American publishers McGraw-Hill. The Open University Press identity is being maintained, and it is continuing to publish books on higher education. Most of these books, including this one, are published in association with the UK-based Society for Research into Higher Education (SRHE). Given that the SRHE also owns two of the higher education journals examined in Chapter 2, it clearly plays a pivotal role in the publication and dissemination of higher education research outside of North America.

While the Open University Press is continuing its work, Jessica Kingsley has recently stopped publishing new books in its series on higher education, while those it has already published are steadily going out of print. The third of the big four players in this area, Taylor & Francis, has also recently been through a bout of amalgamation and reorganization, which brought its two main publishers of books on higher education, Routledge and Falmer, together. While this does mean that the analysis presented here is inevitably something of a snapshot, I do not feel that its conclusions would have been much different if the year chosen for analysis had been a few years earlier or later.

One difference between the analysis presented in this chapter and that in the previous chapter, which looked at academic journal articles, is that most of the books in print in 2000 had been published before that year, whereas all of the articles examined in Chapter 2 were published in 2000. Hence the analysis in this chapter has something of a flavour of contemporary history about it. Table 3.2 details the publication dates of the 284 books in print in 2000. It indicates an annual output of 40 to 50 books on higher education, with over half of the books in print in 2000 having been published since 1997. Some books, however, clearly stay in print for rather longer than this – over ten years in a few cases. Whether this is because they are popular, and keep being reprinted, or, conversely, they are not popular, and it takes time to sell off the initial print run, is difficult to say without access to publishers' internal information. What we can say, though, is the majority of the books in print are very contemporary.

The flip side of being a contemporary literature is that much of it has a relatively short life. Only ten (less than 4 per cent) of the books in print had gone into a second or later edition: six were in their second edition,

Table 3.2 Publication Dates of Books in Print in the Year 2000

Year of Publication	No. of Books	% of Total
2000	42	15
1999	54	19
1998	30	11
1997	30	11
1996	23	8
1995	21	7
1994	33	12
1993	14	5
1992	11	4
1991	6	2
1990	10	4
1989	6	2
1988	2	1
1987	2	1
Totals	284	100

three in their third and a single book was in its fourth edition (Cannon and Newble 2000). Most such books were more practical, 'how to' guides, rather than academic monographs. Interestingly, a substantial minority, 120 (42 per cent), of the books were edited rather than authored: this is clearly a feature of academic literatures that is not so common in book publication in general.

The books in print varied considerably in terms of their length, price and publication format. Their length ranged between a minimum of 91 pages and a maximum of 993 pages, with a mean of 220 pages. The great majority of books, 198 or 70 per cent, were between 160 and 260 pages in length.

Price and publication format are clearly closely related. A total of 114 (40 per cent) books were published only in paperback, with 76 (27 per cent) only in hardback, and 94 (33 per cent) in both formats. Paperback prices varied between £11.99 and £35.00, with a mean of £18.96. The modal paperback prices were £18.99 and £19.99, both just below the psychological barrier of £20.00 (psychology probably also explains why the great majority of paperbacks were priced as £–.99 or, less commonly, £–.95). Hardback book prices varied between £18.95 and £225.00 (the latter was, of course, the 993 page book: the next highest priced was only £75.00), with a mean of £50.57. The modal hardback prices were £60.00 and £50.00 (almost all hardbacks were priced simply in pounds).

Themes and issues

Table 3.3 categorizes the 284 books in print in 2000 in terms of both the themes or issues they cover and the methods or methodologies applied. Compared to academic journal articles, books offer much greater scope for coverage of themes or issues, and for applying a greater range of methods or methodologies. While they have been categorized in Table 3.3 in terms of the dominant theme and method evident, in some cases a variety of themes were addressed and a variety of methods used.

If we examine the bottom row of Table 3.3, it is clear that two of the eight themes dominate, with books focusing on course design or system policy together accounting for 45 per cent of the total books in print. Both the topics emphasized, and the scale of the emphasis, match the patterns identified in Chapter 2 for journal articles (see Table 2.2), confirming a general emphasis in the higher education research literature on these areas.

By comparison, published books on the other six themes or issues identified are less common, though in each case there is an identifiable literature. Thus, there are healthy literatures focusing on institutional management, the student experience and teaching and learning, in each case totalling about half the number of books in print on either course design or system policy. There are somewhat smaller literatures on academic work and quality, with the smallest of all sub-literatures, as in the case of journal articles, dealing with knowledge. It seems interesting that there were more books in print on the topic of knowledge than there were journal articles on it published in 2000. It may be that many of the questions posed within this theme lend themselves to more extended discussion.

Table 3.4 charts the themes or issues covered by the books in print in 2000 in terms of the publishers involved. The leading publisher in this field, the Open University Press, was the only one that published books, and in every case significant numbers of books, on all eight of the key themes identified. The other three major publishers each had books in print on seven of the eight themes identified, but in each case their lists were rather thin in a number of areas.

The books on higher education published by these four main publishers each showed an emphasis on one or both of the leading themes – course design and system policy – but also reveal what might be called a specialist emphasis on other themes. Thus, the Open University Press also appears to be particularly strong in the area of institutional management, where it has developed the *Managing Universities and Colleges: guides to good practice* series. Kogan Page has an impressive set of books focusing on teaching and learning, and Jessica Kingsley published a range of books on the student experience.

Table 3.3 Books in Print in 2000 Categorized by Themes and Methods

	Themes and Issues								
	Teaching/ Learning	Course Design	Student Experience	Quality	System Policy	Institutional Management	Academic Work	Knowledge	Total
Method/ology									
Biography						2	1		3
Critical							1		1
Phenomenography									
Conceptual		4	1	2	3		2	5	17
Multivariate		2	6	1	4	3	2		18
Interviews	2	6	7		4	6	2	1	28
Comparative		2	3	2	17	5	1	2	32
Documentary	27	51	13	16	36	18	16	8	185
(of which 'how to')	(19)	(13)	(1)	(5)		(6)	(6)	(4)	(54)
Totals	29	65	30	21	64	34	25	16	284

Table 3.4 Books in Print in 2000 Categorized by Themes and Publishers

Publisher	Themes and Issues								Total
	Teaching/ Learning	Course Design	Student Experience	Quality	System Policy	Institutional Management	Academic Work	Knowledge	
Open University Press	11	20	12	9	17	22	12	8	111
Kogan Page	13	30		4	5	2	4	5	63
Jessica Kingsley		5	10	6	18	4	4	2	49
Taylor & Francis	4	6	3	2	7	1	3		26
Ashgate		1	3		6	1			11
Elsevier		1			7	2	1		11
Cassell	1	2	2			1		1	7
Oxford University Press					4	1	1		6
Totals	29	65	30	21	64	34	25	16	284

Collectively, the lists of the remaining four, more minor, publishers look rather thin by comparison. Three of these publishers – Ashgate, Elsevier and the Oxford University Press – appear to focus mainly on one theme, system policy.

Methods and methodologies

Looking again at Table 3.3, and focusing on the right hand column, it is clear that one method/ology has been identified as dominant, with four others present in smaller numbers, and the remaining three only minimally present or absent.

To some degree, but only marginally, this is an artefact of the classification process. Some books, as already indicated, may adopt a range of methods or methodologies. Only a handful of those reviewed here could truly be described as 'multi-method', however, which is why I have not sought to separately identify them. In Table 3.3, the books in print have been categorized by the most prevalent method or methodology evident. Given the reliance of much academic writing on reviewing the existing research literature, and also in many cases the policy literature, it is hardly surprising, then, that the dominant method/ology should turn out to be documentary analysis.

The majority, 185 (65 per cent), of the books in print have been classified as relying primarily on documentary analysis. Documentary analysis was also the leading method/ology identified in the analysis of journal articles presented in Chapter 2 (see Table 2.2), though it did not occupy such a dominant position. This is partly because, while the analysis of articles only examined those published in refereed academic journals, this review of books in print covers all books on higher education (with the exceptions noted earlier in this chapter). While all of these books may be said to be research-based or empirically-based, in some sense, the database, therefore, includes many guides to, or summaries of, academic practice as well as more directly research-based analyses. This sub-literature is commonly referred to as the 'how to' genre, a term I will also adopt (and, since I have contributed to this genre myself, I can honestly say that I mean no slur in using this term).

In total, 54 (19 per cent) of the books in print in 2000 could be categorized as belonging to the 'how to' genre; though quite a number of others categorized under documentary analysis displayed aspects of this genre. Since all of these books rely, often implicitly as well as explicitly, to a large extent on existing documents and practices, they have been categorized here as applying documentary analysis. If they were excluded from the analysis, documentary analysis would not appear to be quite so dominant a method/ology, accounting for 131 of 230 (or 57 per cent, rather than 65 per cent) of the books in print. This is still, however, an impressive proportion.

The penultimate row of Table 3.3 indicates how the 'how to' genre is distributed between themes. Two themes, teaching and learning and the student experience, are clearly the most attractive for writers and publishers within this genre, together accounting for 59 per cent of all the 'how to' books identified. There are also, however, significant numbers of such books focusing on four of the other key themes – academic work, institutional management, quality and knowledge (in this last case, these consist chiefly of 'how to research' books aimed at academics). The student experience, by comparison, seems an under-explored theme for this genre. It is perhaps not surprising that there appears to be no 'how to' literature covering system policy, though it might be interesting to speculate what such a literature would contain.

If the 'how to' books are taken away from the figures for documentary analysis presented in Table 3.3, most of the books relying on this method/ology can be seen to focus on two of the eight key themes – course design and system policy – the same two that dominate overall. There are, however, a healthy numbers of books in print applying documentary analysis for exploring all of the other key themes, with the exception of knowledge.

Table 3.3 shows that comparative analysis is the next most popular method/ology in books on print on higher education (accounting for 11 per cent of the total). Indeed, it appears to be more popular as a method/ology for books than it is for journal articles (see Table 2.2). This is largely, no doubt, because the book format offers the extended scope which comparative analyses tend to require – much like academic writing on the theme of knowledge. More than half of the books applying comparative analysis focused on the theme of system policy.

There are significant numbers of books in print relying mainly on three of the other method/ologies identified: interviews (10 per cent of the total), multivariate analysis (6 per cent) and conceptual analysis (6 per cent). Interviews and multivariate analyses are far less commonly the focus for whole books than they are for journal articles (compare Table 2.2). They are, however, applied rather more widely – and frequently together in the same book – but in a less prominent and more supportive role (for example as the basis of one or two chapters), than these overall figures suggest. Conceptual analysis, like comparative analysis, though still a minor method/ology, appears to lend itself more to the extended book format rather than the journal article.

The other three method/ologies identified – biographical analysis, critical analysis and phenomenography – form the basis for tiny numbers of published books on higher education, and, in the case of the last named, appear to be absent entirely. As with interviews, multivariate analysis and conceptual analysis, this rather over-states the position. Many books, for example, contain biographical and/or critical elements: indeed, it could be argued that it is impossible to write a book without including something biographical or critical, whether explicit or not. Even in the case of phenomenography, there were books in print in 2000 that contained such analyses in one or two chapters (e.g. Prosser and Trigwell 1999), and since then at least one book has been published where this is the dominant method/ology (Brew 2001b). It has to be stated, however, that these method/ologies remain under-developed in book format.

Table 3.5 breaks down the books in print on higher education in 2000 in terms of method/ologies and publishers. This shows that books based on documentary analysis dominate in the lists of six of the eight publishers. In two cases, however, Jessica Kingsley and Elsevier, books applying comparative analysis appear in significant numbers, with these two publishers together accounting for 88 per cent of all the books in print relying upon this method/ology. The Open University Press dominates in the areas of conceptual analysis (76 per cent) and interviews (57 per cent).

Only three of the eight publishers were involved in publishing 'how to' books, with the two largest publishers of books on higher education, Kogan Page and the Open University Press, dominating this market. Indeed, 38 per cent of Kogan Page's higher education list falls into this genre.

Level of analysis

Tables 3.6 and 3.7 relate the themes explored, and the methods used, in the books in print on higher education in 2000 to the level at which the analysis was pitched. They both show that the dominant level at which analysis is pitched is the national level, which accounts for 120 (42 per cent) of the books in print. This is similar, though slightly more marked, to the findings with respect to journal articles (see Table 2.5). Unlike the analysis reported for journal articles, however, international (90 books, 32 per cent of the total) and system level (61 per cent, 21 per cent) analyses are the next most prevalent. Clearly, the book format allows scope for a literally larger level of analysis, while the journal article is better suited for institutional or course level analyses (or is more accessible for those researching at these levels). Thus, of the 284 books in print in 2000, only 10 (4 per cent) were focused on the institutional level, with only one each at individual, course and departmental level.

Table 3.6 shows that the national, international and/or system levels of analysis dominate, though in differing combinations, in all of the key themes or issues identified. Only six cells in this table account for more

Table 3.5 Books in Print in 2000 in terms of Methods or Methodologies and Publishers

| | Methods or Methodologies | | | | | | | | |
	Documentary ('how to')	Comparative	Interviews	Multivariate	Conceptual	Phenomenography	Critical	Biography	Totals
Publisher									
Open University Press	74 (21)	3	16	5	13				111
Kogan Page	58 (24)	19	6	7	3			2	63
Jessica Kingsley	16	1	1	3	1				49
Taylor & Francis	19 (9)		2	2			1	1	26
Ashgate	7		1						11
Elsevier	1	9	2						11
Cassell	5		2						7
Oxford University Press	5			1					6
Totals	185 (54)	32	28	18	17	0	1	3	284

Table 3.6 Books in Print in 2000 Categorized by Themes and Level of Analysis

	Themes and Issues								
	Teaching/ Learning	Course Design	Student Experience	Quality	System Policy	Institutional Management	Academic Work	Knowledge	Total
Level of Analysis									
Individual			1						1
Course		1							1
Department						1			1
Institution		2	3	1		3	1		10
National	8	28	13	11	27	19	8	6	120
System	19	21	1	2	4	2	9	3	61
International	2	13	12	7	33	9	7	7	90
Totals	29	65	30	21	64	34	25	25	284

Table 3.7 Books in Print in 2000 Categorized by Method/ologies and Level of Analysis

Level of Analysis	Methods or Methodologies								
	Documentary	Comparative	Interviews	Multivariate	Conceptual	Phenomenography	Critical	Biography	Totals
Individual			1						1
Course			1						1
Department			1						1
Institution	5		5						10
National	90		17	8	2		1	2	120
System	46		1	1	13				61
International	44	32	2	9	2			1	90
Totals	185	32	28	18	17	0	1	3	284

than half of the 284 books categorized: international and national level studies of system policy, national and system level studies of course design, national level studies of institutional management, and system level studies of teaching and learning.

The concentration of the books categorized is even more marked in Table 3.7, with three cells – national, system and international level studies based on documentary analysis – accounting for 63 per cent of the total. However, three other close associations are also worth drawing attention to. Not surprisingly, all books based on comparative analysis have also been categorized as international in level. Perhaps more interestingly, there is a clear relationship between conceptual analysis and system level studies, with 76 per cent of the former falling into the latter category. Interview-based studies – the only method/ology identified at all seven levels of analysis in the database – are particularly prevalent at the national level, which accounts for 61 per cent of the books in print based on this method/ology.

Authors' and editors' location, sex and institutional base

The 284 books in print in 2000 which focused on higher education had a total of 513 authors or editors, an average of 1.8 per volume (slightly higher than the average for journal article authors). The maximum number of authors/editors for one volume was seven, but the great majority had only one (141 books, 50 per cent of the total), two (86, 30 per cent) or three (36, 13 per cent). The 120 edited volumes (42 per cent of the total) had between 3 and 49 contributors, with a mean of just over 17 contributors per volume. This section focuses on the book authors and editors, rather than the books themselves, and in particular on their location, sex, institution and departmental locations, and job titles.

The 513 authors or editors were located in a total of 24 different countries. The largest proportion, indeed a clear majority, 335 (65 per cent), were located in the United Kingdom (see Table 3.8). This is a much greater concentration than was found for journal articles (compare Table 2.8). With most of the leading book publishers based in the United Kingdom – though they all have representatives and/or offices in other countries – it may be that it is simply easier for UK-based authors to pitch their ideas to potential publishers. The UK also represents the largest English language market outside of North America, so publishers might also be more inclined to go with established British authors. For those coming from a non-English speaking background, of course, writing a book will represent a more extended challenge than an article.

Table 3.8 Location of Authors and Editors of Books in Print

Location	No. Authors/Editors	% of total
United Kingdom	335	65
Rest of Europe	60	12
Australasia	43	8
North America	27	5
Asia	5	1
Africa	0	0
Latin America	0	0
not disclosed[1]	43	8
Total	513	100

[1] Curiously, while journals almost invariably provide these details for authors of articles, this is not always the case with book publishers.

Outside of the United Kingdom, the most notable contributions came from authors based in Australia (38, 7 per cent), the United States (23, 4 per cent) and Germany (21, 4 per cent). The rest of Europe together accounted for 60 authors or editors, 12 per cent of the total. Compared to journal articles, the spread of authors or editors was less global, with none based in Africa or Latin America, and only five (less than 1 per cent) in Asia.

In terms of sex, of 513 authors and editors, 323 (63 per cent) were men, 182 (35 per cent) were women, and in eight cases their sex was unclear. These proportions are very similar to those found for the authors of journal articles (see Table 2.9).

In terms of individual authors, the output of books on higher education appears more concentrated than that of journal articles. Perhaps fewer academics are capable of the more extended analysis required to produce a book, or perhaps fewer of them have the time required. A total of 21 individuals contributed two or more books as authors or editors (that is, they had authored or edited two books on their own that were in print, or the equivalent in terms of co-authored or co-edited books divided equally amongst all the named authors or editors). Of these:

- seventeen were based in the United Kingdom: Kate Ashcroft, Ron Barnett, Tony Becher, Sally Brown, Robert Burgess, Peter Denley, Claudius Gellert, Mary Henkel, Peter Knight, Maurice Kogan, Ian McNay, Jennifer Moon, Phil Race, Tom Schuller, Peter Scott, David Warner and David Watson;
- two were based in Australia: Paul Ramsden and Ortrun Zuber-Skerritt; and
- one each were from Germany (Ulrich Teichler) and New Zealand (Graham Webb).

Only four of these names – Ron Barnett, Peter Knight, Maurice Kogan and Ulrich Teichler – were also identified as amongst the most prolific authors of journal articles in the year 2000 (see Chapter 2), though most of these authors/editors are found in both databases. Clearly, the demands of writing prolifically in these different formats are more than most can manage consistently.

Five of these prolific book authors or editors were women, a much higher proportion than amongst prolific journal article authors. The single most prolific contributor, Ron Barnett, had six books in print in 2000 under his individual authorship, plus a further co-edited book. The next most prolific, Sally Brown, had an authorial or editorial hand in even more books in print, 11 in total, but in each case as a co-author or editor. The list includes a number of authors/editors who specialize in the 'how to' genre, as distinct from the more academic monograph, such as Kate Ashcroft, Sally Brown and Phil Race, and some who do both (e.g. Peter Knight), though most focus exclusively on the academic monograph.

In terms of their institutional location, 20 universities or colleges each accounted for six or more of the authors recorded. Of these:

- sixteen were located in the United Kingdom: Canterbury Christ Church and Westminster colleges, Brighton, Brunel, Durham, East London, Edinburgh, Lancaster, Leeds, Luton, Northumbria, Open, Oxford, Warwick and West of England universities, plus the Institute of Education in London;
- two were in Australia: Griffith and Sydney Technology universities; and
- one each were in Germany (Kassel University) and the Netherlands (Twente University).

Only five of these institutions are common to the list produced in Chapter 2 for the institutional locations of journal article authors, suggesting again that interest and involvement in higher education research is fairly widely dispersed.

This conclusion is supported if the departmental affiliations of the authors are also examined (though this detail was only recorded for about 60 per cent of authors). About two-thirds of these authors were located in either generic education departments, specialist education departments focusing on adult or higher education, or academic practice centres. This is a larger proportion than was found for authors of journal articles, suggesting that disciplinary (or, if you prefer, subject) expertise is more important in producing or overseeing the more extended analyses required by the book format. Whether discipline or subject, however, the names given to the locations of this group were very diverse. Authors based in academic practice centres, in particular, operated under a huge variety of titles, and, in some cases, it was impossible to tell simply from the department or centre title whether the focus was on teaching, research, development or all three of these activities.

Most of the remaining third of authors were located in social science departments, with business and management, economics, politics, psychology and sociology particularly well represented (as they were for journal article authors). Authors of books in print on higher education were also to be found, however, in engineering, humanities, professional and science departments, as well as in university administrative and service departments.

Information on job title was available for nearly three-quarters of book authors or editors. As with departmental affiliations, a huge variety of job titles was in evidence. However, the authors and editors were split fairly equally between professors (by far the single most popular job title, accounting for 27 per cent of those providing job titles), other academic titles (that is lecturer, senior lecturer, principal lecturer, associate professor, reader and so on), and administrative titles (for example dean, director, head, pro-vice-chancellor). This is a similar split to that found for journal article authors, confirming the substantial engagement of university managers and administrators in higher education research.

Conclusions

A series of conclusions may be drawn from the analysis presented in this chapter. I would wish to draw particular attention to the following:

- the limited number of publishers involved in producing books based on higher education research, and the somewhat volatile nature of this business;
- the great popularity of edited, as opposed to authored, books on higher education;
- the dominance of books focusing on the themes of course design and system policy;
- the dominance of books based primarily on documentary analysis;
- the strength of the 'how to' literature, as compared to the academic monograph, particularly in writing on teaching and learning and related topics;
- the focus of the great majority of books published on the national, international or system levels;
- the stronger emphasis on United Kingdom based authors, when compared to journal articles; and
- the dispersion in involvement in higher education research amongst education, staff development, social sciences and other university departments and functions.

Part II

Issues and approaches in researching higher education

The eight chapters in this part of the book have been organized in terms of the key themes or issues identified and explored in the first three chapters. The chapters successively focus on researching:

- teaching and learning (Chapter 4);
- course design (Chapter 5);
- the student experience (Chapter 6);
- quality (Chapter 7);
- system policy (Chapter 8);
- institutional management (Chapter 9);
- academic work (Chapter 10);
- knowledge (Chapter 11).

Each chapter has been organized in a common format:

1. The theme under consideration is introduced, and recent research on it is categorized and discussed.
2. Three case studies – summaries of and commentaries on examples of recently published research in higher education – are presented. The case studies have been chosen so as to be illustrative of the range of approaches taken to researching the theme. Most of them take the form of articles in academic journals, though a few are books. The majority – 17 of the total of 24 case studies – are reprinted in a *Reader* (Tight 2003a) which should, therefore, form a useful companion to the present volume. Each case study is analysed in terms of its: themes and issues, methods and methodologies, level, analytical/theoretical framework, related literatures, argument and conclusions.
3. Some ideas for areas for future research are then outlined.

4

Researching teaching and learning

Introduction

The business of teaching and learning may be seen to be at the core of the higher education enterprise. Lecturers teach and students learn, or, at least, that is what should happen if the former are doing their jobs properly and the latter are paying attention. But this is, of course, to over-simplify.

As the organization of this book should make clear, teaching and learning is but one, albeit an important, aspect of higher education. It is, of course, very closely linked to some of the other themes and issues identified here, notably course design (Chapter 5), the student experience (Chapter 6) and academic work (Chapter 10). Some of the topics, and some of the texts, discussed in this chapter could have been discussed in other chapters as well; and, indeed, some are. Thus, the book by Laurillard (2002) – analysed in this chapter as Case Study 4.2, for its examination of student learning and how this informs the design of learning experiences – is also discussed in Chapter 5 for what it has to say about the use of learning technologies.

And, as the analysis presented in Chapters 2 and 3 illustrates (see in particular Tables 2.2 and 3.3), research and writing focusing specifically on teaching and learning is less common than that on most of the other main themes or issues identified. This is partly because – rather like knowledge, discussed in Chapter 11 – the theme of teaching and learning, at least in the way I have defined it, is one of the most theorized and conceptualized. Alongside this more theoretical concern, there is also, though, an extremely practical element of the literature, concerned with how to teach and how best to get students to learn. And there is, as just indicated, the more applied research and literature that examines how to organize and deliver the curriculum, discussed in the next chapter.

Key questions stimulating research into teaching and learning in higher education would include:

- What methods for teaching are available, and how should these be used most effectively in different circumstances?
- How do students go about learning, and what variations are there in this?
- How can we encourage students to learn in the ways we would like them to?
- Do students with different characteristics tend to learn in different ways?
- What do new academics need to know in order to discharge their teaching roles effectively?

In short, then, this chapter focuses on how we understand teaching and learning in higher education, and how we go about it.

Research into teaching and learning

While the analysis in this chapter might have been organized in any number of different ways, I have chosen to structure it in terms of four main sub-themes or genres in the research literature:

- student learning;
- different kinds of students;
- teaching in higher education;
- the 'how to' genre.

Each of these sub-themes or genres will now be exemplified and discussed in turn.

Student learning

If the whole theme of teaching and learning is one of the more theorized areas of research and writing on higher education, the sub-theme focusing on student learning is where this theorization appears to be strongest. This topic for research is particularly associated with the Swedish researcher Marton, and those who have collaborated with and followed on from him (Marton et al. 1997). Two foci for research have been on how students and their teachers conceive of, and how students approach, learning. A wide range of methods and methodologies has been employed in exploring these issues.

Three examples will be given of research into conceptions of learning:

- In a study published in 1993, Marton and his colleagues (Marton et al. 1993) interviewed a small sample of social science students at the United

Kingdom Open University at the beginning and end of their studies about their view of learning. Through phenomenographic analysis (see Chapter 12 for a discussion of this methodology) of the interview transcripts, they identified six qualitatively different student conceptions of learning: increasing one's knowledge, memorizing and reproducing, applying, understanding, seeing something in a different way, and changing as a person. There is clearly both a hierarchy, and an implied preference, in this listing.

- Prosser et al. (1994), by contrast, undertook a phenomenographic analysis of academics' conceptions of science learning and teaching. They identified five different conceptions: accumulating more information to satisfy external demands, acquiring concepts to satisfy external demands, acquiring concepts to satisfy internal demands, conceptual development to satisfy internal demands, and conceptual change to satisfy internal demands. There is some relation to the previous list, but an obvious focus on learning as the acquisition of concepts, and on competing external (that is, assessment) and internal (that is, personal) demands.

- Tynjala (1997), in another longitudinal study, focused on 31 educational psychology students taking a course on theories of learning and development. Essays were written on their conceptions of learning before and after the course, with the students taught in two different, 'traditional' or constructivist, groups. Phenomenographic analysis of the essays identified seven different student conceptions of learning: learning as an externally determined event/process, learning as a developmental process, learning as a student activity, learning as strategies/styles/ approaches, learning as information processing, learning as an interactive process, and learning as a creative process. Here, the emphasis is very much on the nature of the learning process, and on changes in conceptions over time.

Clearly, then, both students and academics may hold very different, and often conflictual, views of what learning is about. These may develop over time (Devlin 2002), and may be related to academic achievement (McLean 2001). Part of our responsibility as academics may, therefore, be seen, as implied by Marton et al.'s (1993) analysis, as being about encouraging the development of more advanced and more effective conceptions of learning in our students and colleagues.

The research on students' approaches to learning – or what others have referred to as learning styles or learning strategies: though some would recognize distinctions between these terms – is closely related. The key finding of this research has been the contrast drawn between deep and surface approaches to learning. Students employing the latter strive to memorize sufficient material to pass a given assessment task, while those applying the former seek to understand and make personal sense of what is being studied. In a way analogous to the research into conceptions of learning, the aim of research on this topic is then to enable academics to develop deep approaches to learning amongst their students.

Much of the research into approaches to learning has been multivariate in nature, making use of now well-established questionnaires, such as the Approaches to Study Inventory (ASI), Inventory of Learning Styles (ILS) and Study Process Questionnaire (SPQ). Students are asked to give their reactions on a scale to a series of statements about learning and studying. The data collected is then analysed making use of techniques such as regression, factor and cluster analysis. Thus, Severiens et al. (2001) report on two longitudinal studies (most research into this topic tends to be cross-sectional in nature) designed to test whether learning strategies change over time, as well as between contexts. They find evidence suggestive of this, but concede the need for further, including qualitative, research.

Meyer and Boulton-Lewis (2003: see also Meyer and Vermunt 2000) have recently drawn together a series of quantitative and qualitative studies focusing on dissonance in student learning. Dissonance may be exhibited in a variety of ways, as between, for example, conceptions of and approaches to learning, or between learning approaches and contexts. They argue that:

> It is clear from the data that dissonance in learning patterns exists in small groups of students in a range of contexts. For some students dissonance appears to be a stable continuing pattern of learning that is not changed by a new learning context whilst for others dissonance may be a temporary phenomenon caused by the challenges in a new environment. Generally, students with dissonant patterns of learning do not succeed as well as other students in their studies. (Meyer and Boulton-Lewis 2003: 3–4)

The book by Prosser and Trigwell (1999), discussed later in this chapter as Case Study 4.3, is a good example of a summation of the different areas for research identified under this sub-theme. While they make use of a range of qualitative and quantitative techniques for data collection and analysis, Prosser and Trigwell are clear in seeing their research as having practical objectives and applications. Thus, they conclude by setting out four principles for university teachers:

1. *Teachers need to become aware of the way they conceive of learning and teaching within the subjects they are teaching.*
2. *Teachers need to examine carefully the context in which they are teaching and to become aware of how that context relates to or affects the way they teach.*
3. *Teachers need to be aware of and seek to understand the way their students perceive the learning and teaching situation.*

4. *Teachers need to be continually revising, adjusting and developing their teaching in the light of this developing awareness.* (p. 173)

Clearly, then, there is a strong connection between the more theorized research into teaching and learning in higher education, and the more practically oriented, 'how to' expositions made widely available to university and college lecturers.

Different kinds of students

While much research into student learning focuses on young under-graduate students, and can seem at times to treat them as if they were a largely homogeneous group, other researchers have consciously set out to investigate whether different kinds or groups of students approach learning in different ways. A similar strategy can be seen in research into the student experience (see Chapter 6).

Amongst the different kinds of students examined are those of different gender (e.g. Severiens and Ten Dam 1998), age (e.g. Macpherson 2002) and nationality (e.g. McNamara and Harris 1997; Ramburuth and McCormick 2001), and those studying at-a-distance instead of face-to-face (e.g. Lawless and Richardson 2002; Richardson 2000). The article by Kember (2000), examined later in this chapter as Case Study 4.1, is an example of this sub-theme for research. Three of these studies will be summarized as examples.

Severiens and Ten Dam (1998), in exploring the relations between gender and learning, seek to test and compare Vermunt's (1996) ideas about students' learning conceptions with Baxter Magolda's (1992) think-ing on ways of women's knowing and reasoning. While they could find links at a conceptual level between these two theories, their empirical study, using interviews and questionnaires, did not confirm these relations.

Macpherson (2002) administered a survey to 193 undergraduates at one Australian university, with the intent of investigating the relations between problem-solving ability, cognitive maturity, age, gender, year of study and previous qualifications. While conceding the limitations of her study, she concluded that:

> . . . *when speaking of cognitive maturity, Age is the primary determinant; when speaking of problem-solving ability, Highest Academic Qualification is the most important correlate.* (p. 20)

Ramburuth and McCormick (2001) set out to compare the learning style preferences and approaches to learning of international students from Asian backgrounds studying in Australia with Australian students. They administered the SPQ and the Perceptual Learning Style Preference Questionnaire to samples of both groups at one university. They came to mixed conclusions (compare Kember 2000):

The results of this study suggest that, in their overall approaches to learning, the Asian international students may not be very different from Australian students. The evidence refutes, to some extent, anecdotal and stereotypical claims in the literature suggesting that international students from Asian backgrounds employ more surface approaches to learning than Australian students. At the same time, there is no support for the proposition . . . that Asian students are generally higher in their deep approach to learning when compared to Australian students. However, significant differences between the Australian and international students on several learning constructs investigated in the study, serve to draw attention to the nature of learning diversity present in Australian tertiary classrooms. (p. 346)

These findings would support the arguments of Prosser and Trigwell (1999), discussed in the previous sub-section, on the need for academics to be aware of the perceptions of and approaches to learning adopted by their students.

Teaching in higher education

The last two sub-themes to be discussed in this chapter, research into teaching in higher education and the 'how to' genre, are closely connected. Indeed, the two literatures could be said to merge into each other, with some researchers and authors contributing to both and some books offering elements of each (e.g. Biggs 1999, 2003; Brookfield and Preskill 1999; Cowan 1998; Evans and Abbott 1998; Knight 2002a; Rowland 2000). Here, however, we will discuss some of the more explicitly research-based studies of the teaching role, before moving on to examine examples of the more pragmatic guidance literature. The former can be seen as either the obverse or the companion of the research into student learning discussed earlier in this chapter, since developing or improving learning may be seen as indelibly linked to developing or improving the teaching that feeds into it.

The literature within this sub-theme typically focuses upon the use of particular teaching techniques, and the evaluation of their success in given settings (there is an, understandable if regrettable, absence of research and writing about teaching innovations or interventions that didn't work). As in the previous sub-section, I will focus on three examples. While these operate at different levels, each involves personal and reflective elements.

Macdonald (2001) evaluates the growth and application of the teaching community model in Australian universities. This model describes 'the situation where a group of staff responsible for teaching a subject or programme meet on a regular basis to discuss student learning and good teaching' (p. 157: compare the discussion of writing groups in Chapter 10).

He identifies – from interviews with some of the academics involved and observation of meetings – a range of, generally positive, outcomes, and links teaching communities to notions of quality management (see Chapter 7). He concludes that 'the Teaching Communities are a learning environment, in which academic staff are learning about good teaching principles and learning how to engage their students in a meaningful educational experience' (p. 164).

Penrose (1999) has produced what is, to me, a particularly stimulating article, in that it demonstrates how fruitful a small-scale and personal study can be. She uses and analyses one of her own lectures to illustrate how personal research experiences can be used to teach the significance of socially constructed categories such as race, gender, sexuality and disability:

> . . . the key concern is to give students an opportunity to think about the signifi-
> cance of categories to understandings of the world in which they live. Further,
> instead of simply telling them that the categories are socially constructed it is
> important for them to explore this construction process, and its consequences, for
> themselves. Finally, by offering them the opportunity to think creatively about
> other ways of conceptualising and applying both categories in general as well
> as specific categories, students can be actively pushed beyond the relatively
> simple act of critical deconstruction towards the more difficult task of construct-
> ive reconceptualisation. (p. 238)

Walker (2001) and her contributors offer an account of a project similar to that analysed by Macdonald. They provide 'the story of a higher educa-tion project', in which six academics 'set out to establish a community . . . concerned to work collaboratively in researching their own teaching, and in supporting and challenging each other through a shared critical dialogue about higher education' (pp. ix–x). Key terms in their exposition are action research, critical professionalism, communities of practice, complexity and multiple voices. The particular topics addressed include mentoring, critical thinking, performance measurement and project work. Walker categorizes the group as struggling 'to practise a professionalism which seeks to develop different forms of agreement-making, through dialogue and action with each other and with students, regarding the ends and purposes of learning in the university'. Revealingly, she notes that this 'is at odds with managerialism and a performance culture characterized by aims, objectives and efficiency gains' (pp. 191–2).

The 'how to' genre

In this chapter, unlike the others in this part of the book, the 'how to' genre – that is, the literature that sets out to provide practical guidance and support on different academic roles and tasks – has been identified as a specific sub-theme for discussion. This is not to say that this genre is unimportant for the other themes or issues identified, as it is discussed in passing in a number of other chapters, but to recognize its particular significance within this theme (see Table 3.3).

Two things about the 'how to' genre should be stressed at this point. First, it would be wrong to dismiss it as in some way as of lesser value than the research-based literature on higher education. I would say this, of course, as I have myself contributed to the 'how to' genre (Blaxter et al. 1998c, 2001). The point is, however, that planning and writing 'how to' texts may be just as demanding as carrying out and writing up empirical research, while, if sales figures are anything to go by, the former attract a much wider readership and usage.

Second, it would be false to dismiss the 'how to' genre as not research-based. On the contrary, it makes extensive use of personal experience, observation and reflection, of case studies of innovations in practice, and of other published research studies. So this is a literature as worthy of study as any, and has its own stories to tell about contemporary higher education. The focus in the remainder of this sub-section will be on 'how to' books, in which the genre reaches its fullest flowering, though there are also a number of professional or practitioner journals – such as *The New Academic* and *Perspectives* – which publish material of this kind.

'How to' books on teaching and learning are available in substantial numbers (e.g. Armitage et al. 1999; Cannon and Newble 2000; Chalmers and Fuller 1996; Cox 1994; Cox and Heames 1999; Dawn et al. 2000; Fry et al. 1999; Nicholls 2002; Race 1998, 1999; Ramsden 1992). This literature has grown in response to the growth of higher education, the increased attention being devoted to teaching quality, and the widespread establishment of initial and continuing teacher training courses for academics. While most training courses are generic in nature, some focus on more specific themes, including dealing with large classes, preparing teaching materials and supporting older students. Two examples of this literature will now be considered in a little more detail.

First, Cox (1994), in a book which evolved from staff development provision at Aston University, 'aims to provide university teachers with practical suggestions for efficient and effective teaching and assessment of students and evaluation of teaching quality' (p. 9). He starts from the premise that 'University teachers receive little or no training in teaching' (p. 10), and seeks to remedy that deficiency through a series of chapters organized in terms of the plan/prepare/present/assess/evaluate stages through which teaching is portrayed as typically progressing. The text is carefully structured, and complemented by plentiful lists and diagrams.

Second, Nicholls (2002), in a more recent book, starts from a recognition of the changing higher education climate: 'The increasing demands for teaching excellence in higher education have led to new academics needing induction into what it is to teach and how students learn' (p. 1). Her book is specifically designed to address the six basic generic issues identified by the United Kingdom's Institute for Learning and Teaching: planning and preparation; conducting teaching and learning sessions; assessment and evaluation; reviewing and improving teaching; academic administration, management and leadership; continual professional development. The style is more developed than in the book by Cox, offering many more lists and diagrams, as well as boxed 'points for consideration' and references to the research literature.

Case studies

The three case studies considered in this chapter comprise:

- a multivariate analysis of the learning experiences of Asian students in the light of the predominantly Western research literature on teaching and learning in higher education;
- a conceptual examination of how students learn, and how learning experiences may be designed to make effective use of available learning technologies; and
- a multivariate analysis of students' views of learning, the learning environment and their approaches to learning.

Case Study 4.1

David Kember (2000) Misconceptions about the Learning Approaches, Motivation and Study Practices of Asian Students. *Higher Education*, 40, 99–121.

Themes and Issues

In this article, David Kember sets out to dispel a series of myths about Asian higher education students:

> When I first went to Hong Kong, over twelve years ago, I talked to many people about the students. I was given a list of characteristics with a high level of consensus. I was informed that the students:

> Rely on rote-learning
> Are passive
> Resist teaching innovations
> Are largely extrinsically motivated, which is usually regarded negatively
> Have high levels of achievement motivation
> Are high achievers
> Are good at project work
> Are willing to invest in education (p. 99)

As Kember points out, these perceptions were somewhat contradictory:

The students were portrayed as rote learners, which is associated with poor academic outcomes in Western universities. A preference for passive over active learning methods also tends to be associated with low level outcomes. Yet the students were recognised as high academic achievers by my new colleagues in Hong Kong. (p. 100)

Kember's concern, which forms the key theme of the article, is to challenge these perceptions, using research to explore the actual learning and studying characteristics of Asian students.

Methods and Methodologies

For the purposes of the analysis reported in Chapter 2, I categorized this article as adopting a multivariate methodological approach. While the studies described use a variety of methods, most commonly questionnaires and interviews, multivariate techniques dominate. The article might also be said to adopt a comparative perspective, in that its key focus is on comparing the learning experiences of Asian students with the predominantly Western literature on teaching and learning in higher education. Kember himself labels his methodological approach as action research (see Chapter 12), and the article makes use of his experience of working on 90 action research projects in his own and other Hong Kong universities.

Particular use is made of the Study Process Questionnaire (SPQ) to survey students' use of deep, surface and achieving approaches to studying. Students' scores on the SPQ's scales are compared with their year of study and the relative age of their courses. The responses of staff and students to innovative methods of teaching are also reported, as are students' opinions – revealed through interviews – on the career preparation and relevance of their courses.

Level

I have categorized this article as focusing on the institutional level, in that all of the research projects referred to were concerned with exploring and/or improving the learning experiences of students within specific universities in Hong Kong.

Analytical/Theoretical Framework

Two related areas of theory are used to provide a framework for the article and its argument. One has to do with different forms of motivation, variously categorized as achieving, career, intrinsic and collective. The other has to do with approaches to learning and teaching, in particular the distinction that has been made between surface and deep approaches to learning, as well as what have been called strategic or achieving approaches. Both of these constitute major areas for research into teaching and learning in higher education.

Related Literatures

The key literature within which Kember locates his research is that on approaches to learning and teaching, an area to which both multivariate and phenomenographical methods have been extensively applied (e.g. Biggs 1999; McLean 2001; Marton et al. 1997; Prosser and Trigwell 1999; Ramsden 1992; Richardson 2000; Severiens et al. 2001). To date, however, there have been only a few other studies which have sought to explore differences between students from different cultural backgrounds (e.g. Ramburuth and McCormick 2001).

There is another related literature, however, having to do with the experience and treatment of overseas or international students in higher education; that is, students studying outside their native country (e.g. Campbell 2000; Grey 2002; Kinnell 1990; Littlemore 2001; McNamara and Harris 1997). While Kember makes no explicit reference to this literature – his focus is, after all, on Hong Kong students studying in Hong Kong – one of the references which he gives (Richardson 1994) does provide a link.

Argument and Conclusions

Kember argues that matters are rather more complex than the simplistic perceptions with which he begins his article would suggest. Asian students may appear as relatively passive and make much use of memorization as an aid to learning, but that has much to do with the ways in which they have been taught at school, and with underlying socio-cultural patterns of behaviour. Memorization may be used as a means to developing understanding, leading to deep learning, rather than the surface forms of learning it tends to imply with Western students. Similarly, Asian students are not simply motivated by the desire to achieve good marks and qualifications in order to get better jobs, but may combine this with both intrinisic motivation and more collective behaviours.

One of the key messages of the article has to do with the close relationship between the higher education curriculum, teaching and learning. Courses may be taught or delivered in different ways, but time needs to be allowed for the students on these courses – whether Asian or otherwise – to adapt to changed ways of learning in order for them to get the greatest benefit. As Kember himself concludes:

> It is clear that common mis-perceptions of the learning approaches and preferences of Asian students have resulted in the adoption of didactic teaching methods and assessment and examinations which test recall. If the academics concerned realise that Asian students are capable of more active forms of learning and benefit from curricula which demand higher forms of learning, the performance could be better still. (p. 117)

Case Study 4.2

Diana Laurillard (2002) *Rethinking University Teaching: a conversational framework for the effective use of learning technologies.* London, RoutledgeFalmer, second edition.

Themes and Issues

The argument of this book is that effective use can only be made of learning technologies if we understand how students learn. The book is, therefore, organized in three parts, examining successively how students learn, what learning technologies have to offer, and how learning experiences may be designed to make effective use of available technologies. The focus of this case study is on the second part of the book, in which Laurillard offers an analysis of the media available for learning and teaching.

Methods and Methodologies

The part or aspect of the book on which I am focusing can be categorized as taking a conceptual approach to the examination of learning technologies.

Level

This book is pitched at the system level of analysis.

Analytical/Theoretical Framework

Laurillard develops her own framework for analysis. She first identifies a four-fold pedagogical classification of educational media – discursive, adaptive, interactive and reflective. These are applied in what she terms a 'conversational framework' to illustrate the activities needed to complete the learning process. Laurillard then recognizes five categories of educational media: narrative, interactive, communicative, adaptive and productive. These are then related to different kinds of learning technologies and learning experiences.

Related Literatures

There are evidently two main literatures within which this discussion may be placed: that focusing on teaching and learning (e.g. Biggs 1999; Chalmers and Fuller 1996; Marton et al. 1997; Prosser and Trigwell 1999), and that examining different learning technologies (e.g. Hawkridge 1993; Mason 1994, Richardson 2000). Laurillard makes effective use of both.

Argument and Conclusions

Having established her analytical framework, Laurillard devotes one chapter to the discussion of each of her categories:

- In considering narrative (linear presentational) media, the focus is on lectures, print, audiovision, television, video and DVDs.

- Interactive media ('essentially linear media delivered in an open, user-controlled environment' (p. 107)) include hypermedia, web resources and interactive television.
- Adaptive media ('computer-based media capable of changing their state in response to the user's actions' (p. 126)) include simulations, virtual environments, tutorial programs and simulations, and educational games.
- Communicative media (which have 'the specific task of bringing people together to discuss' (p. 145)) include computer-mediated conferencing, digital document discussion environments, audioconferencing, videoconferencing and student collaboration.
- Productive media (which 'enable students to produce their own contributions' (p. 161)) include microworlds, productive tools and modelling environments.

In each chapter, checklists are provided of the characteristics of the specific educational media under discussion, and examples are given of how they might be applied within conversational frameworks of the learning process.

Having thus 'covered most of the technological media likely to be used in the service of education' (p. 173), Laurillard concludes that:

> none of the current learning media covers the full iteration between reflective and adaptive discussion and interaction in the way that a teacher in a practical session could. However, they cover the majority of learning activities, and in combination, they cover all the essential activities in the learning process, as defined by the Conversational Framework. (p. 173)

She then proceeds to discuss the practical business of how to use different educational media for effective teaching and learning.

Case Study 4.3

Michael Prosser and Keith Trigwell (1999) *Understanding Learning and Teaching: the experience in higher education*. Buckingham, Open University Press.

Themes and Issues

The key question which Prosser and Trigwell set out to address in this book is 'how can university teachers improve the quality of student learning?' To do this they make extensive use of research data and analysis they have gathered in studying learning and teaching in universities.

Methods and Methodologies

The studies which the authors make use of in this book adopted a range of methods and methodologies, including interviews, multivariate forms of analysis, phenomenography and conceptual analyses. Of these, I would say that the multivariate approach is most common, as it is in the chapter I will focus on here, which examines students' perceptions of their learning situation.

Level

This book is focused at the system level.

Analytical/Theoretical Framework

The authors' basic framework is provided by the research on learning approaches:

> the research describes students as approaching their learning in two qualitatively different ways. In one approach (a deep approach) students aim to understand ideas and seek meanings. They have an intrinsic interest in the task and an expectation of enjoyment in carrying it out ... In the other (surface) approach, students see tasks as external impositions and they have the intention to cope with these requirements. They are instrumentally or pragmatically motivated and seek to meet the demands of the task with minimum effort. (p. 3)

Having established this framework, the authors proceed to 'explore the relations between students' conceptions of learning, their perceptions of the learning environment, their approaches to learning and learning outcomes in higher education' (p. 5). Their argument is that a knowledge of these relations can help improve students' learning.

Related Literatures

As well as their own research, Prosser and Trigwell make extensive use of the now substantial literature on understanding learning and teaching in higher education (e.g. Biggs 1999; Marton et al. 1997; Ramsden 1992).

Argument and Conclusions

In their chapter on 'students' perceptions of their learning situation', the authors start by discussing existing qualitative research on this topic. They then move on to quantitative studies, which dominate the chapter (and loom large throughout the book). Several examples of published research are discussed, each making use of questionnaires and/or inventories to measure and then categorize students' perceptions:

- A study by Ramsden et al. (1997) of the relationship between different forms of academic leadership, learning and teaching. Over 8000 students in 51 subjects were surveyed using versions of two established questionnaires: the Course Experience Questionnaire and the Study Process Questionnaire. Two multivariate techniques – factor analysis and cluster analysis – were used to explore the relationships between students' perceptions of their learning environment and their approaches to study.
- In a study of student learning in first year physics classes, the authors (Prosser et al. 1996, 1997) administered the same two questionnaires at the beginning and end of the first term (getting 144 responses in total). Cluster analysis was used to examine the relations between students' prior conceptual understanding, approaches to study, perceptions of the learning environment and conceptual understanding at the end of the term. This led to the identification of four different groups of students.

- In a third study, Crawford et al. (1998) administered the Study Process Questionnaire and three other subject-specific questionnaires (approaches to studying, perceptions of studying, conceptions of the subject) to 274 first year mathematics students. Cluster analysis was again used to identify different groups of students, and to explore the relationships between the issues researched.

The authors conclude that:

> within the same class, there is a substantial variation in the way students perceive the quality of teaching, clarity and meaning of the goals, the amount of work required, the nature of assessments, etc . . . these perceptions are systematically related to the approaches to learning adopted by the students . . . Thus university teachers, in designing learning and teaching contexts and in engaging in their teaching, need to be continually aware that each student is situated differently within that context and will perceive his or her situation differently. (pp. 81–2)

Ideas for further research

The analysis presented in this chapter indicates several potential directions for further research into teaching and learning in higher education:

- analyses of teaching or learning initiatives that didn't work, and of why;
- research into the usefulness of the 'how to' literature on teaching and learning to academics;
- studies of the learning approaches adopted by older or mature students;
- research into the changing conceptions of learning and teaching held by academics during their careers;
- more qualitative research into changing conceptions of learning and teaching, as held by both academics and students; and
- evaluations, over time, of the effectiveness of academic development programmes focusing on teaching and learning.

This listing is not meant to delimit the possibilities, however, and you may well think of other ideas for further research (including the replication of existing pieces of research in different settings).

5

Researching course design

Introduction

The analysis presented in Part I of this book demonstrated that, along with system policy (see Chapter 8), course design is one of the two most popular, of the eight themes identified, for research into higher education. This popularity is evident in the number of academic journals that chiefly focus, though not exclusively, on this theme. These include *Active Learning in Higher Education, Assessment and Evaluation in Higher Education, Studies in Higher Education* and *Teaching in Higher Education,* as well as the subject-specific *Journal of Geography in Higher Education* (see Tables 2.3 and 2.10).

The obvious reason for this popularity is the centrality of course design to the higher education experience: how we plan, deliver and assess our provision impacts immediately on one of our main 'customers', our students. Course design issues also lend themselves to small-scale research by 'insider' researchers: that is, by the academics running the courses themselves. The short article or report, which describes and evaluates the effectiveness of an innovation in the design of a particular course, is one of the standards of the higher education literature.

Key questions driving contemporary research into course design issues include:

- What are the fairest or most effective ways of assessing student performance?
- How can students be encouraged to develop the kinds of transferable skills that employers say they look for in graduates?
- How may developing information and communication technologies be used to extend and improve the higher education experience?
- Which learning techniques should we use in putting together our courses?

- What does, and should, the higher education curriculum look like?
- What particular considerations should we bear in mind in designing postgraduate courses?

This chapter, then, reviews how higher education researchers have explored these and related questions, and what conclusions they have come to.

Research into course design

For the purposes of this discussion, contemporary research into course design will be considered under five sub-themes:

- the higher education curriculum;
- technologies for learning;
- student writing;
- assessment;
- postgraduate course design.

Each of these sub-themes will now be exemplified and analysed in turn.

The higher education curriculum

Research and writing on the higher education curriculum is characterized by a relatively small number of books and articles that take a general overview, and a large number that focus on specific approaches to or elements of the curriculum and course design.

The article by Barnett et al. (2001), reviewed as Case Study 5.1 later in this chapter, which relates to a study of curriculum organization and change in United Kingdom universities, is an example of the first style of research and writing. Possibly the most thorough overview of this area for research, though now inevitably a little dated, was that carried out over a decade ago by Squires (1987, 1990). The latter book provides a description of what the university undergraduate curriculum looked like at the time in the United Kingdom, and then analyses this in terms of theories of knowledge, culture and student development. Squires' basic argument was that 'Unless we understand what it is we are producing, for whom and in what context, we are unlikely to be able to manage it effectively' (Squires 1990: 162).

That management challenge is also reflected in other general writing on this topic (e.g. Bocock and Watson 1994). Others take a more nuts-and-bolts approach to the issues associated with course design. Thus, Toohey (1999) offers a general guide to course design, informed by existing research and writing and her own experience. She emphasizes the pressures towards change in the higher education curriculum, and the importance of encouraging deep rather than surface learning (see also the discussion in Chapter 4). As well as providing an overview of the course design process, she gives guidance on the role of values, goals, content, structure, flexibility, units of study, teaching strategies and assessment.

Hannan and Silver (2000) take a more directly research-based approach, reporting on an interview-based study in 15 British universities, and examining the processes of innovation in the curriculum. They looked at individual, institutional and national policy-driven innovations, and related their progress to institutional and departmental cultures.

As indicated at the beginning of this sub-section, however, studies that focus on particular aspects of, or approaches to, the curriculum and course design are far more common. This research and writing is so diverse as to almost defy categorization. The following alphabetical listing is an indicative attempt, though it must be stressed that there are many linkages and overlaps between the headings identified (and between their application in higher education and cognate fields, notably adult education and training: see Tight 2002). One characteristic of developing fields of study and practice is the way in which advocates repeatedly attach their own, and thus different, labels to what are essentially the same processes. Another key characteristic to note is the existence in this area of a large 'how to' literature (see Chapter 4) to complement the more research-based writing.

- Accreditation and the modular curriculum (e.g. Allen and Layer 1995; Betts and Smith 1998; Jenkins and Walker 1994; Watson et al. 1989). Much of the emphasis here has been on describing and supporting contemporary moves towards credit-based and modular curricula, but there have also been some questioning and critical accounts of these policies. For example, Morris (2000) carried out an interview-based study of business schools in ten English universities, concluding that:

  > . . . the results . . . would appear to indicate that none of the claimed advantages of modularisation and semesterisation had been fully realised in the case study institutions, and, while the majority of disadvantages had not appeared either, the increased costs associated with semesterisation outweighed any benefits associated with this change. (p. 257)

- Competency-based approaches (e.g. Edwards and Knight 1995; Winter and Maisch 1996). Again, the focus of much writing on this topic has been towards explaining and justifying policy shifts directed at making the curriculum more vocationally explicit, though there are also rather more critical accounts available (e.g. Lum 1999, Usher and Edwards 1994).

- Experiential and independent learning (e.g. Boud et al. 1993; Boud and Miller 1996; Evans 2000; Tait and Knight 1996). These, and related strategies like action learning and self-directed learning, have to do with individualizing the curriculum and transferring responsibility for learning from lecturer to student. There is a limited critical literature (e.g. Hughes 1999).
- Flexible curricula (e.g. Hudson et al. 1997; Thomas 1995; Wade et al. 1994). As in the case of experiential learning and modularization, which can be seen as examples of more flexible curricula, the intention is to simultaneously offer more choice to the learner while reducing, or at least not adding to, lecturers' workloads. Once again, there is a small evaluative or critical literature (e.g. Nicoll 1997).
- The use of learning contracts, learning journals and records of achievement (e.g. Assiter and Shaw 1993; Cook 2000; Moon 1999a; Stephenson and Laycock 1993), again, both to allow more flexibility and to ensure greater individual student engagement and responsibility. Cook provides a very interesting account of the effectiveness of student journal writing as part of a radical 'border' pedagogical strategy for delivering a course on multicultural historical geography.
- Peer tutoring (e.g. Falchikov 2001; Goodlad 1998), a technique for involving students directly in the teaching process.
- Portfolio development (e.g. Bullard and McLean 2000; Klenowski 2002), an increasingly popular means, not least in academic staff development (see Chapter 10), for demonstrating achievement of assessment requirements.
- Problem-based learning (e.g. Boud and Feletti 1997; Fenwick 2002; Savin-Baden 2000; Schwartz et al. 2000), a popular curricular approach for educating professionals. Nevertheless, Savin-Baden argues that 'the potential and influence of problem-based learning is yet to be realised in the context of higher education' (p. 8) because 'knowledge generation in the contexts of students' lives rarely receives acknowledgement in the academe' (p. 148).
- Professional curricula (e.g. Boud and Solomon 2001; Bourner et al. 2000; Cree and Macaulay 2000; Taylor 1997). Taylor's book is based in part on a three-year longitudinal study of students taking a social work education course and then going into practice, using techniques of action research, participant observation and illuminative evaluation. She sees the purpose of such courses as being about the facilitation of independent and interdependent learning as preparation for professional practice.
- The role of reflection (e.g. Boud and Walker 1998; Brockbank and McGill 1998; Moon 1999b; Stewart and Richardson 2000). In some areas of the higher education curriculum, including health care and social work, this is intentionally developed as part of good professional

practice, while in others it may simply be encouraged (e.g. through the use of learning journals). Stewart and Richardson report on a study of a health care programme which sought to assess students' reflective practice, making use of staff interviews and student focus groups. They concluded:

> . . . in order to promote reflection for practice within the students' learning experience, we should move away from assessment by faculty and focus on the process of reflection in trying to engender reflective skills in our students . . . The formal assessment of reflection can then reside within clinical scenarios where the application of the skills of reflection alongside clinical reasoning skills is necessary to complete the assignment. (p. 379)

- Skills development in the curriculum (e.g. Assiter 1995; Bennett et al. 2000; Fallows and Steven 2000), where the purpose of higher education is seen as being more about developing transferable generic skills in students rather than imparting disciplinary knowledge. Bennett et al. report on an interview-based study of samples of academics, students, graduates and employers in the United Kingdom. They arrive at some devastating conclusions:

> The discourse on generic skills, and all its variants, is confused, confusing and under-conceptualised . . . Allied to the above is evidence of the lack of a common language of skills between higher education and employers . . . Improving the nature and quality of discourse, of training and of institutional policy making are all essential but all require an ingredient that, to date, has been sadly lacking – the utilisation of a defensible theory of learning. (pp. 175, 177)

Within all of these related sub-fields there remain plentiful opportunities for further small- or large-scale research projects.

Technologies for learning

Interest in the application of information and communication technologies to higher education has mushroomed in recent years. This interest is partly a consequence of the rapid development of these technologies themselves, and partly because they have come to be regarded as a major element of the solution to the problem of how to deliver mass higher education effectively and at an affordable price. There is a huge literature on learning technologies – evidenced in the existence of specialist journals such as *Open Learning, Distance Education* and *Innovations in Education and Teaching International* – a good proportion of it focusing on levels of education other than higher education.

Like the higher education literature, the distance education literature also contains many examples of both small-scale evaluative case studies (the journal *Innovations in Education and Teaching International*, in particular, seems to specialize in these) and largely descriptive reviews of system policy (e.g. Harry 1999). There is also a strong 'how to' component (e.g. Lockwood 1994). In addition, and largely because the earlier versions of information and communication technologies, correspondence and distance education, were developed in separate, specialist institutions outside the educational mainstream (e.g. the Open University in the United Kingdom), there is a proselytizing element as well (e.g. Daniel 1996; Freeman et al. 2000).

Most recently, however, the distinctions between distance and conventional forms of education have been breaking down as new learning technologies have been applied in all kinds of institutions. Thus, in a review of developments in distance education over the last 30 years, Rumble (2001) identifies five linked trends:

Firstly, and technologically, the period opened with the establishment of one of the most successful of the multi-media based distance education systems, the UK Open University, but ends with the rush towards online education. This technological change underpins a second change, a pedagogical shift within distance education from a transmission model of education towards a constructivist model exploiting computer-mediated communication . . . The third change has been the growing acceptance of distance education, and with this, its expansion. Linked to this is the fourth change – the change in the way distance education is perceived. It has moved from low status to acceptance, with increased confidence as its methods are adopted across education as a whole. Finally, distance education can be seen to be evolving from an essentially modernist form of education into a post-modernist phenomenon with a focus on the student as consumer, on flexibility and global reach. (p. 31)

Much of the contemporary research literature on learning technologies in higher education is concerned with the application and effectiveness of online, computer-mediated or distributed learning instead of and/or alongside more conventional forms of instruction (e.g. Dysthe 2002; Lea and Nicoll 2002; Lockwood and Gooley 2001; Sunderland 2002; Thorpe 2002). It should be noted, of course, as with many developing fields of practice, that there is a wealth of overlapping and confusing terminology in this area. Three examples of this literature will now be considered.

Williams (2002) provides a literature review of this area of research and writing, and concludes by identifying the key issues and challenges to be faced in the development of online learning:

. . . the three main issues to consider when designing and implementing electronic courses are those of pedagogy, participation and access. Courses need to be redesigned to be interactive, and conferencing and on-line tasks should be incorporated in order to take advantage of the pedagogical benefits

offered by Internet technologies . . . decisions need to be made in terms of whether or not to make participation in the electronic learning environment an essential part of the course . . . the issue of access must be considered and students must be provided with adequate computer facilities, or ownership of the necessary technology should be made a prerequisite for entry to the course . . . With the right kind of training and support, successful electronic learning environments can improve the learning experience, and students tend to be enthusiastic about using the new technologies. (pp. 270–1)

Cornford and Pollock (2003) report on a four-year ethnographic research project, which examined how four English universities were going about putting themselves online. They focus on the work involved in constructing online courses and their relation to the physical campus, critique the notion of the university as an informational institution and the issue of standardization, and examine the relationship between online universities and other organizations. They come to an interesting conclusion:

. . . the process of putting the university online results in the online university. But . . . things are more subtle than this. The important (and desirable) outcome of the process is a new kind of university. It is not, however, one that is distinguished from its former self in terms of technologies, structures or processes, but rather it differs in terms of its degree of self-knowledge. (p. 112)

Laurillard (2002: aspects of this book are discussed as Case Study 4.2 in the previous chapter) offers what she terms a 'conversational framework for the effective use of learning technologies', which she applies to the analysis of teaching and learning as a whole. She argues that effective use of learning technologies can only be made if we understand how students learn. With the latter knowledge, it is then feasible to review the available educational media, and reach reasoned decisions on which to use, in which combinations, to promote desired learning and activities. This is a much more measured conclusion than the apparently simple solutions offered by many promoters of the use of new information and communication technologies for learning.

Student writing

By comparison with the research and literature on learning technologies, that concerned with student writing is smaller and more tightly focused. The article by Scott (2000), examined as Case Study 5.3 later in this chapter, is an example of this literature. In focusing on just one essay written by just one student, it shows how such research be both very tightly focused but also engaging and useful. The literature on student writing may, of course, be usefully linked to that on academic writing (discussed in Chapter 10).

Lea and Street (1998: see also Lea and Stierer 2000) report on a study of student writing, which adopted an ethnographic approach, and involved in-depth interviews with samples of staff and students in two English universities. They approach their analysis from the perspective of academic literacies, which they argue is preferable to the alternative perspectives of study skills or academic socialization:

> *This approach sees literacies as social practices . . . It views student writing and learning as issues at the level of epistemology and identities rather than skill or socialisation . . . It sees the literacy demands of the curriculum as involving a variety of communicative practices, including genres, fields and disciplines. From the student point of view a dominant feature of academic literacy practices is the requirement to switch practices between one setting and another, to deploy a repertoire of linguistic practices appropriate to each setting, and to handle the social meanings and identities that each evokes.* (Lea and Street 1998: 159)

Much of this literature focuses on how students write and the problems that they face in doing so. Thus, Campbell et al. (1998) interviewed 46 students on a BEd course to explore how they conceptualized and constructed their essays. They used the SOLO (structure of observed learning outcomes) taxonomy, which grades outcomes in terms of five levels of response, to analyse their essays. They found major differences between students and evidence for a developmental process in underlying conceptualizations of the essay writing process, and use this to argue for greater support for students to help them to better understand what is being sought.

Torrance et al. (2000) employed questionnaires to examine undergraduate essay writing strategies, administering them to both cross-sectional and longitudinal samples on a psychology degree course. They identified four different writing behaviours – minimal drafting, outline and develop, detailed planning and think-then-do strategies – but found no evidence of changes in strategies over time.

Lillis and Turner (2001) apply the discourse of transparency and a cultural-historical perspective to examine student essays and tutors' comments on them (compare the approach adopted by Scott (2000) in Case Study 5.3). They argue that:

> *When student texts match the academics' expectations of what academic writing should be, i.e. when they match the institutionally embedded socio-rhetorical norms of scientific rationality, language remains invisible. When texts don't match such expectations . . . it is the student-writers' language use that becomes the 'problem'.* (Lillis and Turner 2001: 65)

Such taken-for-granted academic conventions, they conclude, need to be challenged.

Read et al. (2001) have a similar agenda, but base their research on interviews with final year undergraduates in four universities. They focus on the power relationship between academics and students, and the difficulties that students face in developing and presenting their voice. They conclude that:

> ... *much needs to be done for students, both in enabling them to understand the 'rules of the game' in essay writing and for them to feel that they are able to present their own 'voice' in a way that facilitates the process of learning and understanding ... we must find ways for students to feel assured that their opinions or viewpoints will be fairly assessed despite their divergence from the views of their markers.* (p. 398)

Assessment

Writing on assessment, like writing on course design as a whole, is split between that which is clearly research-based and that which adopts a descriptive and/or 'how to' approach. The latter specializes in summarizing contemporary good practice and in offering guidance to academics on what forms of assessment to use when (e.g. Brown et al. 1997; Brown and Glasner 1999; Brown and Knight 1994; Cox et al. 1998; Freeman and Lewis 1998; Heywood 2000; Knight 1999; Morgan and O'Reilly 1999). The focus in this sub-section will be on the former. While we will be examining assessment here from the perspective of the academic and their institution, it may also be viewed from the perspective of the student and their experience (see the discussion in Chapter 6, particularly of the article by Norton et al. (2001) in Case Study 6.2).

The research-based literature on assessment in higher education appears to adopt one of two main directions. That is, either it argues that contemporary assessment practices are problematic, and perhaps begins to suggest what might be done about this, or it (following up the 'how to' literature) explores the impacts of utilizing alternative forms of assessment.

Two small-scale studies will be used to illustrate the latter approach. Pope (2001) reports on the use of peer rating for formative assessment on a master's course in an Australian university. Relating his findings to the theory of consumption values, he argues that the innovation led to improved student motivation and learning, but increased stress. Cook (2001) explored the consequences of changing the assessment practice on a large economics course, such that an assignment and mid-semester examination were no longer compulsory, and students could choose between four alternative assessment packages. She reviews the choices the students made and queries whether it had much of an impact on their grades, but concludes that the added flexibility was well received and (unlike the previous example) reduced student stress.

Research which problematizes assessment seems to be increasingly common. Thus, Leach et al. (2001) critique the existing hegemony in assessment practices, and argue the need to take on board students' perceptions. Holroyd (2000) argues that improving assessment practices is part of the growing professionalization of academics. Mutch (2002) suggests the importance of developing assessment strategies at a variety of levels within institutions of higher education. Knight (2002c) argues that our summative assessment practices are in disarray, pointing out a range of problems, including assumptions about knowledge, limits to reliability and stability of judgements, transferability, limitations of criterion referencing, curriculum skew, the misuse and opacity of number, blindness to the learning process and lack of utility. He suggests that we need 'to explore assessment as complex systems of communication, as practices of sense-making and claim-making' (p. 285).

Maclellan (2001) carried out a small-scale project that illustrates some of the problems with assessment practices. She examined how they were differentially experienced by staff and students in one higher education institution, by distributing a questionnaire to samples of both. Issues covered included the purpose of assessment, what was assessed, the timing of assessment, and procedures for marking and reporting. She found inconsistency:

> *Staff declared a commitment to the formative purposes of assessment but engaged in practices that militated against formative assessment being fully realised. Similarly, staff maintained that the full range of learning was frequently assessed yet the dominant mode of assessment was the traditional, academic essay, thereby attenuating the idea that students were engaging in authentic assessment which could enhance their learning . . . Overall the student view of assessment is a depressing one. The students do not exploit assessment to improve their learning and, furthermore, appear to have a very underdeveloped conception of what assessment is.* (p. 317)

Postgraduate course design

While most of the research and writing on course design focuses, implicitly if not always explicitly, on undergraduate provision, there is also a growing body of work examining postgraduate courses. The article by Johnson et al. (2000), considered later in this chapter as Case Study 5.2, is an example of this work. The postgraduate student experience, including the key issue of the supervisory relationship, is considered in more detail in Chapter 6. Here, we will focus on the organization and design of postgraduate courses and research.

It is a curious feature of research on postgraduate courses that little attention has been given to taught master's courses, despite their substantial growth and diversification in recent years (Knight 1997; Taylor 2002). Even general treatments of postgraduate education (e.g. Becher et al. 1994; Burgess 1994), as well as most specialized discussions (such as Johnson et al. 2000), focus exclusively on research degree provision. That focus will inevitably be reflected in the discussion in this subsection. Two particular topics for research will be discussed: the influence of discipline on postgraduate provision and the development of new types of research degree.

Johnson et al. (2000) make clear the influence of varying disciplinary traditions on the ways in which the research student experience is designed and delivered – though, as their discussion suggests, at least in recent history, the use of the term 'design' is perhaps generous. Parry (1998) focuses squarely on this topic, in examining linguistic conventions in doctoral theses in different disciplines; and her research may be seen as linked to that on student writing, discussed earlier in this chapter. She examined 24 doctoral theses, identified as exemplary, from the sciences, humanities and social sciences, analysing them in accordance with the principles of systemic functional linguistics. She found significant differences in terms of overall characteristics, structure of argument, linking ideas, citation and critique conventions, and use of tacit knowledge. She:

> . . . shows how the nature of the knowledge base and the etiquette for communicating knowledge are reflected in patterns of language use . . . students do learn the linguistic rules of the game, even though neither they nor their supervisors seem able to articulate what those rules are. (p. 296)

Smeby (2002) also examines the impact of discipline on postgraduate education, focusing on master's degree students in Norway. His study involved a substantial questionnaire survey, the results from which were subjected to regression analyses, and a more limited sample of structured interviews. The aim was to examine the organization of master's studies, and the extent to which students were linked to academics' research projects:

> The data indicate that organising master's degree students in projects has positive effects on the frequency of supervision, students' collaboration with other students, and the extent to which students finish their study on time. There are, however, important differences between fields of learning that may be related to characteristics of the knowledge structure, the organisation of research and the content of projects in the respective fields. (p. 145)

Research into different kinds of research degree has mainly focused on documenting the rapid expansion of so-called professional doctorates during the last decade. Professional doctorates, modelled on North

American practice, involve a more structured and common programme of learning, and place less emphasis on the individual thesis, than the more conventional PhD. They have become particularly popular in disciplines such as business administration, clinical psychology, education and medicine, and most British universities now offer them (Bourner et al. 2001). There is, however, a great deal of variation between subjects and institutions in what is required for a professional doctorate, and in the extent to which they differ from conventional doctorates. Neither is the situation stable, with further development expected (Green et al. 2001).

Case studies

The three case studies considered in this chapter consist of:

- a conceptual analysis of the higher education curriculum and of curriculum change;
- a critical examination of the relationship between research students and their supervisors; and
- a critical analysis of the notion of 'critical thinking', as manifested by one essay produced by one student.

Case Study 5.1

Ronald Barnett, Gareth Parry and Kelly Coate (2001) Conceptualising Curriculum Change. *Teaching in Higher Education*, 6, 4, 435–49.

Themes and Issues

This article relates to a larger research project, funded by the Economic and Social Research Council (ESRC), which explored changing patterns in the undergraduate curricula.

Methods and Methodologies

This article may be categorized as adopting a conceptual approach to the analysis of course design. It involved interviewing academic staff in five subject areas in six British higher education institutions. While the data collected by that project is used to illustrate the argument of the authors, the focus of the article is primarily on discussing models of the curriculum and of curriculum change.

Level

The article is focused at the national level.

Analytical/Theoretical Framework

The authors make particular reference to the work of the French postmodern theorist, Lyotard, especially his concept of performativity, which stresses the importance of higher education in preparing students for the labour market. They present a curriculum model consisting of three domains – knowledge (subject specialism), action (competences acquired through 'doing') and self (the student's developing educational identity). They then illustrate the different domain emphases apparent in three contrasting knowledge fields: science and technology, arts and humanities, and professional subjects.

Related Literatures

While the authors note the relative absence of recent studies of the higher education curriculum, there are at least three contemporary literatures to which their study may be related. One of these focuses on the variations in practices between different academic disciplines, and is particularly associated with the research of Tony Becher (e.g. Becher 1999; Becher and Trowler 2001; Neumann et al. 2002). A second, to which Barnett himself has made notable contributions, has examined the changing nature of knowledge and knowledge development in higher education (e.g. Barnett 1990, 1994, 1997, 2000; Barnett and Griffin 1997; Delanty 2001; Gibbons et al. 1994; Jacob and Hellstrom 2000; Nowotny et al. 2001). The third takes a more pragmatic approach to the issues of course design (e.g. Toohey 1999).

Argument and Conclusions

Having set up their framework, Barnett and his co-authors then discuss the changes taking place in each of the three curriculum domains. These changes include changing knowledge structures, new topics within knowledge fields, new techniques for studying knowledge fields, the use of new technologies, the greater attention paid to the development of students' skills, the closer relationship with the world of work, and the increased responsibility being placed upon students for their own development. On this basis, they distinguish between different kinds of performativity: epistemological, pedagogical, educational and self-monitoring.

Though their emphasis is on curriculum change, the authors do also note two strong forms of continuity in higher education practices: the importance of lectures within the teaching/learning transaction, and the dominant relationship being between single lecturers and groups of students.

Case Study 5.2

Lesley Johnson, Alison Lee and Bill Green (2000) The PhD and the Autonomous Self: gender, rationality and postgraduate pedagogy. *Studies in Higher Education*, 25, 2, 135–47.

Themes and Issues

This article focuses on what has hitherto been an under-researched and essentially 'secret' area of academic life, but one which is now being subjected to an increasing amount of research: the supervisory relationship between research students and academics. The nature of this relationship varies significantly between disciplines, with research students in the laboratory sciences typically experiencing much more regular, even day-to-day, supervision as part of a research group. This article, however, examines the experience in the humanities and social sciences, where the supervisory relationship is more typically individualized, and research students often pursue a lonely road, perhaps only meeting their supervisor every month or so.

Methods and Methodologies

This article was categorized in the analysis presented in Chapter 2 as adopting a critical perspective to course design. As the authors indicate, it forms part of a larger project exploring the history of PhD practices in Australia, and is based on oral history interviews with both established academics and contemporary supervisors. The article is very carefully written, contextualizing the experiences of selected interviewees, as illustrated through quotations, within existing writing on supervision, changing academic practices and feminist perspectives.

Level

The article focuses at the individual level.

Analytical/Theoretical Framework

The authors stress the contested nature of the concepts of autonomy and independence, which underlie many understandings of the supervisory relationship, and highlight its gendered aspect.

Related Literatures

As suggested, a growing number of recent publications have focused on the research student experience and the supervisory relationship. These can be divided into two kinds – the more analytical (e.g. Bartlett and Mercer 2000; Delamont et al. 2000; Heath 2002; Hunt 2001; Parry 1998; Tinkler and Jackson 2000) and those adopting a 'how to' approach, offering guidance on good practice (e.g. Cryer 1996; Delamont et al. 1997; Murray 2002; Phillips and Pugh 2000; Potter 2002). There are also increasing numbers of studies on postgraduate education – taught as well as research – in general (e.g. Becher et al. 1994; Burgess 1994; Knight 1997; Smeby 2002; Taylor 2002).

Argument and Conclusions

The authors present and analyse a number of alternative models for supervision: an 'always-already' independent model involving benign neglect or tough-mindedness from a typically male supervisor; an 'invisible pedagogy' model, involving more subtle forms of regulation; and possible feminist responses to these.

While only three interviewees are directly referred to in the article, a range of issues is raised regarding the supervisory relationship. The article offers an example of how to make the most of your data.

Case Study 5.3

Mary Scott (2000) Student, Critic and Literary Text: a discussion of 'critical thinking' in a student essay. *Teaching in Higher Education*, 5, 3, 277–88.

Themes and Issues

In this article, Mary Scott provides a detailed analysis of one essay by one student – of English literature – a student she has never met. It is an example of how a small-scale, focused piece of research can nevertheless yield much of interest and use, provided it is harnessed to theory and/or practice, and handled with clarity and reflection.

Methods and Methodologies

This article was categorized in the analysis presented in Chapter 2 as adopting a critical perspective on course design, though it also clearly includes elements of biographical analysis.

Level

The article focuses at the individual level.

Analytical/Theoretical Framework

Scott provides a theoretical framework for her analysis of critical thinking through her use of Bakhtin's concept of dialogic text. Trends in literary criticism are referred to in the text, in particular what is called modern theory, as well as feminist critiques.

Related Literatures

The main higher education literature which offers a context for Scott's analysis is clearly, as she indicates, that focusing on student writing (e.g. Campbell et al. 1998; Cook 2000; Lea and Stierer 2000; Lea and Street 1998; Lillis 2001; Read et al. 2001; Torrance et al. 2000). There is a more practical, 'how to', element of this literature (e.g. Fairbairn and Winch 1996; Thomson 1996). There is also a parallel literature, however, on academic writing (e.g. Grant and Knowles 2000).

Argument and Conclusions

Scott's concern is with the notion of critical thinking, a commonplace expectation in the evaluation of student essays in the humanities and social sciences, yet one that is rarely explained by lecturers with clarity. She explores one student's understanding of critical thinking through an examination of one of her essays. She notes that the student's tutor judged that this essay was not sufficiently critical, and thus awarded it a poor mark. Scott argues, however, that it does display critical thinking of a sort, but that it could not have satisfied the tutor's expectations because of the student's evident lack of knowledge of a significant literature. Scott concludes her article by indicating some of the pedagogical implications of her argument for tutors, and by offering some self-reflexive comments.

Ideas for further research

The discussion in this chapter suggests a series of possible directions for future research in this area:

- historical studies into why the curriculum has developed in the way it has;
- comparative analyses of curricula and practices;
- critical reflections on the impact of national curricular innovations;
- honest accounts of local curricular innovations that didn't work, and why;
- surveys of the extent to which new learning technologies are being applied and used;
- inter-institutional studies of the use and effectiveness of alternative forms of assessment;
- longitudinal studies of the research student experience; and
- analyses of different approaches to master's course design, and of their changing role with postgraduate provision.

You may, of course, think of and wish to pursue other directions for researching course design.

6

Researching the student experience

Introduction

The previous two chapters have examined contemporary research into teaching and learning (Chapter 4) and course design (Chapter 5) in higher education. Here, the attention turns towards the students' perspective, and to how they experience the higher education that has been designed for them. Clearly, this is – or should be – an area of great interest to those working in or concerned with higher education. We need to know whether the courses and support systems we have devised are working in the ways intended, or whether there are aspects of our provision that could be changed or improved. More generally, we also need to keep in touch with what it feels like to be a student in contemporary institutions of higher education.

Some of the key questions stimulating research into the student experience are:

- How do students choose whether to enter higher education, and which institutions and courses to apply to?
- What factors influence how successful students are in their courses, and whether or not they complete them?
- How does the experience of student life vary amongst different groups of the population: e.g. in terms of gender, class, ethnicity and age?
- What kinds of support systems do institutions of higher education need to provide for their students?
- How is the transition between higher education and employment or further education or training managed?
- How is the student experience changing with time?

This chapter, then, focuses on how contemporary higher education researchers have sought to understand student life, and make suggestions for how it might be improved.

Research into the student experience

The discussion in this section has been organized in terms of six main sub-themes:

- accessing higher education;
- the on-course experience;
- success and non-completion;
- the postgraduate experience;
- the experience of different student groups;
- the transition from higher education to work.

As can be seen, this is essentially a sequential form of organization, following students through the higher education experience from entry to exit (or re-entry).

Accessing higher education

While the focus of this chapter is on the student experience, this can be examined from the perspective of the student or of the institution they are applying to or studying at. This is certainly the case when we consider the access or entry experience or procedure. Thus, from the perspective of the institution, or of the funder, the key issue will be about the characteristics of those students who enter higher education. From the perspective of the prospective student, however, the issue is more about how they choose which institution to go to and which course to take.

To take the latter perspective first, we may usefully compare recent British and Australian research. The article by Ball et al. (2002), discussed as Case Study 6.1 later in this chapter, reports on an interview-based analysis of how prospective students choose which institution to study at. It makes particular reference to the role of significant others – parents, friends, teachers – and of social class (see also Archer et al. 2003; Baxter and Britton 2001) in influencing, or limiting, such choices.

In a related piece of work, the same group of authors (Reay et al. 2002) examine the factors affecting the choice of mature students on an access course (that is, a course designed to prepare older students, who lack conventional university entrance qualifications, for higher education). They set their analysis against the context of national policy, supposedly encouraging of increased access to and wider participation in higher education, and find a gap between the rhetoric and actual experience:

> *. . . the story of access remains one of grand designs and inadequate realisations, despite the dedication and commitment of many access tutors. As with all education policy, despite the superficial noisy welter of innovation, at a deeper, more inpenetrable level, certain structures remain much more resistant to change . . . Class inequalities of access to universities endure despite the many access initiatives designed to attract working-class students. Yet there is no uniformity of class conditions, practices and outcomes. Class is always mediated by ethnicity, marital status and gender, and these meditations are played out in mature students' negotiations of the HE process.* (p. 17)

These negotiations take place against what Williams (1997) and her colleagues have described as a 'discourse of selectivity and equity', within which a range of stakeholders take up alternative positions on access.

Gayle et al. (2002) have examined the same question, of what influences young people to enter higher education, through the analysis of a large, quantitative, data set (the Youth Cohort Study of England and Wales). They looked at the impact of a range of factors, including social class, gender, ethnicity, parental education and independent schooling. While they did find that these factors had an effect, this was less than they had expected, and their main conclusion relates to the need for further research to better understand the complexity of what is going on.

James (2000, 2001) has been researching much the same issues from an Australian perspective, using questionnaire surveys. As in the United Kingdom, recent Australian government policy has sought to increase the participation in higher education of those who have not traditionally taken up the opportunity. So called 'equity groups' – such as the disabled, indigenous students and those from the lower social classes, non-English speaking backgrounds, rural and isolated areas – have been identified, and targets set for increasing recruitment (see also Dobson 2003). While some progress may be being made, James argues that:

> *Australia still has a higher education system significantly stratified by social class. Students' earliest decisions about the possibility of higher education are in no terms 'equal', but hinge on the social and economic circumstances of their families and communities and on their geographical locations. These differences are unlikely to be resolved by reliance on the invisible hand of the market and by shallow appeals to the sovereignty of student choice – to put it crudely, some people have very limited choices.* (James 2000: 112)

In a country with the size and population distribution of Australia, geography clearly assumes importance, along with social class, in influencing student choice.

To turn the issue around, then, which students are chosen by institutions of higher education? This perspective can be illustrated by Ahola and Kokko's (2001) survey of students seeking entry to business departments in Finnish universities. With four times as many applicants as there are available places, the issue there for the institutions is how to select the best possible students, making extensive and collaborative use of entrance examinations.

Croot and Chalkley (1999) have analysed national admissions data for another discipline, geography, in England and Wales, in an effort to map patterns of undergraduate enrolment. They found two trends that caused them some concern. One was a recent downturn in recruitment, after a longer period of steady expansion; the other was an increasing tendency for students to opt for universities closer to their homes. Their message – which could be seen as complementing those of Reay et al. (2002) and James (2000) quoted above – was about the need for geography to market itself more effectively to potential students if it is not to loose out in an era of widening participation.

The on-course experience

Research and writing on the student experience after entry to university covers a wide and varied field. There is a generic literature, which attempts to provide an overview of the whole experience, either by taking it theme by theme (Haselgrove 1994) or by reporting on in-depth data collection with students themselves (e.g. Silver and Silver 1997). There is an auto-biographical literature, through which students report upon their experiences directly (e.g. Arksey et al. 1994; Tolmie 1998). There is a 'how to' and/or analytical literature that focuses on students' health, and on how institutions of higher education may best support and counsel their students (e.g. Earwaker 1992; Peelo 1994; Rana 2000; Wolfendale and Corbett 1996). There are studies of the relative success of those students completing higher education, and of the reasons why some do not complete (e.g. Smith and Naylor 2001; Yorke 1999), which are considered in the next sub-section. And, while all of the foregoing focus on under-graduate students – what might be called the mainstream of higher education – there is also a growing body of research on the experience of postgraduate, and particularly research, students (e.g. Delamont et al. 2000), considered in the next but one sub-section.

Silver and Silver start their book by noting 'how little research exists on students as "real people" ' (1997: 2). Their research was based on interviews with academic and student representatives, and the study of archival sources, in a range of British universities (a smaller comparative study of two American universities was also completed). They focus on how students' lives have changed during the last 30 years or so, considering their living arrangements, opinions and attitudes, issues of representation and action, their employment and the extent to which there can be said to be a student community. Their emphasis is on the complex and contextual nature of students' lives:

We have largely bypassed aspects of students' lives which have become so significant a part of modern student mythologies – the promiscuities, misbehaviours, idiocies, illegalities, and so on. It has been sufficient for our purposes to suggest the ambiguities of adolescence, education for responsibility without having responsibility. Whatever the pressures on full-time students, there inevitably also remains something of the sense of a 'time between'. Making allowance for these features of many students' lives, it is difficult to judge how substantially students differ from large numbers of the rest of society. The complex balances between the academic and extra-curricular lives of students, in the immense variety of campus and sub-campus cultures, also make it difficult to arrive at a suitable imagery. (pp. 164–5)

On a smaller scale, Montgomery and Collette (2001) report on a diary-based study of students' experiences within one department, of Women's Studies. They argue that this methodology worked very well:

We feel that the diaries revealed to us very fully that student lives did impact on their learning and vice-versa and at times led to changes . . . The students gained an ability to reflect in greater depth . . . we gave voice to the students . . . although, on reflection, perhaps not as much as we had hoped . . . We had valued the student experience and this gave us greater understanding of their problems in attempting to do a degree, while getting on with their own lives. (p. 307)

The article by Norton et al. (2001), reviewed as Case Study 6.2 later in this chapter, is another example of a smaller-scale study, in this case of what students regard as acceptable behaviours when placed under stress by course assessment expectations. An important area for research into the student experience is currently developing in countries such as Australia and the United Kingdom, where the financial support arrangements for students have recently been revised, shifting more responsibility onto the student. Such research is focusing upon the impact of increased financial responsibility, working while studying and debt on student satisfaction and performance (e.g. Callender 2003; Christie et al. 2001).

Research focusing on students' experience during their first year of registration – viewed, naturally enough, as a particularly critical period – has been part of the North American corpus for some years, and has recently begun to spread beyond there. McInnis (2001) provides a literature review of Australian research on this topic. He notes two main needs for future research:

There is a clear need, sooner rather than later, for some systematic research on the effectiveness of the many and varied innovations and intervention strategies aimed at improving the first year experience . . . In addition, there is a need for longitudinal studies to follow cohorts from the school years through to, at least, the completion of the first degree and possibly beyond. (p. 112)

The latter, in particular, would, of course, be relatively demanding and expensive to undertake.

Success and non-completion

Research that seeks to explain why students succeed, and why they sometimes leave higher education without completing their studies, is of long-standing interest. Both institutions and funders of higher education would like to be able to predict, with as much accuracy as possible, which students it would be most worth investing in and which it would be better to counsel against entering higher education. Unfortunately, the answers to their questions are frequently not that surprising and difficult to do much about.

McKenzie and Schweitzer (2001) report on a study of the factors predicting academic performance at one Australian university. They studied 197 first year students, making use of both questionnaire and documentary data, and looked at both academic and non-academic (psychosocial, cognitive, demographic) predictors. They found that academic performance at this stage in a student's career was associated with previous academic performance, integration with the institution, self-efficacy and employment responsibilities, and concluded by making a series of recommendations for universities and colleges to take on board.

Also in Australia and focusing on one university, Cantwell et al. (2001) researched the academic achievement of students who entered by 'traditional' and 'non-traditional' means. The study made use of institutional documentary sources, subjecting the data used to basic and statistical analyses. They come to a positive conclusion:

> *Given that most students entering university through enabling programmes would not have gained entry in other circumstances, the fact that their performance is only slightly below those entering through traditional means indicates the usefulness of the enabling programme. The most salient finding is the relative success of non-traditional entry when combined with maturity and its relative failure when combined with youth. Importantly, the success of mature-aged non-traditional entry appears independent of socio-economic background, and relatively independent of area of study.* (p. 233)

Smith and Naylor (2001) report on a larger-scale study, analysing archival data on all the students who left university in the United Kingdom in 1993. They carried out an ordered probit regression, relating students' degree classifications to selected variables, including subject studied, personal characteristics, academic background and gender. They concluded that:

> *... degree performance is influenced significantly by personal characteristics such as age and marital status. We also find that degree performance is*

influenced positively by A-level score, positively by occupationally-ranked social class background, and is significantly lower both for students who previously attended an Independent [i.e. private] school prior to university entry and for male students. We find that, with few exceptions, the sign and significance of these effects are robust across separate regressions of degree performance on distinct population sub-samples. (p. 58)

As with all statistical analyses, the interest and difficulty is then in working out causal explanations for these findings.

Yorke (1999, 2000) stands out amongst recent researchers who have examined the reasons why some students do not complete their courses, and what might be done about this. He carried out a questionnaire survey in six higher education institutions in the north-west of England. There were contrasting findings for full-time and part-time students:

Three main influences on withdrawal dominate the responses of the full-time and sandwich students. Roughly equal in frequency of citation were the wrong choice of the field of study and financial problems, with matters relating to the quality of the student experience a little further back ... For the part-time students who responded to the surveys, the demands of employment were the most cited influence on withdrawal and were cited twice as often as the needs of dependants, the magnitude of the workload and financial problems. (Yorke 1999: 53, 67)

Of course, as Yorke himself points out, caution has to be exercised in interpreting the findings of research relying on self-reporting, as respondents may be less than wholly honest, may change their opinions, or may give the answers they suspect the researcher is looking for. After discussing the costs of non-completion to the state and the individual, and what it might be said to say about the institutions concerned, Yorke concludes by making some suggestions as to how institutions might improve completion rates (see also Moxley et al. 2001).

The postgraduate experience

One of the most notable features of the massification of higher education is the feed-through effect from undergraduate to postgraduate provision. As first degrees have become an increasingly common qualification amongst the younger labour force, having a postgraduate degree has become an expectation for more and more professions and jobs. While much of the expansion has been in Masters degree provision (Knight 1997), most of the research interest has been in research degrees (see also the discussion of postgraduate course design in Chapter 5). Two key areas for research into the latter – paralleling the work on undergraduate education – have been into the nature and quality of the research degree experience, and into whether and how it leads to a successful outcome.

To take the former area first, researchers have looked at the training programmes provided for new research students, and their access to departmental and other research cultures while studying (Deem and Brehony 2000), but the main focus has been on the supervisory relationship. Research students typically have one or two academic supervisors, and it is obvious that the quality and success of their work will depend to a considerable extent on how well the supervisory relationship works. Researchers have adopted both qualitative and quantitative strategies towards exploring this issue (e.g. Acker et al. 1994; Burgess et al. 1994; Gurr 2001; Heath 2002; McWilliam et al. 2002; Styles and Radloff 2001).

Delamont and her colleagues (2000: there is also a 'how to' version – Delamont et al. 1997) carried out over 200 in-depth interviews with research students and supervisors in a range of United Kingdom universities. Their focus was on how the research degree process functioned in different disciplines – in the natural and social sciences – to develop the next generation of academics and researchers. They note the existence and importance of different traditions of undertaking research: e.g. the role of fieldwork in social anthropology, of bench experiments in laboratory science, and of the construction of models and simulations in computer science:

> *Each way of knowing does more than just solve particular kinds of puzzles. Each helps to define a particular kind of identity for students and established academics alike.* (Delamont et al. 2000: 175)

But they also identify a number of common features in the research student experience across disciplines:

> *. . . the extent to which the graduate student is, or should be, treated as an independent, autonomous member of the community, or whether he or she is to be placed in a subordinate position . . . the recurrent theme of* isolation *among research students – a mixture of social and intellectual isolation . . . Doctoral research is in many ways a* liminal *experience. The students stand on the threshold of their academic career . . . For students and their supervisors alike, there is a strong component of* faith *in undertaking doctoral research . . . Such articles of faith rest on a fundamental, usually unspoken, faith in disciplinary knowledge.* (pp. 176–7)

Another way of looking at the same issues is in terms of the pedagogies involved in the research student/supervisor relationship. Bartlett and Mercer (2000) offer a reflective, feminist analysis of their own supervisory relationship. They note the movement of the relationship from an initial mother/daughter model to more of a big/little sister model, and offer three metaphors as ways of thinking further about postgraduate pedagogies: creating in the kitchen, digging in the garden, and bushwalking. In another Australian contribution, Johnson et al. (2000: discussed as Case Study 5.2 in the previous chapter) report on their interview-based research into the history and practices of the PhD in the humanities and social sciences, paying particular attention to the gendered component of the supervisory relationship. They stress the continuing 'centrality of the ideal of the autonomous, independent scholar to postgraduate pedagogy' (p. 143), while arguing for the development of new images of the scholar.

The issue of the success or otherwise of the research student process – that is, whether the student survives to achieve a PhD – has been of growing concern to governments and their agencies in a number of countries (Becher et al. 1994; Burgess 1994, 1997; Burgess et al. 1998; Colebatch 2002). This issue can also be seen behind the development of alternative, professional, routes to research degrees, incorporating more taught components (Bourner et al. 2001; Green et al. 2001).

An important consideration here is how the PhD is examined, something that varies considerably from country to country, and has recently become a topic for research. Thus, Tinkler and Jackson (2000: see also Jackson and Tinkler 2001) have argued that, in the British system, the PhD examination process is lacking in both transparency and consistency. Clearly, then, more research and developments in practice can be expected at this level of higher education.

The experience of different student groups

The bulk of research into the student experience, understandably, focuses on undergraduates, and, in particular, on the young, full-time undergraduates who make up the core of most universities' populations. In addition to the research on postgraduate students considered in the previous section, however, there are also literatures focusing on particular – often called 'non-traditional' – kinds of undergraduate students. These include adult, mature, part-time and distance students, women students (now in the majority overall in most developed systems), students from minority ethnic groups, and international students.

The research and writing on adult, mature, women, part-time and distance students may be seen as overlapping. Part-time (Schuller et al. 1999) and distance (Harry 1999) forms of provision are designed for, and appeal particularly to, mature or adult students. Such students will typically have other responsibilities to balance with their involvement in higher education. Research into the higher education experience of minority ethnic groups is relatively limited (but see Bird 1996). We will focus in this section, therefore, on two main student groups: mature and international.

Research into mature students in higher education is linked to that on how higher education is accessed (Hayton and Paczuska 2002: see also the sub-section earlier in this chapter). It also relates to research on over-arching ideas like lifelong learning, the learning society and widening participation (Davies 1995; Knapper and Cropley 2000; Schuetze and Slowey 2000; Watson and Taylor 1998: see also the discussion in Chapter 8). Research into mature women, as opposed to men, places particular emphasis on their complex roles in juggling caring (for children and older relatives) and work responsibilities alongside their educational involvement (Coats 1994; Hughes 2002b; Lunneborg 1994; Merrill 1999; Pascall and Cox 1993).

As an example of this broad area for research, we may consider Burke (2002), who carried out an ethnographic study of 23 students returning to education through access courses in England. She focuses on what these students' autobiographies reveal about contemporary discourses of widening participation, and what impact their educational participation has on them. She stresses the importance of collaboration, both in her methodology and in the pedagogies she researched, and her agenda is explicitly political:

> *Access education must seek to transform the dominant discursive practices of further and higher education that maintain social exclusion. This does not mean simply opening spaces to fit 'non-standard' students in. It requires effecting change by legitimising a diverse range of ideas, experiences, values and perspectives within the academic world.* (pp. 148–9)

The research on international students – that is, students who are studying in a country other than that in which they live – is less extensive and more focused than that on mature students. Part of this research effort is concerned with charting the growing numbers of international students and where they are studying. Another part is focused on the assessment of the effectiveness of collaborative schemes – such as the European Union's ERASMUS and SOCRATES programmes – designed to encourage international movements (Burn et al. 1990; Maiworm et al. 1991; Opper et al. 1990; Sullivan 2002). The major emphasis, however, is probably on the needs of international students, and on how universities and their staff should adjust and adapt their provision to address them (Campbell 2000; Kinnell 1990; McNamara and Harris 1997).

Two small-scale but thoughtful examples of this kind of research are those of Littlemore (2001) and Grey (2002). Littlemore's concern is with the use of metaphors in lectures, how these are commonly misunderstood by international students, and what might be done to rectify this state of affairs. She argues for the need to raise metaphoric awareness amongst both staff and international students. Grey got international students to produce drawings of their concerns in their undergraduate experience at different stages during one semester, and then identified the recurring themes that emerged. She concluded:

The issues raised by the students in this case study through their 'visual state-ments' show that the students have real social and academic concerns . . . where the students are involved in a critical pedagogical process which not only aims at transformation, but also engages them in fundamental issues relating to difference, identity and culture, students can question dominant discourses and valuable shared learning can take place. (Grey 2002: 165–6)

The transition from higher education to work

The end result of the student experience in higher education, and one of its main preparatory functions, is conventionally seen as the transition to work. Of course – as the discussion in previous sub-sections of both postgraduate provision and lifelong education makes clear – increasingly the undergraduate experience is not an end to higher education, and workers may return to further their education on a number of occasions (Moore 2000).

Contemporary European research into this aspect of the student experience is particularly associated with the name of Teichler, who – together with his colleagues from the Centre for Research on Higher Education and Work at Kassel in Germany – has published widely on the issues concerned (e.g. Maiworm and Teichler 1996; Teichler 1999a, 1999b, 2000a, 2000b; Teichler and Maiworm 1994). An example of Teichler's work is considered as Case Study 6.3 in this chapter. In the British context, Brennan and his colleagues (Brennan et al. 1993, 1995) have also been notable contributors.

Teichler's concern has been to explore and understand the changing natures of both higher education and work, and to suggest how their inter-relationships may be strengthened and improved. He argues:

Institutions of higher education and responsible governments, in reflecting the future challenges from the world of work, are clearly in need of improved information on employment and the work of graduates; on the impact of study provisions and conditions of future employment and work; and on indications for long-term technological, economic and social changes . . . Observations of labour market trends and graduate employment, however, are often too narrowly interpreted in the search for recipes . . . Improved regular communication among all those involved in shaping the future of links between higher education and the world is . . . needed. (Teichler 1999a: 308)

The importance of change in the relationship between higher education and work is emphasized by many researchers. Thus, Harvey (2000) stresses the growth of the employability agenda within higher education, and the increasing stress being placed on producing flexible and empowered graduates. In his analysis:

The 'New Realities' that ask searching questions about the relationship between higher education and employment are, incidentally, asking about the purpose and structure of higher education. In particular, emphasising the need for the development of critical, reflective, empowered learners raises fundamental questions about traditional forms of teaching in higher education and the priorities of higher education institutions and governments. (p. 14)

Kivinen and Ahola (1999) add to this debate an analysis of the surrounding rhetoric of human capital, the information society, boundaryless careers and entrepreneurial work. Also addressing the issue of human capital, but from an economic perspective, Ashworth (1998) questions whether, with increased participation in higher education, the rate of return on this investment continues to be worthwhile, either to individuals or society as a whole.

Other researchers have looked at what happens to graduates after they leave the university. Thus, Egerton (2001a, 2001b) has carried out an extensive quantitative analysis of the occupational attainment of mature graduates, making use of data from the General Household Survey in the United Kingdom. Her focus was on occupational attainment and the impact of social class:

. . . although mature graduates are less successful occupationally than early graduates, they are more successful than matriculates, and clearly most of them make a successful transition into graduate careers. The occupations they enter seem to give opportunities for promotion. However, they mainly work in the public sector, where relative rates of pay and conditions of employment have deteriorated over the past two decades. Generally, they seem to follow a distinctively different trajectory than those followed by early graduates. (Egerton 2001a: 146)

. . . it is clear that mature study has become an accessible avenue to intergenerational social mobility for manual class women and men. The effects are slightly less pronounced for women than for men. (Egerton 2001b: 283)

Jenkins et al. (2001) have, by contrast, taken a smaller scale and qualitative approach in trying to assess the long-term effects on graduates who took a particular degree course, but they broaden the analysis to consider its effects not just on work but on life as a whole. They interviewed 18 graduates who had started the course between 1979 and 1994, adopting a life story approach and asking about the higher education experience as a whole. They stress both the commonalities (gains in skills, awareness and confidence) and the individuality of the student experience after graduation, and pose the questions of 'when you should evaluate a degree, how you should evaluate it, and what you should evaluate' (p. 159).

Case studies

The three case studies considered in this chapter consist of:

- an interview-based study into how prospective higher education students choose which higher education institutions to study at;
- a questionnaire-based examination of students' behaviours when faced with demanding assessment tasks; and
- a comparative overview of European data on graduate employment.

Case Study 6.1

Stephen Ball, Jackie Davies, Miriam David and Diane Reay (2002) 'Classification' and 'Judgement': social class and the 'cognitive structures' of choice in higher education. *British Journal of Sociology of Education*, 23, 1, 51–72.

Themes and Issues

In this article, Stephen Ball and his co-authors report on the analysis of data collected as part of a research project funded by the United Kingdom's Economic and Social Research Council (ESRC). The focus of the authors is on how prospective students choose – assisted and influenced by their parents, friends and teachers – which higher education institutions to study at, and on the role of social class in such choices.

Methods and Methodologies

I would categorize this article as adopting an interview-based methodology to researching the student experience. In total, 120 prospective students were interviewed in six schools and colleges in and around London, together with 15 teachers and 40 parents. The study was not wholly interview-based, however, and might more strictly be described as multi-method. Questionnaires were also administered to a larger sample of prospective students, with 502 responses, and a limited amount of observation was carried out within the institutions surveyed.

Level

In terms of level, the study goes beyond the merely institutional, in targeting a number of institutions for study, albeit all within a limited area. While, therefore, in terms of my typology, it is institutional, this is an example of a study for which the term regional might be a better descriptor.

Analytical/Theoretical Framework

For their theoretical framework, the authors refer to the work of the French sociologist Bourdieu, and, in particular, his concepts of 'classification' and 'judgement'. Within this framework, a number of themes are developed and stressed:

- the status differentiations evident between UK higher education institutions, and the perceptions of these held by prospective students and others;
- the continuing under-participation of those of working class origin in higher education, and the influence of previous family experience on this;
- the relation between social class, school attended, school examination performance and participation in higher education, the kind of higher education institution attended, and the kind of course chosen; and
- the notion of the choice of which kind of higher education institution to attend as being a lifestyle choice.

Related Literatures

The article may be placed in relation to a number of literatures, not all of them referred to in the text. First, there is the authors' own previous work on the issue of choice in post-compulsory education (e.g. Ball et al. 2000; Gewirtz et al. 1995; Reay et al. 2002). Then there are related studies by others focusing on young people's choices within post-compulsory education (e.g. Gayle et al. 2002; Hodkinson and Sparkes 1997; Moogan et al. 1999), the matching literature on how institutions recruit and select students (e.g. Ahola and Kokko 2001; Croot and Chalkley 1999), and analyses of participation rates (e.g. James 2001).

But there are at least two other literatures of interest. One consists of longitudinal studies (e.g. Banks et al. 1992; Jenkins et al. 2001) into young people's experiences and choices, which can be relatively expensive and time-consuming to carry out, and are thus comparatively rare. The other is a kind of parallel literature, which has focused on mature rather than young entrants into higher education, and within which a particular interest in working class and women mature students is evident (e.g. Edwards 1993; Pascall and Cox 1993; Williams 1997).

Argument and Conclusions

A distinction is made between prospective higher education students who pursue 'normal' and 'choice' biographies. In the former case, prospective students from families with experience of higher education typically see university entry as the normal route to take on completion of school, so their decisions focus on which university and course to attend. In the latter case, prospective students from families with little or no experience of higher education will have to make a very conscious choice to do something different.

As the authors conclude:

Many students, especially working-class students, never get to the position where they can contemplate HE [higher education]. Others are qualified to do so but exclude themselves. Others who do apply avoid certain institutions. Conversely, for working-class and minority ethnic students, for a combination of negative and positive factors, other institutions are attractive. (p. 70)

Case Study 6.2

Lin Norton, Alice Tilley, Stephen Newstead and Arlene Franklyn-Stokes (2001) The Pressures of Assessment in Undergraduate Courses and their Effect on Student Behaviours. *Assessment and Evaluation in Higher Education*, 26, 3, 269–84.

Themes and Issues

This article may be read as the coming together of the research interests of two groups of researchers based in two different higher education institutions. As such, it builds upon their earlier, independent researches (Newstead et al. 1996; Norton et al. 1996).

The authors have a general interest in the relations between approaches to studying and assessment practices, and in exploring how the latter influence students' strategies for the former. In this article, they focus in particular on students' essay writing tactics and cheating behaviours, examining how these are correlated (this is a quantitative piece of work) with approaches to studying.

Methods and Methodologies

This article may be categorized as adopting a multivariate approach to researching the student experience. It presents the results of a survey of 267 third-year undergraduate psychology students in four United Kingdom higher education institutions. Each student was required to complete three separate questionnaires:

- a 'rules of the game' questionnaire (Norton et al. 1996), devised to assess students' essay writing tactics, in particular how these are adapted with a view to impressing the academics who will assess them;
- a cheating questionnaire (Newstead et al. 1996), listing '21 behaviours which might be considered to be cheating', and asking whether the student had ever made use of them; and
- the Approaches to Studying Inventory (ASI), devised by Entwistle and his colleagues (Entwistle et al. 1979), and subsequently much used and modified, in a version devised by Richardson (1990).

Level

The article may be classified as institutional in level, in that it focuses on four United Kingdom higher education institutions.

Analytical/Theoretical Framework

The analysis proceeds by, first, presenting the results from the three questionnaires separately, detailing frequencies of responses, means and standard deviations. Then, after converting the responses to the three questionnaires into indexes, correlations were calculated between all three questionnaires, in pairs, to explore whether the students' behaviours they measure are related.

Related Literatures

The main literature within which this study may be located is clearly that on approaches to learning and teaching (e.g. Biggs 1999; Marton et al. 1997; Prosser and Trigwell 1999; Ramsden 1992; Richardson 2000). There is a related literature on students' academic performance, and the reasons for variations in this (e.g. Cantwell et al. 2001; McKenzie and Schweitzer 2001), and another on student non-completion (e.g. Yorke 1999, 2000). The literature specifically focusing on students' assessment tactics and cheating behaviours is more limited, but growing (e.g. Ashworth et al. 1997; Shevlin et al. 2000).

Argument and Conclusions

The authors found evidence that many of the students surveyed were using essay writing tactics and cheating behaviours, findings that they link with the assessment pressures faced by these students. However, their analysis of studying approaches produced 'rather disappointing' results, with many students adopting surface or strategic, rather than deep, approaches to studying. Correlations between approaches to studying and essay tactics and cheating were mostly small.

> The findings from this research suggest that psychology students do feel under pressure by the assessment system and respond by using a variety of stratagems such as cheating, and using 'rules of the game' ... if these results are an indication that students actually are affected by assessment demands in this way, the implications for lecturers are profound. (p. 281)

Case Study 6.3

Ulrich Teichler (2000b) Graduate Employment and Work in Selected European Countries. *European Journal of Education*, 35, 2, 141–56.

Themes and Issues

This article stems from a project funded by the European Commission, and examines the quality of the available international statistics on graduate employment in nine Western European countries. It comments on the difficulties of comparative analyses, the usefulness of surveys of this kind, and what might be done to improve matters in the future.

Methods and Methodologies

This article was categorized in the analysis discussed in the introductory chapter as adopting a comparative approach to researching the student experience. The facet of the student experience being considered is primarily its outcome: what students do after they have finished being students.

Level

As a study of European data, the study focuses at an international level.

Analytical/Theoretical Framework

As a piece of research, the article offers an evaluation of two sets of secondary data – the term social scientists commonly use to refer to previously collected information that they haven't gathered themselves. Teichler focuses in particular on two existing data sets published each year: that compiled by EURYDICE, the European Commission agency responsible for collecting educational data, and that compiled by the Organisation for Economic Co-operation and Development (OECD).

The key statistics examined include: enrolment rates in higher education, the proportion of graduates in their age group, the percentage of adults who have completed higher education, and the variations in these statistics in terms of age, gender and field of study. Teichler then goes on to look at key employment statistics, including unemployment and labour force participation rates, and the relative earnings of those who have completed higher education.

Related Literatures

The main literature to which this article relates is that substantial body of work dealing with the relation between the worlds of higher education and work. In recent years, Teichler and his colleagues have been responsible for a significant amount of research and publication in this area themselves (e.g. Maiworm and Teichler 1996; Teichler 1999a, 1999b, 2000a; Teichler and Maiworm 1994), though others, of course, have contributed as well (e.g. Brennan et al. 1993; Egerton 2001a, 2001b; Harvey 2000). Two other literatures of interest here are those which deal with making the higher education experience more relevant to the world of work (e.g. Bennett et al. 2000; Boud and Solomon 2001; van Ernst et al. 2001), and with general evaluations of changing national policy (e.g. Kogan and Hanney 2000).

The extension of European Union policy and funding into higher education has also stimulated comparative research into other aspects of higher education policy and practice within Western Europe (e.g. Sullivan 2002).

Argument and Conclusions

Throughout his analysis, Teichler points out problems with the available data and their interpretation: varying definitions of what it means to be a student, differences in the age group typically in initial full-time higher education, what is and is not included within higher education in different countries. He argues that:

> It is very difficult to compare the employment and work situation of higher education graduates and the relationships between higher education and the world of work in the various European countries. (p. 141)

In the final third of the article, he goes on to consider some more generic issues, including the relevance of the graduation rate in an era of mass higher education, and recent graduate employment problems. He ends the article with some suggestions for improving international, and particularly European, higher education statistics.

Ideas for further research

This review of contemporary research into the student experience suggests a number of topics for future research:

- examinations of the experiences of master's degree students, and of the role the master's degree plays in their lives;
- studies of the experiences of students from minority ethnic groups, and other under-researched groups, such as those with disabilities;
- more longer-term analyses of the effects of higher education on the students undertaking it;
- a greater emphasis on researching the non-vocational, rather than the vocational, impact of participation in higher education;
- studies of people who make repeated use of higher education during their lives;
- investigations into the ways in which universities and their component departments select students for entry;
- further research into students' social lives, and their relation to their course experiences;
- analyses of the impacts of changing financial arrangements on students' lives and performances; and
- qualitative studies of the experiences of the increasing numbers of working class students entering higher education.

7

Researching quality

Introduction

With the move towards mass systems of higher education in many countries in the 1980s and 1990s, concerns with the quality, standard and value for money of what was on offer naturally came to the forefront in policy discussions. One consequence was the establishment of what might be called a 'quality industry' within, and on the fringes of, higher education systems, staffed by current and former academics. Another was a rapid growth of interest amongst academics in researching quality in higher education.

Now that quality systems are an established and accepted part of higher education, the level of interest in practice and theory may have peaked, but the volume of research and writing in this area remains high. There is also an academic journal specifically devoted to quality issues, *Quality in Higher Education*, as well as several others that regularly publish articles on this topic.

Key questions driving research into the quality of higher education include:

- How should we evaluate what academics do?
- What forms of quality assurance are most appropriate for higher education?
- Are degree standards common within given higher education systems, and are they constant over time?
- What is the role for performance-based funding in higher education?
- How can the results of quality assurance exercises be best communicated to the users of higher education?
- What are the linkages between assessment practices, standards and quality?

This chapter, then, focuses on how higher education researchers have addressed these and related questions, and how their understanding of what constitutes quality in higher education has developed.

Research into quality

While contemporary research into quality in higher education could be categorized in many different ways, it seemed most useful for present purposes to divide up the field chiefly in terms of the level of interest. Thus, four linked areas for research may be identified:

- course evaluation;
- grading and outcomes;
- national monitoring practices;
- system standards.

Each of these areas will now be illustrated and analysed in turn.

Course evaluation

The most basic level of quality assurance, and hence research into quality, concerns the course, module, individual teaching/learning event or any other aspect of the higher education experience (Aylett and Gregory 1996). The concern here, in terms of practice, is with checking student (or customer) response to, and satisfaction with, what they are receiving. In research terms, the focus is on assessing the validity of course evaluation techniques, with designing more effective ones, and, more fundamentally, with understanding what constitutes quality or satisfaction for the student (Carson 2001; Hill 1995; Johnson 2000).

There can be few academics today who are not familiar with course evaluation questionnaires. Many institutions and departments have standardized questionnaires, which are routinely administered at set times in the academic year, and the results of which feed into module, course and/or departmental reviews. In some institutions, they may also feed into decisions on staff appointments, contracts and renewal. These question-naires vary a great deal in terms of sophistication, from basic 'happy sheets', designed to minimize the workload of course evaluation and/or try and ensure a reasonably 'good' response, to lengthy and thoroughly validated instruments such as the Course Experience Questionnaire. As all experienced social researchers know, however, the answers you get depend upon the questions you ask, while the interpretation you place on the answers is likely to be related to what you want to find.

The article by Shevlin et al. (2000), reviewed later in this chapter as Case

Study 7.3, is an example of a piece of research that questioned whether course evaluation questionnaires really measure what they set out to do. Intriguingly, the authors used a questionnaire to collect the data for their analysis. While few would argue that course evaluation questionnaires could ever be wholly reliable and objective methods for measuring satisfaction, this research suggests just how affected student assessments of their lecturers may be by other factors, in this case whether they perceived their lecturers as being charismatic or not.

Higher education is, of course, a diverse sector of provision, and particular techniques may need to be adapted to evaluate, for example, sub-degree provision, postgraduate courses, professional courses and continuing education (Ashworth and Harvey 1994; Tovey 1994; Zuber-Skerritt and Ryan 1994). Tricker et al. (2001) have examined the particular case of distance education provision, noting that the physical and temporal separation of students and lecturers poses special demands for effective evaluation. Simply getting an adequate response rate can be difficult in these circumstances. Adapting practice from the service delivery industry, they report on the development of a service template for measuring any gaps between what students want and what they perceive themselves as getting.

Lawless and Richardson (2002) were also concerned with distance education, specifically with assessing the relationship between perceptions of academic quality and approaches to study (see also Chapter 4). They administered versions of the Course Experience Questionnaire and the Approaches to Study Inventory to a sample of students at the UK Open University, receiving 1218 useable responses (a 68 per cent response rate). The data were then subjected to factor and correlation analyses. They found a strong association between students' approaches to studying and their perceptions of the academic quality of their courses; though, as this was a correlational result, more research using different techniques would be needed to explore and demonstrate a causal relationship.

Wright and O'Neill (2002) also applied factor and correlation analyses to researching students' perceptions of quality – in this case of an online library service – and how they might be most effectively measured. They, in an analogous fashion to Tricker et al. (2001), adapted an 'importance-performance' technique (that is, an approach that attempts to measure not simply how satisfactory different aspects of a service are, but also which are the more important aspects) from the service delivery industry. They stress that, for evaluation to be meaningful and helpful, the university must start from a detailed understanding of what student requirements actually are.

Grading and outcomes

In one sense, practice and research into grading and outcomes is the flip-side of course evaluation. Rather than students evaluating their universities, courses and lecturers, the focus here is on the more conventional practice of lecturers rating their students. Two recent foci for research here have been on the relationship between course organization, methods of assessment and student grading.

A group of British researchers going under the collective title of the Student Assessment and Classification Working Group have recently produced a series of carefully measured studies on this area (Bridges et al. 2002; Yorke et al. 2002). For one of these studies they looked at student grades on modules in six selected subjects in four universities. They made use of a range of simple quantitative and presentational techniques to explore the relationship between coursework and examination marks: correlation analysis, ring charts, scattergrams and bar charts. They concluded:

> Our evidence, which is drawn from the analysis of over 12,500 student performances at four UK universities, tends to confirm the commonly held perception that the marks awarded for coursework are generally higher than for formal examinations. The differences are small in English and History but are significant in Biology, Business Studies, Computer Studies and Law. The differences range from one-third of an honours class to two-thirds of an honours class (division). Students who elect to take coursework-only modules are advantaged over students who take options that include formal examinations.
> (Bridges et al. 2002: 47)

A related, smaller scale, study – which investigated the impact on performance of the introduction of formative assessment – is reported by Greer (2001).

In a second study, the same group started from the observation that published statistics:

> . . . consistently show a variation between subject areas as regards the spread of degree classifications, science-based subjects tending to show a higher proportion of first and third-class honours than subjects in the Arts, Humanities and Social Sciences. (Yorke et al. 2002: 270)

This is linked to the, somewhat longer standing, concern which – noting the increase in the proportion of students getting higher classes of degree over time – argues that degree standards are falling (Yorke 2002). Yorke and his colleagues then proceed to analyse what effects grading students on a percentage scale or in terms of a less lengthy grading scale might have on their overall classification. While they do not come to any definitive conclusion, they argue that higher education institutions need to know more about how their grading methodologies and award algorithms work.

One area of grading practices that remains peculiar to the British system is the use of external examiners (Piper 1994; Williams 1997), whereby an experienced academic from another university is employed to moderate the marks given to students and provide a check on course standards. Much of the research and writing in this area has been critical. Piper, on the basis of an extensive questionnaire and interview study, notes that external examiners' identities are primarily 'subject-based', and found 'little evidence . . . of more than a handful drawing upon a relevant body of theory and systematically collected evidence about examining in higher education' (Piper 1994: 235). Williams, in questioning whether the external examining system is in demise or not, argues that:

> *The external examiner system has . . . become a means of maintaining a kind of balance between institutional/departmental autonomy, and external inspections on the one hand, and a defence against the encroachment of institutional managerialism on professional and departmental autonomy, on the other.* (Williams 1997: 86)

She concludes that, given the rise of national quality assurance regimes and the increasing pressures on academics, the system will need to be strengthened if it is to remain effective.

National monitoring practices

Moving up from a consideration of student, lecturer and course perspectives, we reach the national level, and its impact on the institution. Much of the focus of attention here has been on analysing and critiquing the systems imposed by governments on higher education for quality assurance purposes (e.g. Drennan 2001; Harman 2000a; Radford et al. 1997; Spencer-Matthews 2001; Wood and Meek 2002). A common theme is that the quality assurance systems in place in different countries are not working as intended.

Drennan interviewed senior academic managers in the 13 Scottish universities, noting the contrast between the strategies adopted for the teaching quality and research assessments:

> *As long as the UK funding councils favour large institutional awards for excellence in research and much smaller rewards for excellence in teaching, individual academics will choose to concentrate their activities in research activity, to the detriment of teaching. Only when the differential between these rewards is narrowed will the tension between teaching and research activity in higher education be reduced.* (Drennan 2001: 177)

Clearly, academics – as individuals and groups – tend to make fairly sensible judgements on what is in their best interests in any given situation. This is somewhat confirmed by Spencer-Matthews' study (2001). She reports on an attempt to introduce a quality management system in one university department, taking an action research strategy to collecting and analysing the data that resulted. She found, not surprisingly, that:

The change was only partially successful with the technical change being achieved with relative ease but the cultural change, a necessary part of the overall change process, proving more difficult. (p. 57)

Academics, as highly educated professionals with a fair degree of autonomy, can prove quite adept at resisting or superficially accepting change they do not 'own'. They can also prove to be pretty good at 'playing the game', as the experience in the United Kingdom with both the teaching quality assessment and the research assessment exercise shows. This is not to say, however, that further development is not required in some of these areas (see, for example, Gibbs 1995; Gibbs et al. 2000).

One particular aspect of higher education quality concerns how this is presented, or marketed, to potential clients: students, parents, employers, politicians and so on. The article by Bowden (2000), reviewed as Case Study 7.1 in this chapter, addresses this issue in exploring the attraction and deficiencies of the university and college league tables which appear increasingly frequently in national newspapers in many parts of the world.

National quality assurance systems, like some other aspects of higher education – for example the experience of academic work (see Chapter 10) and national policies more generally (see Chapter 8) – have also been the subject of international and comparative research studies (Brennan et al. 1997; Craft 1992; Kells 1992; Vroeijenstijn 1994). The international survey of the use of performance-based funding in higher education, discussed in Chapter 8 as Case Study 8.2 (Jongbloed and Vossensteyn 2001), also relates to the topic of quality assurance.

Brennan and Shah (2000) report on a study into the effects of national and institutional quality systems in 14 countries, undertaken for the Organisation for Economic Co-operation and Development (OECD). Their particular focus is on 29 case studies of institutional practices, produced voluntarily by senior staff in the institutions concerned. They consider the methodology of quality assessment, how it impacts, and the implications for academic values and power relations, and conclude that:

. . . the introduction of external quality assessment systems in most European countries, as well as in many other parts of the world, over the past decade has been associated with a shift in the distribution of power within higher education. This shift has favoured the institutional level at the expense of the basic unit. It has also tended to strengthen extrinsic *over* intrinsic *values as both managerial and market concerns have acquired greater importance compared with disciplinary academic concerns.* (p. 347)

Smeby and Stensaker (1999) describe a smaller-scale study of national quality assessment systems in four Nordic countries: Denmark, Finland, Norway and Sweden. Again, the analysis rests on accounts of the four systems produced by national experts. They conclude that, in these four countries at least, change in practices is relatively slow:

> *In Norway and Finland, assessments were given the status of 'policy experiments'. In Denmark, the whole assessment procedure is being evaluated after the first round. In Sweden, where assessment most clearly supports institutional autonomy and the delegation of power from the state to institutions, decentralisation and delegation have a long history* . . . (p. 13)

Clearly, some national governments are more trusting in their higher education sectors, institutions and employees.

System standards

At the system level, the focus of research and writing is on what quality means and how it might be applied in an ideal system. The article by Harvey (2002), discussed later in this chapter as Case Study 7.2, is an example of such research.

We may recognize two related and overlapping genres of work here. One, which is of most interest here, and will be discussed further, takes a research-based and/or analytical approach. We should also note, however, that there is – as in a number of fields, most notably teaching and learning and institutional management (see Chapters 4 and 9) – a significant 'how to' literature on this topic. This sets out good practice and offers advice (e.g. Ashcroft and Foreman-Peck 1995; Ashworth and Harvey 1994; Ellis 1993; Harvey and Associates 1997; Liston 1999; Smith et al. 1999).

Considerable attention has been devoted to exploring what quality, as applied to higher education, might mean (e.g. Barnett 1992; Green 1994; Kekale 2002; Tam 2001). Thus, Harvey and Knight (1996) offer five main interpretations, viewing quality alternatively as exceptional, perfection or consistency, fitness for purpose, value for money or transformation. They also offer three views of standards: academic standards, standards of competence and service standards. Clearly, as they point out:

> *The interrelationship between quality and standards depends on the approach to quality and the particular notion of standard* . . . *The exceptional approach to quality emphasizes the maintenance of academic standards, through the summative assessment of knowledge* . . . *The perfection approach emphasizes consistency in external quality monitoring of academic, competence and service standards* . . . *The fitness-for-purpose approach relates standards to specified purpose-related objectives* . . . *The value-for-money approach places emphasis on a 'good deal' for the customer or client, usually government, employer, student or parents* . . . *The transformative approach uses standards to assess the enhancement of students both in terms of academic knowledge and a broader set of transformative skills, such as analysis, critique, lateral thinking, innovation and communication.* (Harvey and Knight 1996: 17, 23)

Harvey and Knight then present survey and other evidence suggesting that academic staff and students tend to emphasize the quality of the student experience, while employers focus on graduates' employability and governments use quality as a means of controlling higher education. Their own preference, not surprisingly, is for the transformative approach.

Goodlad (1995) takes a different strategy to analysing quality, by seeking to set out what it shouldn't be. He identified 16 forms of what he terms 'heresies': four relating to the curriculum (determinism, academicism, utilitarianism, survivalism), four to teaching methods (pedagogicism, abstractionism, occupationalism, mechanism), four to research (sponsorism, libertarianism, departmentalism, opportunism) and four to college organization (collegialism, monasticism, homogenism, individualism). While declining to offer a single, overarching definition of quality, he provides a checklist of issues that need addressing if poor quality provision is to be avoided.

The meaning you attach to quality in higher education, naturally enough, effects how you go about trying to achieve quality and how you try and measure what has been achieved. While most attention, as we have seen, has been given to the quality assurance systems actually in use – often transferred, with relatively little thought, from manufacturing or service industries – some academics have argued for the introduction of particular systems (e.g. van Ernst et al. 2001; Houston and Studman 2001).

Case studies

The three case studies presented in this chapter comprise:

- a critique of the validity and usefulness of the university league tables produced by newspapers;
- a review of the different kinds of external quality monitoring systems in use in higher education; and
- a questionnaire-based analysis of the validity of student evaluation questionnaires.

Case Study 7.1

Rachel Bowden (2000) Fantasy Higher Education: university and college league tables. *Quality in Higher Education*, 6, 1, 41–60.

Themes and Issues

Bowden's concern in this article is with the proliferation of league tables, ranking British universities and colleges, which are published by national newspapers each year, ostensibly to provide guidance to prospective students, their parents and other interested parties on the relative quality of, and facilities offered by, different institutions. She takes a critical stance towards these league tables, characterizing them in her title as 'fantasy higher education'.

Methods and Methodologies

This article relies on documentary analysis – the university league tables produced by different national newspapers – and is a good example of a critical study of readily available secondary data.

Level

Though there is some reference to the situation in other countries, the article is primarily focused at the national level: that is, the United Kingdom system.

Analytical/Theoretical Framework

The framework for the article is relatively straightforward – the league tables produced by five different publications are first described, and then their accuracy and usefulness are critiqued.

Related Literatures

The advent of university league tables in the popular press has attracted a good deal of academic criticism (e.g. Berry 1999; Tight 2000c; Tomlin 1998; Yorke 1997), as well as discussion in professional journals such as the *Times Higher Education Supplement*. There is also a more general literature focusing on the use of all kinds of performance indicators in higher education (Cave et al. 1997; Johnes and Taylor 1991), which is discussed further in Chapter 8.

Argument and Conclusions

Having described the five league tables being considered, Bowden begins her critique by noting the variation in the positions of individual universities in the published tables, and in the scores given for component criteria. She then reviews the doubts raised concerning the validity of the tables, the quality of the variables included, data errors and methodology. She argues that the utility of the tables is reduced by the omission of some institutions, the focus on institutions rather than courses, and the weighting of the variables included. She concludes that:

> The evidence strongly suggests that the compilers of the university league tables produced to date have exaggerated their claims to provide students with reliable and valid information on the UK's best universities in order to aid their selection of university. (p. 57)

Case Study 7.2

Lee Harvey (2002) Evaluation for What? *Teaching in Higher Education*, 7, 3, 245–63.

Themes and Issues

In undertaking a systematic review of external quality monitoring of higher education, Harvey 'asks who are the quality monitors, what, how and why do they evaluate?' (p. 245)

Methods and Methodologies

The article relies on documentary analysis, referring to and analysing a wide range of writing on the topic.

Level

The focus of this article is at the system level, in that it examines the role of external quality monitoring in a generic sense, while using examples from a variety of different countries.

Analytical/Theoretical Framework

In this article, Harvey develops a series of analytical frameworks for considering quality monitoring of higher education institutions:

- whether monitoring is internal or external, and, if the latter, whether it is statutory or non-statutory, and how independent it is;
- whether the focus of the evaluation is on quality or standards; and
- what use is made in the evaluation of self-assessment, peer evaluation and performance indicators.

Related Literatures

With the increased attention accorded internationally to the quality of higher education over the last two decades, there is now a substantive literature focusing on this issue (e.g. Aylett and Gregory 1996; Craft 1992; Goodlad 1995; Radford et al. 1997). There is also an academic journal, *Quality in Higher Education*, devoted to the theme. Harvey, as the editor of that journal since its foundation, has been one of the leading contributors to this literature.

Argument and Conclusions

Having effectively outlined the scope and variety of quality monitoring practices, Harvey then offers a critique of the process. In this, he draws particular attention to the value of statistical indicators, the honesty of self-evaluation, the training given to peer reviewers, the openness of the procedures and the extent to which game-playing takes place. He comes to a rather depressing conclusion:

> *Most agencies, it seems, have not even considered how their method-led, bureaucratic procedures fail to engage student learning. They have tended to ignore a quarter of a century of research into learning theory, the nature and styles of learning, and classroom innovations. Agency reports fail to act as a conduit for good practice. The only thing most external quality monitoring is useful for is the 'peer reviewers' who learn a lot from the experience. Unfortunately, there is little evidence that this invaluable personal experience is either shared with the reviewers' colleagues or reflected in the experience of the reviewed. (p. 260)*

Case Study 7.3

Mark Shevlin, Philip Banyard, Mark Davies and Mark Griffiths (2000) The Validity of Student Evaluation of Teaching in Higher Education: love me, love my lectures? *Assessment and Evaluation in Higher Education*, 25, 4, 397–405.

Themes and Issues

Student evaluation of teaching is a mainstay of most higher education institutions' quality assurance practices, and it would be an unusual institution, department or course team nowadays that did not pay some attention to the results of such evaluations. In some cases, decisions on lecturers' employment and promotion may be, in part, based on such evaluations. But just how accurate or valid are they? And what constitutes effective teaching? Those are the questions posed in this article by Shevlin and his colleagues.

Methods and Methodologies

This article was categorized in the analysis reported in the introductory chapter as adopting a multivariate approach to researching quality issues. The research involved administering a questionnaire to 213 undergraduate students at one United Kingdom higher education institution. The questionnaire asked the students to rate their lecturer in terms of twelve items: six to do with the lecturer's ability, five concerning the attributes of the module or course they were studying, and a final item assessing whether their lecturer had charisma. The data collected was then subjected to factor analysis, and a model produced of teaching effectiveness and charisma.

Level

With data collection confined to one higher education institution, this can be categorized as an institutional level study, though its implications are obviously broader than that.

Analytical/Theoretical Framework

The authors locate their study within the context of previous research that:

- tried to identify the key characteristics of effective teaching: here little consensus was apparent;

- indicated a relationship between expected assessment grades and reported evaluations of teacher effectiveness.

To this they add, from the business/management literature, the concept of charismatic or transformative leadership. In the business/management literature, perceptions of charisma have been shown to positively affect employees' views of their managers and employers. The authors' hypothesis, then, is that students' perceptions of their lecturers as charismatic will have a positive affect on their assessment of those lecturers.

Related Literatures

There are two literatures to which this interesting study may be related. One is the general literature on teaching in higher education, how to teach, what works and how to assess and evaluate teaching (e.g. Aylett and Gregory 1996; Biggs 1999; Brown and Atkins 2002; Johnson 2000; Knight 2002a; Laurillard 2002; Nicholls 2002; Ramsden 1992; Walker 2001). The other is the developing literature on student behaviours, of which the article by Norton et al. (2001) is an example.

Argument and Conclusions

The model that the authors produce from their factor analysis does suggest that there is a 'halo effect' in students' evaluations of their lecturers produced by the formers' perception of the latter as charismatic. They then, naturally enough, raise the issue of how much reliance should then be placed upon student evaluations.

Ideas for further research

Following on from the analysis presented in this chapter, a variety of topics for further research may be identified. Readers may, of course, wish to add their own ideas to this selection:

- autobiographical and biographical studies of the experiences of those conducting and undergoing quality assessment within higher education;
- more detailed studies of the impacts – foreseen and unforeseen, beneficial and unhelpful – of performance-based funding on academic work;
- analyses of how the different customers of higher education understand its purposes and operation;
- investigations of the possibilities of using more qualitative means for evaluating courses;
- research into why, and how, academics allocate grades to particular pieces of assessed work; and
- more comparative studies of the advantages, disadvantages and operation of alternative quality assessment systems.

8

Researching system policy

Introduction

As the analysis in Part I of this book made clear, system policy is one of the most popular areas for research – among the eight themes identified – in higher education. This popularity is made manifest through the existence of a number of academic journals that specialize in this area. These include both nationally focused journals such as *Higher Education Quarterly* and the *Journal of Higher Education Policy and Management,* and international journals such as the *European Journal of Education* and *Higher Education Policy.*

In part, the popularity of research and writing on system policy is probably because everyone working within higher education, naturally enough, has an opinion on higher education policy, whether they are a higher education researcher or not, and many are not shy of expressing (and publishing) them. More importantly, though, with the government remaining the major funder of higher education in most countries, system policy remains the crucial determinant of higher education practice. It naturally, therefore, forms a key focus for comment and research, with any changes in policy being subject to review and evaluation.

Some of the key questions behind research into system policy include:

- How effective are the changing policies of governments?
- How is policy made, and how might we influence it?
- How do the higher education policies adopted by governments in different countries compare?
- What are the most effective ways of funding higher education provision?
- How might the relationships between governments, their agencies and higher education institutions be best organized?
- How have system policies changed in the light of the move from elite to mass participation?

- How do higher education systems relate to each other internationally?

This chapter, then, focuses on how higher education researchers have attempted to understand, critique and perhaps even influence the policies adopted within different national systems.

Research into system policy

Research into higher education system policy has been categorized into five related sub-themes for the purposes of the present analysis. These are:

- the policy context;
- national policies;
- comparative policy studies;
- historical policy studies;
- funding relationships.

Each of these sub-themes will now be discussed in more detail.

The policy context

Studies of the context for system policy are commonly focused at what I have termed the 'system' level (see Chapter 1). That is, though they may be implicitly grounded in the researcher's knowledge and experience of a particular higher education system (or systems), the discussion is pitched in terms of some idealized system. In method/ological terms, we may also observe something of an elision between a more conventional reliance on documentary forms of analysis and towards the adoption of more conceptual, and sometimes critical, approaches.

Another characteristic of research in this area is its discussion of what might be called grand issues or topics. These topics come and go with time, often re-appearing, suitably or subtly relabelled, under different guises. One easy, but not totally foolproof or inclusive, way of identifying these grand issues is that many terminate in the suffix 'ism' or 'ization'. Thus, we may consider under this heading, for example, research into the ideas and practices underlying:

- diversification;
- entrepreneurialism (Clark 1998; Marginson and Considine 2000);
- globalization (Kwiek 2001; Scott 1998);
- internationalization;
- managerialism (Deem 2001; Trowler 2001);
- marketization (Meek 2000);
- massification (Scott 1995);

- McDonaldization and the McUniversity (Hayes and Wynyard 2002; Prichard and Willmott 1997);
- post-industrialism;
- post-modernism (Raschke 2003; Smith and Webster 1997);
- privatization; and
- the virtual university (Robins and Webster 2002),

as well as the more prosaically titled lifelong learning (Knapper and Cropley 2000) and the learning society (Dunne 1999).

The article by Deem (2001), reviewed as Case Study 8.1 in this chapter, is a good example of this kind of research and writing. She examines contemporary thinking on the concepts of globalization, new managerialism, academic capitalism and entrepreneurialism – as they are applied to higher education systems – through an extended review of two recently published and influential books (Clark 1998; Slaughter and Leslie 1997). In doing so, she raises doubts about the empirical bases and methodological rigour of some studies on these topics.

Scott (1995, 1998) is another key thinker in this area, with successive publications examining massification and globalization. Scott's book on mass higher education is a good illustration of how a single publication may range across different themes, methods and levels. Thus, while it is grounded in an extensive knowledge and experience of the British system, it includes comparative elements. And though it makes extensive use of documentary sources, it might be said to be predominantly conceptual in approach. Scott argues that:

> The two most important features of the structure of mass higher education . . . are fuzziness and permeability. It has become more difficult to distinguish clearly between the four main types of higher education system – dual systems, in which universities stand apart from the rest of post-secondary education; binary systems, where alternative higher education institutions are established to complement or rival the universities; unified systems, in which all higher education institutions are treated (approximately) equally; and stratified systems, characterised by a division of institutional labour. (Scott 1995: 169)

He then goes on to outline the implications of these developments for higher education institutions:

> The impact of massification on institutions has been twofold. First, they have to develop their own distinctive missions. Because of fuzziness and permeability, real and rhetorical priorities can no longer be derived, normatively, from totalising ideas such as the liberal university or, operationally, from sector-wide stereotypes such as the standard polytechnic . . . Second, institutions have become much more complex, in size as the system has expanded, and in scope as it has become more heterogeneous. (p. 170)

Meek (2000) has undertaken a similar study of the impact of marketization on higher education systems, with particular reference to its relation to diversification. As with Scott's study, though Meek draws particular attention to developments in Australia and the United Kingdom, his analysis is more generic. He concludes that the concepts, or rather the practice, of marketization and diversification are in opposition:

> . . . *market competition between institutions in the same policy environment results in emulation and a convergence of academic norms and values . . . the answer to the question of whether or not a nation wants a highly differentiated set of tertiary education institutions, serving the diverse needs of an extremely heterogeneous mass student clientele, rests on a policy decision; it cannot be left solely to the market to resolve.* (p. 37)

Though somewhat contrary, Ritzer's McDonaldization hypothesis (Ritzer 1998, 2000), as applied to higher education (Hayes and Wynyard 2002), might be said to be focused on the impact of the market. Ritzer, however, bases his hypothesis – which presents the highly standardized fast-food industry as an exemplar of modern organizational trends and practices – firmly on an updating of Weber's ideas about bureaucratization, stressing the key issues of efficiency, calculability, predictability and control. Interestingly, Ritzer himself, while noting that higher education is not presently as McDonaldized as the fast-food industry, and arguing that some degree of McDonaldization – or the McDonaldization of certain functions – would be beneficial, emphasizes the need to de-McDonaldize the university:

> *To survive as a means of consumption, the university must learn from the highly successful cathedrals of consumption and find ways of becoming more spectacular . . . While everything around it is growing increasingly McDonaldized, the route open to the university is to create spectacle by deMcDonaldizing its quotidian activities. Inefficient, unpredictable, incalculable education employing human technologies will seem quite spectacular to students, especially in contrast to the numbing McDonaldization that is increasingly found almost everywhere else. The spectacle of the deMcDonaldization of the university's everyday activities will not only be spectacular and attract students, but it will also serve to enhance dramatically the quality of the educational process.* (Ritzer 2002: 31–2)

How, and whether, all universities can de-McDonaldize is obviously a key question.

National policies

Research into the higher education policy of a specific country or nation is, without doubt, the most common form of research in the area of system policy (and one of the most common forms for research into higher education generally). Within this sub-theme, the most popular approach is to offer some reflection, critique or commentary on a recently, or about to be, introduced policy. With higher education systems seen as – and in most cases also being – subject to a considerable amount of policy change in recent decades, this is understandable. Hence, books and articles taking this strategy regularly roll off the printing presses, including many edited volumes (e.g. Coffield and Williamson 1997; Raffe et al. 2001; Schuller 1995; Scott 2000). While these studies are of considerable interest and topicality around about the time they are published – and of some continuing historical interest – their concerns and emphases often soon date.

For example, Watson and Taylor (1998) take the publication of the Dearing Report (National Committee of Inquiry into Higher Education 1997) as an opportunity to provide an analysis of higher education policy in the United Kingdom, and where it might be going. They examine successively history, rates of participation, the curriculum and its organization, resourcing issues and the impact of higher education, and show a particular interest in the possible implications for a lifelong learning policy. It might be argued, with a few more years retrospection, that the impact of the Dearing Report has been minimal, and that its association with the idea(l) of lifelong learning was always marginal. Nevertheless, Watson and Taylor do provide a carefully considered analysis of the position at their time of writing, and one which repays re-visiting.

By comparison, Bessant (2002) offers a more focused, and hence somewhat less time-bound, analysis of a major national policy development in Australia, the higher education reforms introduced in the 1990s by the then Minister John Dawkins. While she offers a summary of the reforms, the focus of much analysis by Australian higher education researchers and writers, her interest is in the use of metaphor and rhetoric in their articulation and justification. Bessant distinguishes between pedagogical (for example policy agenda, private beneficiary), heuristic (for example market place, flexibility) and constitutive (for example human capital, higher education system) metaphors, and traces their use in the presentation of the higher education reforms. She concludes:

Metaphors serve a variety of functions in official political rhetoric. Pedagogical metaphors assist with the task of clarification. Heuristic metaphors are important for those who are attempting to be systematic and objective; they help explain ideas, and build policy and 'educational service delivery models'. Constitutive metaphors frame discourses. As such they also offer insights into the reasons for fundamental differences and disagreements between those in policy-making communities . . . Recognising metaphor in official rhetoric is useful for bringing about change . . . considering the official rhetoric in higher education reform

*offers opportunities to change those accounts and to replace them with entirely
new frameworks for understanding issues around learning, research, teaching,
etc.* (p. 97)

Schuller et al. (1999) take as their analytical focus the state of part-time
forms of higher education in Scotland. Their study is not just a policy
analysis, but an evaluation of contemporary practice as well. Thus, it
includes case studies of practice in four higher education institutions,
and questionnaire and interview data collected from student samples in
those institutions. This is framed, however, by a discussion of changing
national higher education policy and, in particular, the advantages and
disadvantages of part-time and full-time forms of provision.

Kogan and Hanney (2000) provide an analysis of changes in higher
education policy in the United Kingdom between 1975 and 1997, adopting
a political science framework. They make use of documentary analysis
and interviews with key or representative informants, at both national and
institutional levels. In a densely argued text, they come to a conclusion
about the development of national higher education which might be either
worrying or re-assuring, depending upon your perspective:

> *We can offer no clearly schematic picture of how policies emerged and ideologies
> were sponsored. Intentions were forged partly by belief systems, partly by the
> power of circumstances, and partly by opportunistic reactions to what might not
> have been planned or even rationally contemplated.* (pp. 236–7)

This conclusion throws into the air again the question of how policy makers
may best be influenced and persuaded.

Comparative policy studies

Research into comparative higher education policy is well established.
Indeed, it is clearly the best developed area of comparative higher
education research, most probably because – for a methodology that is
particularly demanding in terms of resources required – it is not so
demanding to undertake, particularly in collaboration with colleagues in
other countries. The second and third of the case studies discussed in this
chapter (Jongbloed and Vossensteyn 2001; McBurnie and Ziguras 2001)
are both comparative policy studies.

Comparative policy studies may be categorized in a number of ways. One
obvious classification is in terms of the numbers of countries or systems
compared:

- Comparisons between just two or three countries, particularly if they are
  adjacent or share common histories and languages, can be relatively
  straightforward to undertake, even for a single researcher. Given the
  narrowness of focus, they may also allow the researcher to get into the

issues being explored in much greater depth. Thus, for example, Harman (2000a) compares research infrastructure grant allocation in Australia and the United Kingdom; Maassen (1996) examines governmental steering strategies in Germany and the Netherlands; and Osborne (1996) compares policy in Northern Ireland and the Republic of Ireland.

- Comparisons between several countries in one region of the world are somewhat more complex, though this may, again, be kept within reasonable bounds if the countries considered have cultural or economic factors in common. Europe, particularly the European community, offers fertile ground for this kind of study (e.g. Gellert 1998; Hare 1997; Henkel and Little 1999; Kehm et al. 1997). Indeed, many themed issues of journals like the *European Journal of Education* or *Higher Education in Europe* – taking each issue as a whole – consist of comparative European studies on a particular theme. Europe is not the only region subject to such comparative research, however: East Asia, for example, also offers a group of countries with many similarities (Yee 1995), and even more challenging comparative studies, such as of the circumpolar north (Nord and Weller 2002) are possible.

- Global, or neo-global, comparative studies offer the greatest challenges of all, of course, though these may be kept under control by focusing the study on either developed or developing countries. Of these two strategies, the former, unsurprisingly, is the more common (e.g. Brennan et al. 1999; Goedegebuure et al. 1994; Meek et al. 1996), though the latter also exist, as do some studies aspiring to a truly global reach (e.g. Cowen 1996).

Another way of categorizing comparative research is in terms of how it is carried out and presented. Here, there are two main strategies. The first – and most common, because it is clearly the most manageable – is to produce or commission a series of national studies, to a more or less common format and methodology, and then to 'top and tail' these with a comparative analysis and summary. For example, Goedegebuure et al. (1994 – compare Altbach 1996) produced a comparative study of higher education policy in 11 developed systems (mostly nations, but including two states which exercised policy responsibility for higher education): Australia, California, Denmark, France, Germany, Japan, the Netherlands, Ontario, Sweden, Switzerland and the United Kingdom. They commissioned national experts in each of these systems to produce a report, issuing them with a questionnaire to guide them as to the information required. The key issues of interest to them were: regulation, steering and control; governments, markets and academia; autonomy and academic freedom; federalism and intermediary bodies.

The published report of this study consists, therefore, of an introductory chapter, 11 chapters presenting the findings of the individual system studies, and a final chapter drawing the comparative lessons of the research out. This last chapter focuses on issues of diversity, authority, policy instruments, quality and accountability, and states of transition. The editors offer the following general conclusion:

> ... it does appear that the dual process of relaxing government control, and strengthening institutional management and autonomy, will continue in several countries. This process, it seems, will be accompanied by enhanced institutional competition, a degree of privatization in funding of both teaching and research, and some degree of reliance on market-like regulation. At the same time, institutions will be held more accountable for their quality and services. (Goedegebuure et al. 1994: 347–8)

These conclusions clearly relate to those of Meek (2000), Ritzer (2002) and Scott (1995, 1998), discussed in the section on the policy context earlier in this chapter.

The alternative strategy to producing national studies, and then comparing them, is to carry out thematic research across a number of systems simultaneously. Clearly, this is easier to do the fewer the systems involved, and the more focused the theme being researched (it also helps if the systems examined share a common language), but it is possible.

Historical policy studies

As will be argued in Chapter 9, most historical research on higher education tends to be focused on individual institutions. There are, however, some more general studies, many of which focus on system policy. Clearly, studies on earlier historical periods have to rely primarily on documentary sources (e.g. Bell and Tight 1993; de Ridder-Symoens 1992, 1996), while those covering more recent periods or initiatives may also make use of interviews and observation (e.g. Pratt 1997; White 2001).

Pratt's (1997) study of the 27-year history of the 30 English and Welsh polytechnics, which became universities in 1992, is a good example of the latter genre of research. He set himself two aims:

> .. to produce the first full history of the experiment, to be as comprehensive a record as possible of the events and of the views of those making, taking part and observing them ... to analyse the policy – in terms of its intentions, its outcomes and its implications for the development of higher education systems both in England and Wales and abroad. (pp. 5–6)

He examines the developing policy, the students the polytechnics recruited, the ways they were taught, staff, quality assurance, funding and management. In attempting to reach an overall assessment of how well the polytechnic experiment worked, he argues that, while there were both successes and failures, perhaps the greatest success of the experiment was the impact it had on British higher education as a whole:

> *The polytechnics moved away from some of the purposes set for them, but the universities moved towards the polytechnics in significant respects. The polytechnics had a substantial effect on the university sector, leading to a breakdown of the traditional demarcation between vocational and academic courses that had characterised, albeit imperfectly, the two sectors. The universities increasingly acquired characteristics that had traditionally been those of the polytechnics, for example in developing modular courses and recruiting non-traditional students. The resulting 'unified' system cannot be wholly or accurately described in terms of either of the predecessor sectors.*
> (p. 309)

A similar, though less extensive, evaluative strategy is adopted by Marginson (2002) in his analysis of changing national policy for higher education in Australia since the 1950s. Marginson portrays Australian post-war higher education policy as being concerned primarily with nation-building, strengthening its universities and removing dependence on the British and American systems. He argues that that strategy has been in crisis since the late 1980s, as a result of the pressures of globalization, a declining government commitment and a crisis of academic identity. The Australian system, like those of Canada and New Zealand, is now commonly viewed as part of the 'American periphery':

> *It is widely and deeply felt that Australian institutions should steer more closely to the cost structures and missions, and the separation from government, seen to characterise American universities.* (p. 415)

Marginson, however, argues strongly for an alternative strategy:

> *. . . the primary strategy should not be to imitate American universities, a course of action which is likely to deliver modest returns, but to strengthen the academic identity and place-based identity of Australian institutions, enabling them to make a distinctive contribution to global higher education underpinned by a renewed partnership between nation and university.* (p. 409)

Looking back beyond recent system history, the two volumes edited by de Ridder-Symoens (1992, 1996: two more volumes are in preparation) provide an excellent, and relatively rare, example of a thematic – as opposed to institutional – and comparative history of higher education. Each book has a common organization (compare the discussion of comparative policy studies earlier in this chapter). Thus, different authors examine themes and patterns (including the origins and diversity of universities), structures (including relations with authority, management, resources, teachers), students (including admissions, student life, graduate careers, mobility) and learning (including faculty origins, changing structures of knowledge and the curriculum).

This series is being sponsored by the Conference of European Rectors, as 'a collaborative investigation which would deal with the social setting, the social demands, the structures, and the major problems of the European universities as they have developed and changed in the course of their history' (Ruegg 1992: xxii). The desirability of researching into the history of the university as a European institution is fervently argued:

> *The university is a European institution; indeed, it is the European institution par excellence . . . It is, moreover, the only European institution which has preserved its fundamental patterns and its basic social role and functions over the course of history . . . No other European institution has spread over the entire world in the way in which the traditional form of the European university has done . . . the university . . . has developed and transmitted scientific and scholarly knowledge and the methods of cultivating that knowledge which has arisen from and formed part of the common European intellectual tradition.* (pp. xix–xx)

Each chapter synthesizes, and builds upon, the substantial existing historical literature – largely based on documentary analysis – particularly that covering individual institutional histories and changing national policies and practices.

Funding relationships

The final sub-theme to be considered in this chapter is interesting for being the only one of the five identified to have a specific focus: the other four all examine system policy in general. It is probably not surprising to learn that this sub-theme has to do with funding: how is higher education to be paid for, and how do those paying try and ensure that they are getting value for money?

As with research into other topics, while studies of particular systems dominate, there are also some comparative studies (e.g. Hare 1997; Henkel and Little 1999; Kaiser et al. 1992; Salmi and Verspoor 1994). Three areas for research stand out:

- studies of public expenditure on higher education (e.g. Kaiser et al. 1992);
- studies of the use of performance indicators (e.g. Cave et al. 1997; Johnes and Taylor 1991; Jongbloed and Vossensteyn 2001 – the last of these is discussed as a case study later in this chapter); and
- studies of the relationships between state and higher education institutions (e.g. Henkel and Little 1999; Neave and van Vught 1994), in particular the role of intermediary bodies (e.g. Shattock 1994).

Cave et al.'s book (1997) is unusual, for the higher education literature, in having gone to a third edition. While the focus is on the development and application of performance indicators within the British system, this is set within the context of practice and experience in the USA and other countries. The authors examine performance indicators for teaching and learning, and for research, and look at different models and their application. They argue that, while performance indicators are being applied more and more to different aspects of higher education, they have yet to have much impact:

> *As yet, the evidence is that new measures incorporating more diverse criteria have not been institutionalised and that the dominant forms of evaluation are those of the state rather than those of the market. As we have seen, the main influence on the funding councils' research and teaching quality assessments is that of peer review. The role of PIs in the process is either negligible, as in the case of teaching quality, or unclear, as in the case of research assessment. In each case the criteria adopted appear overwhelmingly to have been those of high academic excellence and reputation, despite policy commitments in the areas of research and teaching to more diverse concepts of quality.*
> (p. 224)

However, Cave et al. hold out some hope, suggesting that 'the development of the quality movement might make it possible for PIs to be used more precisely and more beneficially' (p. 227 – see also the discussion of quality in Chapter 7 of this book).

Henkel and Little's edited collection (1999) draws on a series of research seminars conducted in 1996/97. Their focus is on Western European systems, with a bias towards the United Kingdom. They link recent and ongoing changes in the relationships between higher education and the state primarily to massification (see also the discussion in the section on the policy context earlier in this chapter):

> *Massification has compelled governments to develop new forms of regulation, which, in turn, may imply different degrees of freedom and control for different institutions. Massification entails diversification. It implies a wider range of institutions, of students and of university staff: different inputs will tend to produce different outputs, different types of graduate and different forms of knowledge. There will be more variation between universities as to the functions they perform. So universal regulation and central planning must give way to new forms of control: contracts; institutional self regulation within a more discretionary framework; incentives and sanctions; new and more extensive forms of evaluation; competition in quasi-markets.*
> (pp. 339–40)

Perhaps their most interesting conclusion, however, concerns the diversity and variability of governments' changing strategies: 'governments are to be found speaking in different voices; vacillating between solutions; exerting contradictory pressures; using constructive ambiguity as a tool of policy making' (p. 341). Clearly, as with all complex systems, there is no one simple, stable and obvious solution.

Case studies

The three case studies considered in this chapter comprise:

- a documentary analysis of current thinking internationally on the development of higher education policy;
- a comparative analysis of government policies regarding performance-based funding; and
- a comparative analysis, again based largely on documents, of government policies on the regulation of transnational higher education.

Case Study 8.1

Rosemary Deem (2001) Globalisation, New Managerialism, Academic Capitalism and Entrepreneurialism in Universities: is the local dimension still important? *Comparative Education*, 37, 1, 7–20.

Themes and Issues

This article is essentially a review of contemporary thinking about how higher education systems are developing in the context of social, economic and technological pressures. Or, as Deem herself, puts it, it:

> ... explores some recent analyses of change in universities in Western countries undertaken by scholars using case-study materials about different institutions. (p. 7)

Methods and Methodologies

This article may be categorized as adopting documentary analysis to analyse system policy. It has a comparative element, in that it discusses two analyses of universities in Europe and North America, and was published in a comparative education journal. It is, in essence, though, a review article, critiquing two recently published books, which is why I have characterized it as documentary analysis.

Level

I would categorize this article as focusing on the system level, in that its concern is with how the higher education system is changing.

Analytical/Theoretical Framework

Deem locates her analysis within a discussion of the related concepts of globalization, new managerialism, academic capitalism and entrepreneurialism. In comparing the experiences of universities in Europe and North America, she argues that the importance of the local dimension may have been overlooked in the focus on global changes, and also suggests that there are important linkages between the global and the local.

Related Literatures

This article may be related to both the comparative literature and that dealing with the analysis of key concepts – such as globalization and modernization – particularly as they are applied within national systems (e.g. Kwiek 2001; McBurnie 2001; Meek 2000; Middleton 2000; Scott 1998). For me, though, as indicated, it is a good example of a synoptic, and critical, review article. This is something that a developing field of research, such as higher education, needs more of (e.g. McInnis 2001).

Argument and Conclusions

Deem's analysis centres on two recent, and fairly influential books – Clark (1998) on *Creating Entrepreneurial Universities* and Slaughter and Leslie (1997) on *Academic Capitalism*. She argues that the authors have over-emphasized the degree of convergence between the case study universities examined, and that their methodological approaches lack critique and robustness. She emphasizes the need to adopt robust methodologies and less constraining frameworks in undertaking comparative research into higher education.

Case Study 8.2

Ben Jongbloed and Hans Vossensteyn (2001) Keeping up Performances: an international survey of performance-based funding in higher education. *Journal of Higher Education Policy and Management*, 23, 2, 127–45.

Themes and Issues

Jongbloed and Vossensteyn's theme has to do with the use of performance-based funding in higher education. They set out to try and answer the question: 'do the funding authorities that decide on the universities' teaching and research grants base the size of the grant on measures of institutional performance?' (p. 127)

Methods and Methodologies

This article may be categorized as adopting a comparative approach to researching system policy. While the methodological approach is clear, the actual methods used are not explicitly spelt out. The bibliography, however, indicates that the study was essentially a documentary analysis, analysing reports produced by government departments and agencies in the systems studied. It also clearly makes use of the knowledge built up over recent years by the research centre in which the authors are based.

Level

As an analysis of policy in several countries, the study is clearly focused at an international level.

Analytical/Theoretical Framework

The two authors provide an analysis and comparison of the university funding policies practised by 11 members of the Organisation for Economic Co-operation and Development (OECD). These countries include Australia, Japan, New Zealand and the United States, as well as seven Western European countries. Separate descriptions of the policies pursued in each country are provided along with a comparative analysis.

The article is contextualized in terms of performance indicators and alternative models of performance-based funding, and of input- and output-based funding systems. An expectation here is that, with the growth of mass higher education systems in developed countries, and the increased public expenditure which that implies, governments might be interested in rewarding better performing institutions.

Related Literatures

Comparative studies of this kind are not that common, largely because they are relatively expensive and time-consuming, and also, as the authors of this article make clear, difficult to do (see also the article by Teichler (2000b), discussed in Chapter 6). Comparative studies also frequently take the form of a series of national case studies produced by national experts to a common format, rather than a genuinely comparative and analytic overview. There are, however, some interesting examples of comparative higher education studies (e.g. Braun and Merrien 1999; Brennan and Shah 2000; Enders 2001; Goedegebuure et al. 1994; Harman 2000a; McBurnie and Ziguras 2001; Meek et al. 1996; Smeby and Stensaker 1999).

The other literature of relevance to this article, though it is not explicitly located within it, is that devoted to the quality assurance and evaluation of higher education institutions (e.g. Bowden 2000; Drennan 2001; Gibbs et al. 2000; Harvey 2002; Tam 2001).

Argument and Conclusions

Jongbloed and Vossensteyn's study suggests that their presumption – that governments would be interested in rewarding better performing institutions – is not borne out in most of the systems studied. The funding of university teaching remains largely based on enrolments, that is, on inputs. In the case of research, however, output-based funding is more common. The authors conclude by speculating on why input-based funding should be so popular, and on how it can be made to function more effectively.

Case Study 8.3

Grant McBurnie and Christopher Ziguras (2001) The Regulation of Transnational Higher Education in Southeast Asia: case studies of Hong Kong, Malaysia and Australia. *Higher Education*, 42, 85–105.

Themes and Issues

McBurnie and Ziguras focus on transnational higher education, that is, higher education provided by institutions based in one country through satellite operations in other countries.

Methods and Methodologies

This article may be categorized as adopting a comparative approach to researching system policy. As with the article by Jongbloed and Vossensteyn (2001), discussed as Case Study 8.2, while the comparative methodology is clear, the methods used to collect and analyse the data are not so explicit. Again, however, the research presented evidently rests upon the analysis of documents produced by governments and agencies in the systems compared.

Level

The article focuses on the international level.

Analytical/Theoretical Framework

The authors locate their analysis within the general context provided by globalization – 'Higher education is part of the increasing globalisation of the trade in goods and services' (p. 85) – the World Trade Organisation (WTO) and the General Agreement on Trade in Services (GATS). In terms of the WTO's categorization of modes of international service delivery, their focus is on 'commercial presence'.

Related Literatures

The literature on transnational higher education is relatively limited (e.g. Knight and de Wit 1997), but growing as the phenomenon itself grows in importance. It has connections with the literature on international study, discussed in Chapter 4 along with the article by Kember (2000).

Argument and Conclusions

The region analysed – Southeast Asia – is an interesting one, both for the substantial growth in the demand for higher education, and for the varied approach towards transnational higher education taken by the governments concerned, which range from relatively laissez-faire to highly regulatory. Quality and standards issues are clearly to the fore in their consideration.

The authors provide case studies of three systems – Hong Kong, Malaysia and Australia – in each case discussing the degree of regulation applied, how it operates and the rationale for it. They show that consumer protection is of key importance in Hong Kong, together with transparency in regulations. In Malaysia, by comparison, the chief rationale appears to be the advancement of specific national goals, while in Australia the concern is to protect the local system from recent pressures from overseas institutions.

Ideas for further research

The foregoing review would suggest a series of fruitful avenues for further research:

- research into the transfer of ideas and policies between systems;
- studies which look for evidence of continuity in system policy, rather than simply focusing on and emphasizing change;
- studies of local reactions and adaptations to system policy;
- more smaller-scale, focused comparative research into aspects of system policy;
- more inter-institutional and/or thematic historical research; and
- more focused studies on system policy issues other than those connected with funding.

9

Researching institutional management

Introduction

With the massification of higher education systems (see Chapter 8), and the increasing attention being paid to quality and standards (see Chapter 7), the management of higher education institutions has – like other aspects of higher education – come to be seen as of critical importance. While it may have been possible in the past for smaller colleges to survive well enough under the guidance of a senior academic, with no management training, acting as a 'first amongst equals' within a supportive collegial environment, this would no longer work. Nowadays, what Clark (1998) has termed a 'strengthened steering core' is regarded as essential for a university to thrive in an increasingly competitive market, supported by a range of trained specialist staff at central and departmental levels.

Not surprisingly, then, more and more attention is being paid to researching how higher education institutions are managed, and how this might be improved. This is reflected in the existence of journals specifically focusing on this topic, including both glossy professional journals such as *Managing HE: for decision-makers in higher education* and academic journals like *Higher Education Management.*

Key questions underlying research into the management of higher education institutions include:

- What do managers of higher education institutions do?
- How is management exercised at the departmental level?
- How do the roles of managers of academics and academics-as-managers (a distinction usefully made by Deem (2003)) relate?
- How are the managers of higher education institutions trained and developed?
- What do managerial careers within higher education look like?

- How can the management of higher education institutions be improved?

This chapter explores how higher education researchers have approached these and related issues, and what conclusions they have come to.

Research into institutional management

For the purposes of this exploration, six main areas of research will be recognized:

- higher education management practice;
- institutional leadership and governance;
- institutional development and history;
- institutional structure;
- economies of scale and institutional mergers;
- relations between higher education, industry and community.

These areas could, of course, have been organized differently, but are arguably adequate for present purposes. They will each now be discussed in turn.

Higher education management practice

Research into the practice of higher education management may be characterized in terms of a dichotomy or spectrum. Thus, on the one hand, there is a substantial and growing body of writing which sets out to advise on how higher education institutions might best be managed in contemporary circumstances: the 'how to' literature. Then, on the other hand, there is the more theorized and analytical body of research which seeks to explain how and why higher education institutions are managed in the ways they are. And, of course, there are a multitude of literatures lying between these, somewhat artificial, extremes, embodying varied components of empirical analysis and 'how to' guidance.

The 'how to' literature on institutional management is more developed than that on any other academic role (see Chapter 10), with the exception of teaching and learning (see Chapter 4). Indeed, its recent expansion may be said to parallel that of the 'how to' literature on teaching and learning, though it started later and has not yet caught up. It may be epitomized by the 'Managing Universities and Colleges: guides to good practice' series, edited for the Open University Press by Warner and Palfreyman. This currently includes volumes on managing the academic unit, external relations, financial resources, information, international students, quality and standards, strategy, stress and students (Albrighton and Thomas 2001; Bolton 2000; Edworthy 2000; Elkin and Law 2000; Gledhill 1999; Humfrey 1999; Liston 1999; Thomas 2001; Watson 2000), with further titles planned.

In addition to this very pragmatic series, the same publishers offer several – longer, more theorized, widely referenced and definitely research-based – other books on the management of institutions of higher education, and by much the same set of authors. There is obviously, therefore, a significant market for writing on this area of academic life. These books include both an overview of the field of practice (Warner and Palfreyman 1996), and volumes focusing on more specific topics such as the management of academic staff (Farnham 1999), and of educational property (Warner and Kelly 1994), human resource management (Warner and Crosthwaite 1995), higher education and the law (Palfreyman and Warner 1998: see also Farrington 1994) and income generation (Warner and Leonard 1997).

This second literature might be termed 'middle ground' – midway, that is, between the explicitly 'how to' literature and critical, empirically based studies of higher education management – or 'can do'. We may distinguish between the 'how to' and 'can do' literatures in the following way, while recognizing that in practice there is inevitably some degree of overlap. A 'how to' text is the equivalent of a car repair manual or cookery book: follow these instructions and you should be OK. A 'can do' text, by contrast, is more visionary or missionary in its approach, suggesting that there is a single, best or preferred way of, in this case, managing higher education, which the reader should follow in order not just to survive, but also, hopefully, to achieve something approaching excellence.

As an example of the 'can do' literature, we may consider a recent edited volume of institutional case studies (Warner and Palfreyman 2001). This volume is of particular interest to me because, of the 18 authors included, all but one work, or used to work, for my own university, and the book as a whole is somewhat of a eulogy to what it terms 'the Warwick way'. The chapters included examine management practice in different kinds of higher education institutions within the United Kingdom, the role of external agencies and outward-looking departments within the university, and how institutional change and diversity might best be managed.

In the editors' words, the book:

> . . . *collects together a series of essays written by senior managers who share a common work experience and have reacted to that experience in differing ways. The common thread is the belief in the dynamism of HE [higher education] and the role of managers in helping to achieve the continuous improvement, relevance and development of the system.* (p. 2)

In short, this literature offers analysed examples of higher education management practice, for others to reflect carefully upon and perhaps then emulate, at least in part. There is a strong auto/biographical element (see also Miller 1995; Slowey 1995; Weil 1994).

By comparison with what I have called the 'how to' and 'can do' literatures on the management of institutions of higher education, the empirically based, more theorized and critical literature on this area is less developed. In part, this is probably because researching managers, particularly senior managers, is, at least potentially, a risky business. Two interesting examples of such research will, however, be highlighted here.

First, Deem (2003 – see also Deem 1998; Deem and Johnson 2000; Reed and Deem 2002; and Case Study 8.1) reports on an extensive, interview-based survey of the perceptions on institutional management of academics, manager-academics (i.e. academics acting as managers) and senior administrators in 16 British universities. She casts her analysis in terms of the ideology of 'new managerialism' and differing views of the social relations between managers and academics in contemporary universities. She concludes that:

> *The comparison of manager-academic and managed staff views gives many hints that, whilst few senior manager-academics appear to deliberately aim to be exclusionary in their management practices (indeed some express a fairly inclusive philosophy), many ordinary staff perceive the running and decision making of their institutions as such, even when in other respects they experience a sense of a shared and inclusive community.* (Deem 2003: 121)

Second, Prichard (2000) reports on an interview-based study of 65 senior postholders in four universities and four further education colleges in the United Kingdom. The focus of his research was on his respondents' changing experience of academic work, and, in particular, academic management. He casts his analysis within the context of 'knowledge practices', and argues on the basis of his research that:

> . . . a *'state of hostilities' has tended to exist in this education sector (during the period of the study) between the ascendant managerial knowledge practices and those embedded and variably subordinated (but not erased) academic and administrative knowledge practices.* (p. 199)

Clearly, the analyses of both Deem and Prichard suggest that all is not well with higher education management practice. If higher education managers are using the 'how to' and 'can do' literatures, then they don't seem to be working.

There is a link here, of course, between the higher education management literature and the more general business and management literature. The latter contains a vast range of generic 'how to' writing, of the kind that finds a prominent place on the airport bookstall. But there is also, as with higher education, a smaller, more theorized and critical literature. Within this, there are some examples of business/management academics, like Prichard, analysing the business within which they themselves work (e.g. Parker and Jary 1995; Prichard and Willmott 1997; Willmott 1995).

Institutional leadership and governance

The distinction between research on higher education management practice, and that on institutional leadership and governance, might be said to be a fine one, and these two topics certainly do overlap. While I would not want to argue the difference between these fields for research too hard, as the categorization adopted here is basically a convenience, it does relate to a distinction in the kinds of concepts and literatures referred to.

Case Study 9.2 (Ramsden 1998) is an example of research and writing on this topic. His emphasis is on leadership, seen as one element of the managerial role, and one of particular importance for those in senior managerial positions in higher education institutions. There are elements of 'how to' and 'can do' about the book – and this is clearly something its publishers were keen to promote in the back cover blurb – but it is also based on empirical research by the author and others.

A related, slightly earlier, study is that by Middlehurst (1993). She reviews the general literature on leadership – from early trait theories to more recent ideas of charismatic or transformative leadership – and relates this to the particular context of higher education. She then reports on her own empirical studies of leadership in British universities, making use of questionnaire and interview data. Thus, the different perspectives on leadership of vice-chancellors, pro-vice-chancellors, senior administrators and heads of departments are successively reviewed. These findings are then applied to the question of how leaders of higher education institutions might be developed more effectively. Her view of leadership might best be described as contingent:

> . . . no individual has a monopoly on leadership in a university, although formal leaders at different levels of the institution carry particular leadership functions. The expectation and the potential for leadership are widely distributed . . . different features of leadership are brought to the foreground, or seem most relevant, at different times. (pp. 191–2)

Knight and Trowler (2001) take a broadly similar view to studying leadership within higher education, but focus exclusively at the departmental level. Their study is primarily documentary, though it does make use of some survey data, and applies social practice theory. Knight and Trowler also see leadership as contingent and widely distributed, arguing for an approach that might be called 'distributed conceptual leadership':

> Leadership in higher education at the department level and below is best when it is distributed across the workgroup rather than being located solely in the person

of one individual, although final responsibility usually rests with the formal group leader . . . Good local leaders are in tune with the sociocultural context in which they operate . . . Tuned-in leaders are able to 'read' the likely ways in which proposals and policies will be received . . . good leaders are also able to operate well at the level of 'gut feelings' . . . the actions that constitute 'leading well' will vary from context to context. (p. 176)

The other key approach to researching leadership stresses the concept of governance and the role of the governing bodies of higher education institutions. Thus, Bargh et al. (1996) offer a pioneering study of governors in British universities, based on a questionnaire survey of 745 governors and interviews within four selected case study institutions. They present and discuss collected data on the characteristics of governors, how they are selected, the roles they perform and their relations with key university staff. They argue that governance is becoming a central concern in university management – a way past 'the culture of an anachronistic "donnish dominion" or, its ideological antithesis, imposing an alien "business" culture' (p. 178). Its future success, however, is seen as depending upon making governing bodies more representative, democratic and open (Shattock 2002). There is also a developing comparative literature on this topic (Braun and Merrien 1999).

Institutional development and history

Institutional histories of individual universities and colleges are one of the staples of the higher education literature. Indeed, there can be few institutions of more than two or three decades in age which have not had an institutional history produced (recent examples include, for example, Burgess et al. 1995; Ives et al. 2000; Kolbert 2000; Shear 1996; Smart 1994). Typically, these are either published internally or by the university's own press. There are also a number of journals devoted to this area, such as *History of Universities*, and some generic educational history journals.

Institutions of higher education which have lasted for a hundred years, in one form or another, will have had a series of histories produced (compare, for example, Aldrich 2002 and Dixon 1986 on the history of the Institute of Education in London). Surviving for 500 years can result in a whole book series being produced, as in the case of the University of Aberdeen, whose university press published a dozen volumes in the mid-1990s (e.g. Dukes 1995). The oldest universities are even more fully documented: there are shelves full of books on the history of the University of Oxford and its component colleges, and a massive, eight volume, generic history has only recently been completed (e.g. Brock and Curthoys 2000).

Such histories usually restrict themselves to recording the steady expansion and successes of the university or college in question. Thus, Aldrich's recent (2002) history of the London Institute of Education contains 11 chapters organized chronologically, and with titles such as 'a clash of cultures', 'war and reconstruction', 'expansion and stalemate' and 'into a new century'. It is full of photographs of buildings the Institute has occupied, generations of senior staff, and groups of students doing many of the things that students do (being taught, reading in the library, at degree ceremonies, going on demonstrations). Successive tables chart the growth in numbers of staff and students over the years. The tone of the writing is one of measured, factual reportage.

University histories refer to many aspects of higher education and its development – set in the context of underlying socio-economic changes – including academics' careers, student life and the development of departments or disciplines. The dominant perspective is, however, typically that of management – that is, the overall direction and development of the institution – which is why they are discussed in this chapter. They contain a great deal of information, and are extremely useful to those researching the origins and growth of particular institutions, or looking for a guide to what might be available in terms of original documentary source materials. They tend, though, to lack a truly critical perspective, and inevitably miss a lot out. Thus, for example, the reader rarely gets much of a sense of what it was like to study or work in the institutions in question. Given the in-house nature of most institutional histories, and their frequent use for marking significant institutional anniversaries, this is perhaps not too surprising, particularly where recent history is concerned.

There are rather fewer research studies that do adopt a more critical perspective. Such studies are probably best undertaken by researchers who do not work for the institutions researched. Two examples of more reflective or critical studies are discussed as Case Studies 9.1 and 9.3 in this chapter (Jenkins and Ward 2001; Stensaker and Norgard 2001). Both, perhaps significantly, were not produced by historians, and appear in the higher education – as opposed to the history of higher education – literature. Both cover the last 30 years, with the former offering an intriguing biographical study of the development of one department, while the latter relies largely on documentary analysis to review the development of a new university. Interestingly, the former was produced by former members of the department in question, which seems indicative of a very open or together departmental culture.

Institutional structure

The study of the structure of institutions of higher education is closely linked to the study of the higher education systems in which they operate (see Chapter 8). A classic of this field is Becher and Kogan's work (1992 – itself a second edition), which identified four hierarchical levels within the higher education system – central authority, institution, basic unit (or department) and individual. Three of these levels are to be found, of course, within the institution itself. Using this model, Becher and Kogan note how variable institutional structures may be:

> *In traditional university structures, the basic unit would usually be taken as the individual subject department, rather than the faculty bringing together a number of cognate departments. However, this is not a hard-and-fast rule, since some long-established universities use the term 'faculty' where others would use 'department'. Some more recent institutions have developed alternative structures, in which the constituent elements are more broadly based 'schools of study', 'course teams' and the like.* (p. 87)

Studies of the internal make-up of universities – in terms of, for example, departmental and course identities, emphasis on particular sub-ject areas, levels of study or modes of study – reveal just how diverse, and structurally unstable, these institutions are. Indeed, each university has its own distinct identity, with no two identical (Tight 1996, 2003b). Thus, Huisman (1995), applying quantitative techniques derived from ecology to study the development of higher education programmes (or courses) in the Netherlands over the period 1974–1993, found that:

> *. . . decreasing or fluctuating first-year student numbers encourage study pro-gramme actors to establish new specialisations in existing study programmes and to establish new study programmes . . . the 'softer' the discipline, the more processes of differentiation took place . . . the number of processes of differentiation through time increased.* (p. 199)

Conversely, Scott (1995) has argued that, as a consequence of massifi-cation (discussed in Chapter 8), departmental structures are becoming less reductionist and more flexible and thematic:

> *The tendency for broadly based faculties to be broken down, effectively if not constitutionally, into reductionist departments has been reversed as more and more universities have developed looser academic structures based on schools, often built around theme categories such as European studies or environmental sciences. More recently, as modular and credit systems have become more popular, some institutions have gone further, establishing still looser frameworks which embrace schools, departments and individual academic programmes.* (p. 159)

The other main theme in research into university structures concerns how these are changing in response to the demands of external pressures: from governments, business and industry, local communities and so on (and partly as a consequence of changing structures of knowledge itself, discussed further in Chapter 11). Thus, different researchers have heralded the development of adaptive, entrepreneurial or hybrid universities (Clark 1998; Mouwen 2000; Slaughter and Leslie 1997; Sporn 1999).

Mouwen, to take one example, drawing on the literature on hybrid organizations, notes that: 'A university that earns a *substantial* part of its income on the "market" for higher education and research, is frequently denoted as *hybrid*' (2000: 47). He goes on to distinguish between the task-oriented and market-oriented aspects of such universities, and discusses possible structures and strategies for hybrid universities with different balances of task and market orientation.

Clark (1998 – see also the critique by Deem (2001) discussed as Case Study 8.1 in Chapter 8), to take a second example, based on case studies of five selected European universities, has identified the arrival of entrepreneurial universities:

> *An entrepreneurial university, on its own, actively seeks to innovate in how it goes about its business. It seeks to work out a substantial shift in organisational character so as to arrive at a more promising posture for the future. Entrepreneurial universities seek to become 'stand-up' universities that are significant actors on their own terms.* (Clark 1998: 4)

He goes on to identify five elements which he argues are the minimum requirements for transforming a university into an entrepreneurial university: 'a strengthened steering core; an expanded developmental periphery; a diversified funding base; a stimulated academic heartland; and an integrated entrepreneurial culture' (p. 5).

Economies of scale and institutional mergers

The issues of economies of scale – in terms of the size of universities and colleges and their component departments or units – and institutional mergers are clearly closely related. They were key issues in the 1970s and 1980s, as the massification of higher education systems in many countries across the world got underway, but do not seem to be such topical issues for research at present. In part, this may be because most viable institutional mergers have already been undertaken; though the current discussion in the United Kingdom about further concentrating research and teaching excellence may suggest that another bout is about to start in that country.

A recent, international, review of studies of economies of scale in higher education, conducted by Patterson (2000), came to mixed conclusions:

> *Supporters, advocates and drivers of higher education mergers and other growth strategies do tend to overestimate and emphasise the benefits, but underplay the costs. The findings outlined here at least question several of the most common merger and growth beliefs and assumptions: that small institutions*

are inefficient; that large institutions are most efficient; that institutions should have a broad range of educational offerings; that amalgamations will lead to cost savings. (pp. 267–8)

These conclusions do not apply, however, in the particular field of distance education. Here, Daniel (1996) argues, 'mega-universities' making effective use of developing learning technologies, and serving as large a market as possible, offer the most cost-effective strategy; though it might not necessarily be the most beneficial in other ways. Of course, in conventional universities as well, much attention is currently being accorded to the potential benefits – economic and otherwise – of applying new learning technologies (e.g. Laurillard 2002), as the drive to serving more students and customers with a reduced unit of resource continues.

Recent research on institutional mergers (Harman 2000c; Rowley 1997), while finding that most were, at least in a general sense, successful, also draws attention to the short-term human costs. Whether occasioned by government policy or institutional strategy, mergers are rarely based on a partnership of equals, but typically constitute a takeover by a larger, more powerful institution of a smaller, less viable one. As such, they represent just a special case of the organizational mergers common throughout business. Thus, Rowley, on the basis of a questionnaire survey of British institutions of higher education that had recently undergone mergers, concluded that:

> ... as in industry generally, while most HE mergers were associated with a rational planning process, their outcomes included many unanticipated consequences, some of which were strategically significant ... it seems that HE mergers are much like mergers generally: costly, both before and after the event, and 'messy'. (p. 261)

Relations between higher education, industry and community

A final area for contemporary research into institutional management concerns itself with the relations between individual institutions, industrial and commercial partners and their local communities. The emphasis in these studies has been primarily economic. At least three main, if overlapping, foci for these studies may be identified:

* the developing relationships between universities and industrial companies, in the form of partnerships, science and business parks, and university spin-off companies, and associated issues of intellectual capital and copyright (e.g. Blair and Hitchens 1998; Harman 2001);
* the creation of corporate universities, their practices, and their potential impact upon conventional universities (e.g. Jarvis 2001; Macfarlane 2000); and

- the regional impact of universities on their surroundings, in terms of employment, financial and cultural benefits (e.g. Chatterton and Goddard 2000; Florax 1992; Gray 1999).

In the first of these areas, Harman (2001) reports on a survey of science and technology academics in three Australian universities. He indicates surprise at finding that over one-third of his respondents were in receipt of industrial funding, often from multiple sources, but was reassured to note a widespread awareness of the benefits and risks that such funding brings with it. Blair and Hitchens' (1998) study of university-based or linked companies in the United Kingdom and Ireland is based on series of interviews. They found a great deal of variety in the companies studied and in the strategies of the universities they were linked to, and many of their conclusions are directed towards how universities might better engage in this kind of activity.

Jarvis (2001) offers a system level analysis of the rise of the corporate university. He associates their rise with the linked developments of globalization and the learning society (discussed in Chapter 8 of this book). He argues that:

> ... education, especially university education, has been forced to respond to the pressures of globalisation and where it has failed to do so adequately, corporations have started their own education and training centres, some of which are now known as corporate universities ... the learning society is a learning market in which the established educational institutions no longer enjoy anything like a monopoly. (p. 129)

This leads him towards the conclusion that the oft-heralded crisis of the university (Tight 1994) is about the nature and identity of the university itself. Macfarlane (2000) takes a critical stance on these developments, using data from a small-scale interview-based study of two British business schools. He reports:

> All interviewees expressed concerns about client-based management education programmes. Although the positive, practical and cost benefits of such schemes were acknowledged, in terms of convenience of location for student-managers, for example, interviewees from both institutions focused on a number of recurrent themes or issues largely critical of client-based provision. (p. 55)

The main concerns identified were the extent to which participation was voluntary, the insularity of the learning process, the politics of the classroom, and the greater ambiguity of the lecturer/student/client relationship.

Research into the third area identified has concentrated on measuring and emphasizing the positive contributions that universities make to the communities in which they are based. Thus, chapters in Gray's (1999) edited book argue that universities can thrive locally in a global economy, attempt to measure the economic impact of universities, present case studies of university/community relations, and argue for the further development of the 'community university'. By contrast, I'm not aware of any recent research that has attempted to explore the negative impacts that universities can have – e.g. on employment, housing, traffic and the environment generally – on local communities.

Case Studies

The three case studies discussed in this chapter offer:

- a biographical history of the development of a university department;
- a documentary analysis of leadership in contemporary universities; and
- a documentary analysis of the development of one Norwegian university.

Case Study 9.1

Alan Jenkins and Andrew Ward (2001) Moving with the Times: an oral history of a geography department. *Journal of Geography in Higher Education*, 25, 2, 191–208.

Themes and Issues

This article reports on the 30-year history of a geography department at an English university (see also Jenkins et al. 2001), carried out by an independent consultant who interviewed many of those who had worked in the department over this period. It provides, therefore, an oral history, and one focusing on the teaching function.

Methods and Methodologies

I would categorize this article as adopting a biographical approach to the study of institutional management. It stems from an unusual study and is a very unusual kind of article. Thus, following a few introductory pages, it consists almost entirely of selected quotations from those interviewed.

Level

This article, fairly obviously, focuses on the departmental level.

Analytical/Theoretical Framework

There is very little in the way of linking material or analysis provided by the article's authors, one of whom was also one of the interviewees. In other words, there is little in the way of an explicit analytical or theoretical framework. The story – and it is essentially a story, rather than an analysis – is provided by carefully pasting together the quotations in a particular order. But analysis, through selection and ordering, is clearly involved:

> *The departmental history presented here is our interpretation.* Our *questions shaped the data and our editing produced the final account.* (p. 192)

I think that, on the whole, this works pretty well, and demonstrates what can be done with focused data collection of this kind.

Related Literatures

The inner life of higher education institutions, and of their component departments, has rarely been explored using the kind of biographical or life history approach adopted in this article. University vice-chancellors do occasionally end their careers by producing a volume of memoirs, but these hardly provide a rounded view of what it is like to work in a university. Some studies of academic work have focused on the institutional story (e.g. Potts 1997; Trowler 1998), or on the departmental level (e.g. Knight and Trowler 2001), but these are relatively few.

Argument and Conclusions

To a large extent, the article works because it has a clear and fairly coherent story to tell. The department in question has had, as the authors argue, a shared pedagogic culture over the last three decades, focusing on the encouragement of active learning amongst its students. It has also had a close association with the journal in which the article appeared. And the members of the department have been responsible for many publications concerned with the teaching/learning experience, a sample listing of which is appended to the article.

As the authors point out, the article raises many more questions than it answers, but does provide some of the evidence for seeking answers:

> *Somewhere in these words – or behind these words – are the answers to a number of key questions concerning teaching and teaching methods. How do staff learn to teach more effectively? How do they learn to shift much of the responsibility of learning onto students? How does a departmental culture incorporate innovation? Can that innovative culture be maintained or is it a function of a particular era and a particular group of individuals?* (p. 206)

More auto/biographical research of this kind is to be encouraged, and – particularly at the departmental level – should be very 'do-able'. There are, though, risks to this kind of research. While the authors of this article can provide a generally positive account of a successful department with a shared culture, many departments and institutions are probably not so together.

Case Study 9.2

Paul Ramsden (1998) *Learning to Lead in Higher Education*. London: Routledge.

Themes and Issues

In this book, Paul Ramsden offers an analysis of management and leadership in contemporary universities, together with guidance on how university leadership can be improved.

Methods and Methodologies

The book makes use of a variety of methods and methodologies, including qualitative interviews and quantitative surveys. It has been categorized, however, as making use of documentary analysis, in that it builds up an argument from data taken from both the author's own research and the existing literature on management and leadership.

Level

The book is focused at the international level, in that it considers university leadership in a number of countries, most notably Australia and the United Kingdom.

Analytical/Theoretical Framework

Ramsden provides a framework for his study in terms of the contemporary challenges faced by universities – mass higher education and the growth of knowledge, the waning status of academic work, academic values and culture – and the implications of this for changing models of the university.

Related Literatures

The book may be related to both the growing literature on university management and leadership (e.g. Bargh et al. 1996, 2000; Knight and Trowler 2001; Middlehurst 1993; Prichard 2000; Warner and Palfreyman 1996), and the much broader literature on general management and leadership issuing from business schools worldwide.

Argument and Conclusions

Having reviewed the contemporary pressures being faced by universities, Ramsden goes on to examine both the general literature on leadership and management, and that specific to these functions in higher education. He also makes use of findings from research, including his own, on experiences of leadership in universities, to work towards principles that might be of use to those with leadership roles in universities. He argues that 'leadership, the academic work environment, and academic productivity are linked' (p. 10).

On the basis of his analysis, Ramsden identifies six core principles and four central academic leadership responsibilities. The six principles identified are that academic leadership is a dynamic process, should have an outcomes-focused agenda, be multi-level in its operation, be relational, involve the leader's learning, and be essentially transformative. The four responsibilities cover: vision, strategy and planning; enabling academic people; recognizing and developing performance; learning to lead and improving university leadership. This framework is then used in the second half of the book to explore issues in academic leadership and possible responses to them.

Case Study 9.3

Bjorn Stensaker and Jorunn Dahl Norgard (2001) Innovation and Isomorphism: a case-study of university identity struggle 1969–1999. *Higher Education*, 42, 473–92.

Themes and Issues

Stensaker and Norgard present an analysis of the experience of one Norwegian university, the University of Tromso, from its foundation in 1969 up until 1999.

Methods and Methodologies

I would categorize this article as adopting documentary analysis to analyse institutional management. Like the article by Jenkins and Ward (2001), analysed as Case Study 9.1, it is somewhat unusual in focusing on the organizational experience of higher education. It is also, like that article, historical in approach, though the emphasis is again on recent history.

For data, Stensaker and Norgard make use of institutional documents, two previous external studies, and interviews with 32 staff and students. The emphasis, however, in the article is on the documents rather than the interview data, which is why I have categorized the article in the way that I have.

Level

Unlike Case Study 9.1, the focus in this case is at the institutional rather than the departmental level.

Analytical/Theoretical Framework

The authors contextualize their study in terms of the struggle for organizational identity faced by the University of Tromso. It started life intending to be an innovative organization – in terms, for example, of its structure and governance, and in the use of new teaching and learning methods – making a significant contribution to the life and economy of the northern Norwegian region. Over the 30-year period studied, however, the university had to adapt to survive against pressures to standardize and stabilize its work. The article discusses:

the way in which institutional handling of the pressures for innovation and standardisation may be understood as an identity formation process. (p. 475)

Related Literatures

Within the history of higher education literature, one can find many histories of individual universities and colleges – and even more contemporary analyses (e.g. Warner and Palfreyman 2001) – usually published at the time of some significant anniversary. Understandably, particularly when they are authored by members of staff of the institutions concerned, these tend to be relatively measured in tone and uncontroversial (recent examples include, for example, Aldrich 2002; Ives et al. 2000). Stensaker and Norgard, being external to the institution – though not the system – concerned, have been able to take a more analytical stance.

Other significant areas of research in recent years within the literature on higher education institutions have been concerned with the effects of institutional mergers (e.g. Harman 2002), the organization of higher education institutions (e.g. Becher and Kogan 1992), and institutional leadership (e.g. Bargh et al. 2000; Middlehurst 1993).

Argument and Conclusions

The authors interpret the development of the University of Tromso as a success story. They identify:

an interesting dynamic between innovation and isomorphism, of trying to develop and fulfil innovative institutional objectives while at the same time trying to adapt to external pressure and demands for standardisation. What can be observed is an institution that struggles with, but also to a large extent, has succeeded in integrating these two dimensions. It is our view that the University of Tromso has managed this by 'translating', re-interpreting and 'editing' institutional identity labels to attach meaning to and provide a feeling of coherence when facing organisational change. (p. 489)

Ideas for further research

The discussion in this chapter suggests a whole series of possible areas of institutional management for further research. These would include:

- comparative studies of management practices in institutions of higher education and other organizations;
- more comparative studies of management practices in institutions of higher education in different countries, and over time;
- research into the alternative management strategies adopted within higher education, particularly in relation to size of organization, their benefits and disbenefits;

- research into the practical usefulness of 'how to' and 'can do' literatures and associated training sessions;
- studies of the background, training, development and experience of institutional managers during their careers;
- research into the relationships, negative as well as positive, and particularly non-economic, between higher education institutions and their local communities; and
- studies of the relations between professional managers, academics as managers, and academics within institutions.

10

Researching academic work

Introduction

While it might be argued, at a fairly superficial level, that the idea of academics researching academic work seems a peculiarly introspective form of navel-gazing, further reflection should suggest that understanding the nature of academic work is critical if we are to understand higher education. Academics are, after all, the key to the higher education process; without them, there would be no one to teach and supervise students, to carry out and disseminate academic research, or, to a considerable extent, to run higher education institutions.

Key questions underlying research into academic work, therefore, include:

- What do academics do? And why do they do what they do?
- How does this vary from academic to academic, subject to subject, institution to institution?
- How is academic work changing over time? How satisfied are academics with these changes?
- What do academic careers look like? Is academic work one profession or a number of professions? How mobile are academics between institutions, sectors and countries?
- How can academics be best trained, inducted and developed in their roles?
- How do academics themselves conceive of their different roles, and the relationships between them?

This chapter, then, considers how higher education researchers have explored these and related questions, and what conclusions they have come to.

Research into academic work

There are, of course, many ways in which contemporary research into academic work may be categorized. For the purposes of the present discussion, I will identify six key areas of this research:

- academic roles;
- academic development;
- academic careers;
- women academics;
- the changing nature of academic work;
- academic work in different countries.

These areas will now be examined and illustrated in turn.

Academic roles

One way of looking at academic work is in terms of the different roles which academics perform. In previous research (Blaxter et al. 1998b, 1998c), my colleagues and I identified five key academic roles – teaching, researching, managing, writing and networking (see Kyvik 2000 for a review of alternative ways of categorizing academic roles). Of course, not all academics will perform all of these roles. Their importance may also vary during an academic's career, and at different times of the year, and some academics may specialize in just one area.

Because of the way in which this book has been organized, most of these roles are examined in other chapters. Thus the teaching role is considered in Chapter 4 (Teaching and Learning), the research and networking roles in Chapter 11 (Knowledge), and the management role in Chapter 9 (Institutional Management). In this sub-section, therefore, we will focus on research into the writing role.

Most research on writing within the higher education context focuses on student writing (discussed in Chapter 5). However, the increasing pressure on academics to become and remain research-active, and to demonstrate this activity through regular publication, has led to growing attention being paid – both by academic developers (see next sub-section) and researchers – to the academic writing role. Not surprisingly, then, much of the small but growing literature on academic writing falls into the 'how to' genre. This consists of texts that proffer advice on how to put together a book or an article, and on how to get them published (e.g. Day 1996; Huff 1999; Luey 1995). Similarly, the emphasis in the more limited, explicitly research-based literature is chiefly on evaluating the effectiveness of developmental activities designed to improve the quality, and increase the volume, of academic writing.

The first case study examined in this chapter (Case Study 10.1: Grant and Knowles 2000) is one example of this. Their conclusion was that successful and satisfying academic writing was about changing, or developing, one's identity as an academic:

> For all academics, women and men, the processes of practising writing and be(com)ing a writer are inextricably entangled. If we discipline ourselves to write regularly, 'doing writer' as a daily event, we may contribute to producing ourselves as writers who, finding pleasure in the act, seek more opportunities for it. (p. 17)

In a similar study, but one without a feminist perspective, Morss and Murray (2001) evaluate the successfulness of a 'Writing for Publication' programme in a Scottish university. This six-month programme involved a series of small group meetings, writing practices, the gradual development of an article, and the regular exchange of ideas and drafts with peers. Morss and Murray stress that the programme works through building up the confidence of its participants, and that this is done through a *combination* of activities:

> The experience of running the programme and the evaluation data suggest that confidence grows through a combination of a number of quite different activities: goal setting and deadlines, peer support, structured approach to writing, strategies for regular writing, strategies for making time for writing and protecting it. (p. 49)

Clearly, then, research into writing as an academic role currently displays a very practical orientation.

Academic development

The generic literature on academic development shares many of the key characteristics of that which focuses specifically on the development of academic writing, reviewed in the previous sub-section. As higher education has expanded, and more attention has been given externally to its quality, higher education institutions have naturally begun to devote more attention to the academic development function. Where new academics once learned on the job, perhaps repeating, with little thought, the teaching and other practices they had themselves experienced or had observed being practised by colleagues, they now find themselves engaged in, increasingly compulsory, initial and continuing development activities.

This growth in academic development has been reflected in the establishment of centres for academic practice, staff development, teaching and learning, and a myriad other titles, in most institutions of higher education. While their main focus has been on developing teaching and learning, increasing attention is also being given to the management and research functions. This increased activity has been accompanied by a growing literature on the academic development function, the majority of which, as in the case of academic writing, has had a practical, 'how to' orientation (e.g. Webb 1994).

Parallel to this is, again, a smaller, research-based literature examining what happens in academic development, and how well it works. Thus, a number of recent texts have provided overviews of the function from a policy or philosophical perspective (e.g. Brew 1995; Nicholls 2000; Webb 1996). Brew's (1995) edited book contains 14 chapters contributed by 16 authors working in development centres or functions in the United Kingdom and Australia. Brew outlines the aim of the book in the following terms:

> *It is hoped that the book will be a source of information for managers responsible for the organisational arrangements for staff development and for policy and strategy within their institutions. It is hoped too that it will be an encouragement to new staff developers, and that it will provide a source book for established ones as they increasingly assert their professional identity.* (p. 1)

More recently, Eggins and Macdonald (2003) edited what could be seen as an updated version of Brew's book, re-focused to examine what they term the scholarship of academic development in the context of a varied and rapidly changing field (Fraser 2001; Gosling 2001). Their book contains 15 chapters by 20 authors, all but two from the United Kingdom. Brew herself concludes this book by arguing for substantial changes in, and additions to, the roles of academic developers:

> *. . . in order to be credible as agents for change in a higher and tertiary educa- tion context where the boundaries between research and teaching are breaking down, developers are having to take research and scholarship seriously and become credible as researchers and facilitators of research on teaching . . . as teaching becomes increasingly viewed as a process of developing academic pro- fessionalism and the skills of inquiry in students so that they can cope with a world of complexity, developers need to work towards integrating their own research and teaching.* (Brew 2003: 180)

Other studies have focused on specific aspects of the process and its component practices, such as the use of teaching portfolios (Bullard and McLean 2000). There is an also academic journal devoted to this aspect of higher education, *The International Journal for Academic Development*.

The article by Land (2001), which is examined as Case Study 10.2 in this chapter (and which was published in *The International Journal for Academic Development*), is unusual in taking a theorized approach to understanding the academic development function, and the varied views of change embodied within it. Unusually, he did not portray the aim of his research as being about immediately improving practice; rather, he hoped for 'a better understanding . . . of the conceptions and approaches of academic developers to their practice' (p. 5).

Academic careers

As with the previous two sub-themes, the literature on academic careers contains both 'how to' (e.g. Blaxter et al. 1998c; Graham 2000) and research-based strands. The distinction is, of course, not always that clear, and it has to be acknowledged that the two genres often merge imperceptibly into one another. The latter genre has addressed a range of issues, including the mobility of academics (Blumenthal 1995), their induction and socialization, and the extent to which academics can be regarded as a profession. We may also recognize a further strand, in the auto/biographical accounts produced of some academics' careers.

The third case study reviewed in this chapter (Case Study 10.3: Trowler and Knight 2000 – see also Knight and Trowler 1999; Trowler 1998) is a research-based contribution to understanding academic careers, in this case focusing on academic induction and socialization. In contrast to much of the literature on academic development, which explicitly or implicitly assumes a critical role for formal developmental activities, Trowler and Knight's work emphasizes the importance for new academics of learning informal and tacit knowledge within their workplace:

> . . . *what the higher education institution does about the induction of NAAs [new academic appointees] is far less significant than what happens in activity systems and in the cultures created in communities of practice. In essence, induction is about the discourses and practices of the teams and departments that the NAA is trying to join.* (Trowler and Knight 2000: 28)

But are new academics being socialized into a healthy profession? And is it a single profession or a number of related professions, or perhaps not a profession at all, or one in the process of being de-professionalized or even proletarianized (Dearlove 1997)? On the basis of his studies of the English academic profession, carried out as part of a comparative international survey, Fulton has argued that:

> . . . *whatever the considerable evidence of discontent and even of deprofessionalization, English academics retain a set of attitudes and values which could be benevolently described as both professional and collegial.* (Fulton 1996a: 168: see also Fulton 1996b)

However, conscious as he is of writing at a time of considerable change within the higher education system, Fulton adds a rider:

> *I suspect that British academics have adopted the* principle *of mass higher education* . . . *without fully accepting or understanding the* consequences

that will follow. How long can the single profession survive? (Fulton 1996a: 168)

For those seeking an understanding of varied and changing academic careers, but without the time to collect data directly from academics themselves, these research-based studies may be usefully supplemented by individual auto/biographical accounts written by current or former academics. In the recent past, retiring vice-chancellors and college principals quite often produced dry volumes of memoirs, partly at least to justify their careers, but this genre seems now to have largely dried up. It has been supplanted by livelier auto/biographical collections from a range of academic staff (e.g. Allan 1996; David and Woodward 1998; Frost and Taylor 1996; Griffiths 1996; Richards 1997), that may offer guidance and comfort in roughly equal measure to the academic reader.

Women academics

Research and writing on the position of women academics (and students: see Chapter 6) in higher education is a relatively strong genre, with both feminist and non-feminist components. By comparison, there is little or no literature published outside of North America on ethnic minority academics, or other identifiable social groups, though this is a strong genre in the United States (but see Bird 1996).

The literature on women academics includes some of the auto/ biographical collections referred to in the previous sub-section (e.g. David and Woodward 1998; Griffiths 1996). In addition, the last decade has witnessed the publication of a succession of edited volumes looking at the academy from a gendered perspective (Brooks and Mackinnon 2001; Howie and Tauchert 2002; Malina and Maslin-Prothero 1998; Morley and Walsh 1995, 1996). Most of the contributors to these volumes take an overtly feminist perspective. By contrast, relatively few feminist critiques are published in specialist higher education journals. These tend to appear instead in other journals, notably those specializing in this area, such as *Gender and Education.*

Analyses of the position and experience of women academics typically start from evidenced statements of the inequality that they experience when compared with their male colleagues (Bagilhole 2002). For example:

Academic women have long known that they are not promoted as much or paid as much, and do not, in truth, have equality with their male counterparts. (Halvorsen 2002: 9)

Evidence from the UK and elsewhere points to the fact that institutions of higher education are masculinist institutions, with limited and rigid career patterns for academic women. (Brooks 1997: 1)

As well as mapping the inequality that continues to be experienced by most women academics, research on this sub-theme takes a series of directions. To some extent, this could be seen as mirroring the organization of the generic (i.e. usually implicitly male) literature on academic work. But there is, understandably, an underlying agenda, which is about striving to re-model the academic landscape in a more female-friendly form.

Thus, we may identify literatures focusing on:

- the development of women's and gender studies within the curriculum (e.g. Griffin 1998);
- the application of feminist pedagogies (e.g. Hughes 2002a);
- women academics as leaders and managers (e.g. Deem 1999; Eggins 1997; Meehan 1999);
- women's research careers (e.g. Hatt et al. 1999);
- gendered forms of work within the academy, such as caring roles (e.g. Barnes-Powell and Letherby 1998);
- the experience of combining academic work with caring roles outside the academy (Hughes 2002b);
- experience of harassment and bullying in the workplace (Butler and Landells 1995);
- change strategies for improving the position of women academics (Mavin and Bryans 2002; Price and Priest 1996); and
- the particular position of certain groups of women, notably black women and lesbians (e.g. Mirza 1995 – there is a small parallel literature on the experience of gay male academics: e.g. Skelton 2000).

This listing, of course, should be seen as indicative rather than definitive.

The changing nature of academic work

The idea of major and ongoing change is a key part of the mythology of contemporary higher education. It is usually contrasted, at least by implication, with a previous 'golden age', typically located just before you started working in higher education, when practices were stable, funding at least adequate, relationships collegial and public respect assured. This is not, of course, to argue that change has not been an important factor in higher education – I don't think that anyone would seek to argue that – just that its impact can all too easily be over-stated. Nevertheless, 'change' is a key word in writing on academic work (e.g. Askling 2001; Henkel 2000; Lafferty and Fleming 2000; McInnis 2000a; McWilliam et al. 1999; Marginson 2000; Martin 1999; Smyth 1995; Taylor 1999; Tight 2000b; Trowler 1998).

There are a number of different strategies evident in researching and writing about changing academic work. Seemingly the most straightforward approach involves recording how academic work has changed over a given period, and documenting academics' responses to this. Thus, both

Harman (2000b) and McInnis (2000a, 2000b) have demonstrated, by comparing survey data for different dates, how the Australian higher education system has expanded and diversified, and how academics' roles have become more demanding. While they may have sought to maintain their values in the transition from an elite to a mass higher education system, the pressure and stress upon academics is increasingly evident (Fisher 1994).

Taking this strategy further, some researchers have moved beyond documenting change in academic work to exploring and/or recommending responses or coping strategies. Thus, Martin (1999) starts by using a small-scale, but international, survey of academic staff to illustrate their experience of change. She then offers a selective analysis of some of the literature on learning and teaching, on the one hand, and organizational change and learning organizations, on the other, as a framework for understanding and thinking about contemporary higher education. This is then used as a basis for suggesting strategies for coping with, and encouraging more 'positive', change.

Trowler (1998) takes a slightly different tack, in seeking to examine and understand academics' responses, in one British institution, to change in their working lives – in this case, the adoption of a credit framework and associated developments. He manages to do so without making recommendations. Trowler used a mixture of interviews, observations and documents to collect data for analysis. He argues, in conclusion, that coping with change effectively requires the recognition of the many cultures that operate within universities, rather than the attempted imposition of a single corporate culture:

> To date, thinking about the management of change in universities has tended to adopt a 'policy science' approach, one which takes a 'scientific' standpoint in order to formulate a rational, top-down, prescription for action but which, in the process, loses a grasp on the deeply structured historical, cultural, political, ideological and value issues ingrained in social processes. Policy scholarship approaches, by contrast, situate an understanding of education policy in the context of the cultural and ideological struggles in which they are located and demonstrate the constraining or liberating effects of wider socio-economic and political relationships. (p. 158)

Henkel (2000) reports on a similar kind of study, but one conducted at the national rather than institutional level. She carried out interviews with samples of academics in seven disciplines working in 11 English higher education institutions, focusing in particular on their experience of two policy initiatives in the 1990s: teaching quality assurance and research assessment. Her interest was in 'the extent to which major change in the politics and structures of higher education has also meant major change in what it means to be an academic in the UK' (p. 13). Despite the rhetoric and reality of change, however, Henkel's analysis of academics' changing identities as researchers, teachers and, increasingly, managers places more stress on stability, in particular the continuing centrality of the discipline or sub-discipline in shaping academic identities, careers and lives.

Academic work in different countries

Undertaking a truly international and comparative study is – as is stressed elsewhere in this volume – a major undertaking, so it would hardly be surprising if few researchers or research teams sought to analyse academic work in this way. However, there have been a number of recent studies, which serve to illustrate the challenges and possibilities of such research. Three will be discussed in this sub-section.

In their study, Kogan et al. (1994) did not seek to collect any new empirical data, but to draw together and analyse existing research on higher education staffing in OECD (Organisation for Economic Co-operation and Development) countries. In this way, they reviewed what was known about the changing framework for the profession, changing academic tasks, staffing structures, qualifications, staff development, demography and conditions of service. Their focus was on the implications of these changes for policy makers and managers. They concluded:

> . . . the changed mission of higher education calls for more sophisticated and careful management of human resources than used to be the case. These changes should lead to new thinking about the governance and management of higher education. The new tasks call for new structures which take account of the proliferation and elaboration of roles. They call for more wide ranging and well planned forms of staff development. They should lead to the creation of structures which combine the vertical management and the horizontal collegial modes of governance and for the release of synergy between academic and management values. (pp. 116–17)

The growing tension becoming evident between managerial and academic values is clearly highlighted.

In the early 1990s, the Carnegie Foundation for the Advancement of Teaching organized an international survey of the academic profession, taking in 14 countries (Australia, Brazil, Chile, England, Germany, Hong Kong, Israel, Japan, Mexico, the Netherlands, Russia, South Korea, Sweden and the United States). The strategy adopted involved both commissioning local experts in each country to compile national reports and the administration in each country of a questionnaire survey to a sizeable sample of academics (Altbach 1996). The researchers found many underlying shared values, as well as differences in working conditions related to national policies, and came to an upbeat conclusion:

This portrait of the professoriate [that is, academic staff] depicts a strong, but somewhat unsettled profession. Academics around the world are inspired by the intellectual ferment of the times. The intrinsic pleasures of academic life obviously endure. Academe is facing the future with concern but with surprising optimism. (Altbach and Lewis 1996: 48)

One wonders if the conclusion would be so optimistic if the survey were to be repeated today.

A third, and most recent, example also adopted the strategy of using national experts to write reports to a common framework (Enders 2000, 2001). The focus of the study was on employment and working conditions, staff structure and staffing, and recent developments and changes. Enders came to some interesting interim conclusions, again emphasizing the implications for institutional management:

Although the dynamics and areas of change might differ according to country, at least three major trends might be identified:

- *heterogenisation, as a reaction and withdrawal from the former idea or philosophy of legal homogeneity in higher education institutions;*
- *decentralisation, as a switch in government towards a system of distant steering or state supervision, in which each institution is given a higher degree of autonomy;*
- *marketisation, as an effort to build up a market-like resource allocation system as well as to strengthen competition between and within higher education institutions.*

In effect, control of higher education institutions has shifted to some extent away from academic oligarchy towards, paradoxically enough, more market and more state control. (Enders 2000: 29)

Case studies

The three case studies discussed in this chapter offer:

- a biographical analysis of the experience of women academics developing as writers;
- a conceptual analysis of different strategies adopted for academic development; and
- an interview-based study of how academics are socialized into their work roles.

Case Study 10.1

Barbara Grant and Sally Knowles (2000) Flights of Imagination: academic women be(com)ing writers. *The International Journal for Academic Development*, 5, 1, 6–19.

Themes and Issues

In this article, Grant and Knowles discuss how to make writing pleasurable as well as productive for women academics. This is seen as not just a matter of making time and space for writing, but also of making imaginative space and developing one's understanding of oneself as a writer.

Methods and Methodologies

This article has been categorized as adopting a biographical approach to the study of academic work. With its feminist concerns, it might also have been described as taking a critical approach, but has been classified as biographical because of its focus on the experiences of the women concerned (including the authors themselves).

Level

The article may be categorized as course focused, in that it examines the experience on two writing programmes (though it might also be termed international, as the two programmes were in different countries).

Analytical/Theoretical Framework

The analysis is set within the context of women's place within the academy as being largely subordinate and subject to the assessment and appraisal, predominantly, of men.

Related Literatures

The article may be related to two kinds of higher education literatures. One of these deals specifically with academic writing, and how it may be developed (e.g. Morss and Murray 2001). There are links here, of course, to the literature on student writing (e.g. Maclellan 2001). The second literature of relevance is that focusing on the position of women within higher education institutions (e.g. Asmar 1999; Brooks 1997; Brooks and Mackinnon 2001; Eggins 1997; Howie and Tauchert 2002)

Argument and Conclusions

The authors describe two interventions which they led in different institutions in their role as academic developers. One of these took the form of a one-week writing retreat, involving seven participants from three New Zealand universities. The other was a peer mentoring group of six women at one Australian university, which met fortnightly for two hours over two semesters. The accounts are illustrated by feedback comments from the women involved.

They demonstrate the motivational and supportive elements that such interventions can provide to stimulate writing.

Case Study 10.2

Ray Land (2001) Agency, Context and Change in Academic Development. *The International Journal for Academic Development*, 6, 1, 4–20.

Themes and Issues

This article explores alternative ways in which the academic development process is conceived and practised, and the relation between these differences and alternative views of change.

Methods and Methodologies

This article has been categorized as adopting a conceptual approach to the analysis of academic work. It makes use of 31 interviews with academic developers working in UK higher education institutions, a group the author describes as 'a fragmented community of practice'. While extracts from these interviews are used as illustrations, the focus of the article is, however, on identifying and explicating different models and theories of, and orientations towards, academic development. That is why I have characterized it as a conceptual piece, rather than an example of an interview-based piece of research.

Level

The article is focused at the national level (in this case the United Kingdom).

Analytical/Theoretical Framework

It is relatively uncommon, in the higher education literature, to find the level of engagement with concepts and theories that is present in this article. The use of terms like agency and context is indicative of a sociological base for the analysis.

Related Literatures

Land's study is unusual in focusing on the academic development function, an area for research which is only gradually being opened up as academic development becomes a standard and accepted part of academic life (e.g. Macdonald 2001). Publications in this area tend to take either a more theorized or a more 'how to' approach (compare Webb 1996 and 1994 respectively). However, Land contextualizes his study in terms of the literature on university cultures (Becher 1989, McNay 1995, Trowler and Knight 2000).

Argument and Conclusions

Using his data, Land first identifies 12 orientations to academic development practice, including the managerial, entrepreneurial, romantic, reflective practitioner and vigilant opportunist. He then maps these on to a two-dimensional model of academic development, in terms of whether the focus is on the individual or the institution, and whether what he terms domesticating or liberating strategies are adopted.

The second half of the article then categorizes academic developers' attitudes to change, each of which is exemplified by quotations from Land's interviewees. Nine varieties of attitude are identified, namely systemic models, empirical-rational strategies, disjointed incrementalism, the 'garbage can' model, cybernetic models, diffusion models, opportunistic change, Kai Zen and chaotic theories. Finally, links are made between orientations to academic development and change conceptions, and associated theorists are identified.

Case Study 10.3

Paul Trowler and Peter Knight (2000) Coming to Know in Higher Education: theorising faculty entry to new work contexts. *Higher Education Research and Development*, 19, 1, 27–42.

Themes and Issues

The focus of the study is on how new academics are inducted and socialized into their roles.

Methods and Methodologies

This article has been categorized as adopting an interview-based methodology to researching academic work. It makes use of three sets of interview data: 24 interviews conducted with new academic staff in England and Canada, 50 previous interviews in one English university, and a re-examination of data produced for three North American studies (so there is also, at least implicitly, a comparative element as well).

Level

As it makes use of data from three countries, this article will be categorized as international in scope.

Analytical/Theoretical Framework

The authors contextualize their study with reference to two related theoretical frameworks: activity systems theory as developed by Engestrom (1987), and communities of practice as developed by Lave and Wenger (1991). Becoming an academic is then seen as entering and coming to know an activity system or a community of practice. They illustrate their argument with lots of illustrative quotations.

Related Literatures

Trowler and Knight argue in their article that research on university culture and organization lags behind that in other organizations, and that in schools (see Knight 2002b) in particular. Nevertheless, there are developing higher education research literatures in these areas. They include not only the work on academic cultures, particularly associated with Tony Becher, to which Trowler has contributed (Becher and Trowler 2001; Tuire and Erno 2001; Valimaa 1998), but also research into the changing nature of academic work, both in particular countries (e.g. Askling 2001; Cuthbert 1996; Henkel 2000; Lafferty and Fleming 2000; McInnis 2000a; Prichard 2000; Taylor 1999; Tight 2000b; Trowler 1998) and internationally (e.g. Altbach 1996; Enders 2001, Kogan et al. 1994).

Argument and Conclusions

Trowler and Knight usefully contrast the rational-cognitive model of learning, which underlies most formal induction processes, with the need of new academics to learn what they refer to as 'embedded' knowledge, which includes also the informal or tacit routines by which things get done in any organization. In these circumstances, transfer of necessary knowledge may not be easy because those who possess it may not be aware of it. There are clear implications here for academic practice, which the authors set out at the end of their article.

Ideas for further research

On the basis of this review, a series of areas for further research may be identified. This is, of course, my selection only, to which other ideas may be added:

- research into the experiences of academics at different stages in their careers, enabling both generational and life cycle differences to be analysed;
- research into those who have moved into and out of academe in mid-career, or who split their career between academe and, for example, another profession (for example accounting, law, medicine, social work, teaching);
- studies of academics working together in departments or institutions, focusing on their collective experience and inter-relationships (e.g. Potts 1997);
- studies of specialist academics, such as those pursuing research careers and those exercising managerial or administrative functions;

- research into academics involved in their networking and dissemination roles;
- studies of the experience of ethnic minority and foreign academics; and
- research into the impact of new and more extensive staff development regimes, both on new and older academics.

11

Researching knowledge

Introduction

The last of the key themes or issues to be considered in this book, that of knowledge, is in many ways the most fundamental, and the most theorized, but the least researched. That statement may seem to be rather contradictory, but a little thought suggests that it is not that surprising. Knowledge – its discovery, expansion, analysis, interpretation, transmission and dissemination – is at the heart of what higher education is all about. To those working in higher education, both academics and students, and to those outside who share a concern with higher education, the centrality of knowledge to higher education will probably seem obvious. As such a shared concern, it may hardly seem worth researching: after all, we all know what knowledge is and what we are about. But this is not the case, and knowledge remains a highly contested arena.

Why, then, is knowledge relatively under-researched? Partly, I think, because it is not such an immediate concern as, for example, improving the student experience, managing a course or responding to changing government policy. In other words, it is not something that the individual academic or researcher feels they can do much about in the short term. Partly, also, because knowledge is a highly theorized and conceptualized area for research, and thus not as accessible to new researchers. And partly because researching knowledge involves working across and between disciplines, rather than within them, and is thus particularly demanding.

Key questions driving research into knowledge include:

- What counts as valid knowledge within different disciplines?
- How do practices vary between disciplines?
- How does research produce knowledge?

- How does the research function relate to other academic roles, most notably teaching?
- What different kinds of knowledge, or knowledges, are they?
- What is the role and meaning of higher education, or the university, within contemporary society?

This chapter will focus on the treatment of these and related questions.

Research into knowledge

The discussion in this section is organized in terms of four main sub-themes:

- the nature of research;
- disciplinarity;
- forms of knowledge;
- the nature of the university;

Each of these sub-themes will now be illustrated and analysed in turn.

The nature of research

Contemporary research into the nature of research has focused on two closely related topics: how research is understood and experienced by academic researchers in different disciplines and institutions, and, in particular, how this understanding and experience is related to their understanding and experience of teaching. Case Study 11.1 (Brew 2001a) in this chapter is an example of research into the former topic, while Case Study 11.3 (Robertson and Bond 2001) is an example of the latter. There is one other sub-literature worth mentioning – offering guidance on 'how to' do research (e.g. Blaxter et al. 2001) – though this will not be considered further here.

Brew's study (2001a), discussed as Case Study 11.1, identified four different categories of research experience amongst the senior researchers she interviewed. There were those who saw research as a series of tasks ('domino'), as a social phenomenon emphasizing products ('trading'), as the excavation of reality ('layer'), and as an experience that transforms the researcher ('journey'). She stresses that individual researchers may combine elements of two or more of these approaches, and that their perspectives may change over time.

In a more extensive study, Brew (2001b) makes use of documentary analysis as well as her phenomenographic analysis of interview data. She relates research to ideas about knowledge and scholarship, and, in particular, to prevailing higher education policies emphasizing the economic, applied purposes of research (see also Whiston and Geiger 1992, and the discussion of system policy in Chapter 8 of this book). As part of that study, she offers four other conceptualizations of research:

> *The most powerful and pernicious influences on academic research currently in focus are output views of research with their emphasis on performativity, enshrined most particularly in government policies and funding formulas. The products of research are viewed as commodities within such an economic model. . . The view of research as a process of personal and social learning is left out of the economic model . . . Individual and social learning come together through teaching. In the broadest sense the aim of research is to teach . . . the nature of the language used to talk about research supports the interests of those who have power in defining research agendas.* (Brew 2001b: 12–13)

These commodity, learning, teaching and discourse conceptualizations of research do not map directly onto the domino, trading, layer and journey variations identified in her other study, though there is a clear link between the dominant commodity and trading perceptions. The power of these different labels, however, is in helping us, as research practitioners, to better understand what we are doing, the contexts within which we are working, and the prospects for change.

Research into the actual, possible and/or desirable relations between the research and teaching functions (see also the discussion of academic roles in Chapter 10) has assumed greater urgency in recent years as governments have explored different funding models for higher education. At one extreme, there are those who argue that research (or at least scholarship) and teaching are, or should be, indelibly linked in any quality higher education experience, so that students are taught by those actively engaged in researching their fields. At the other extreme are those who argue for concentrating research (and to a lesser extent teaching) funding into a limited number of the 'best' institutions and departments. Such policies would lead to the explicit (arguably they already exist in some cases) establishment of research-only or teaching-only institutions and departments (Hughes and Tight 1995; Jenkins 2000; Jenkins et al. 2003).

The study by Robertson and Bond (2001), reported as Case Study 11.3, offers – in a way analogous to Brew's (2001a) study – a phenomenographic analysis of academics' experiences of the relations between teaching and research (see also Neumann 1992). Five different perceptions of this relationship are identified, seeing research and teaching as incompatible or as little connected at undergraduate level, or as connected through the teaching of new research knowledge, by encouraging a research-based approach to learning, or through a symbiotic relationship.

Coate et al. (2001) report on a larger scale project, funded by the Higher Education Funding Council for England (HEFCE) to inform its deliberations on funding policy. They focused on four representative subjects (business studies, chemistry, engineering and history) in eight sample institutions, carrying out semi-structured interviews with heads of departments, and focus group interviews with samples of staff and students. They found evidence for six possible relationships between teaching and research – integrated, positive (either research influencing teaching or vice-versa), independent or negative (again, either research impacting on teaching or vice-versa). They concluded:

> The assumption that good researchers will also be good teachers has been described as a 'myth' of higher education, and so too is perhaps the belief that research enhances teaching. Yet these are pervasive beliefs that we encountered frequently in our fieldwork. Teaching and research can exist in a range of relationships with each other, and these relationships are shaped by the value-orientations of academic staff and the management of available resources. The volumes of teaching and research activities, and the values accorded to them, have shifted over time, although there have been two fairly consistent drivers within the contemporary higher education system: the generally declining unit of resource and the high value of research. These drivers present particular challenges to those academics who are in the position of trying to maintain a balance between teaching and research activities. (p. 172)

Disciplinarity

The study of the different disciplines that together make up the map of knowledge in higher education – how they develop, their varied traditions, methodologies, ways of thinking, linkages and forms of dissemination – is particularly associated with Becher. His original study (Becher 1989) has now been updated, extended and supplemented by Trowler (Becher 1999; Becher and Trowler 2001; Braxton and Hargens 1996), and developed further in particular directions (e.g. Neumann et al. 2002). Other researchers have focused on particular disciplines, or groups of disciplines (e.g. Fuller 2000).

Becher's original work was based on interviews with over 220 academics, in 12 disciplines in 18 higher status institutions in the United Kingdom and the United States. He examined the nature of disciplines and the specialisms within them, how they relate to each other and beyond, and how academics get on within them and develop careers. He started from the assumption that 'there are identifiable patterns to be found within the relationship between knowledge forms and their associated knowledge communities' (Becher 1989: 150).

Becher concluded by categorizing disciplines in terms of a series of dichotomies – 'hard/soft and pure/applied in the cognitive realm; convergent/divergent and urban/rural in the social' (Becher 1989: p. 153) – while stressing that these distinctions were relative, and that disciplines might change their characteristics over time. He argued that:

> *In so far as the distinctions are accepted as observational realities rather than theoretical artefacts, they can be argued to have significant implications for the management of higher education and the policies of individual institutions within it . . . the overall picture is of academic institutions made up of basic organisational units whose constituent faculty members have relatively little mutuality of research interest.* (pp. 162–4)

In updating and extending Becher's work, Trowler also made use of interview data he had collected in the United Kingdom and Canada (Trowler 1998). While Trowler notes the impact of a variety of more contemporary developments, such as managerialism and marketization, the argument and conclusions remain much the same.

Becher's work has been influential, though he has been criticized for, amongst other things, his emphasis on higher status institutions and departments, and his lack of attention to more professional disciplines (a criticism in part addressed in a later work: Becher 1999). The attraction of his fairly simple classification of disciplinary characteristics remains strong. Thus, Neumann et al. (2002) have applied the fourfold categorization of disciplines into hard pure (e.g. chemistry, physics), soft pure (e.g. anthropology, history), hard applied (e.g. engineering) and soft applied (e.g. education, management) to explore different approaches to curriculum, assessment, cognitive purpose, teacher characteristics, teaching methods and student requirements. They make use of a range of previous research projects, both published and unpublished. They use their analysis to suggest implications for policy and practice in staff development, teaching innovations, student assessment and quality assurance.

Clearly, one area for future work would be to relate these categorizations of disciplinary characteristics to the varied conceptions of research, and its relation to teaching, discussed in the preceding section.

Forms of knowledge

The debate on forms of knowledge (Gibbons et al. 1994; Nowotny et al. 2001), largely based on conceptual analyses of changing policy and practice, has sought to argue that we are witnessing a major change in the ownership, development and use of knowledge. Thus, Gibbons et al. have argued that what they call 'Mode 1 knowledge' is being superseded in importance by 'Mode 2 knowledge', and that this has profound implications for both disciplines and universities. They state:

By contrast with traditional knowledge, which we call Mode 1, generated within a disciplinary, primarily cognitive, context, Mode 2 knowledge is created in broader, transdisciplinary social and economic contexts . . . The emergence of Mode 2 . . . is profound and calls into question the adequacy of familiar knowledge producing institutions, whether universities, government research establishments, or corporate laboratories. (Gibbons et al. 1994: 1)

It may be questioned, however, just how new and significant these developments are. They would imply, for example, the development of new forms of academic units under the influence of, and in co-operation with, institutions external to the university. The widespread development by universities of business and science parks, enabling entrepreneurs to work in close liaison with academic researchers (Gray 1999: see also Chapter 9 of this book), and of tailored postgraduate courses for particular companies, provide supporting evidence. Whether these are having a general impact on universities, or only on a minority of disciplines and departments, is less clear.

Thus, Askling et al. (2001), in an examination of the impact of lifelong learning policies on concepts of knowledge and university organization, concluded that:

At most universities, the role of disciplines and the related structure of faculties and departments, as well as the disciplinary organisation of curricula, are still strong. Typical for most institutions included in our sample was lifelong learning policy in which initiatives and activities were either left to individual academic staff members or concentrated in mostly smaller, sometimes bigger, but often isolated, central units for continuing education. (pp. 348–9)

Similarly, analysis of the organization and naming of academic units has found 'much evidence of the contemporary strength of what may be termed "traditional" forms of departmental and disciplinary organisation' (Tight 2003b: 267).

Yet, while Mode 2 developments may not be impacting much, or at all, on many, perhaps most, of those who work in universities, their contemporary and future significance remains high. Thus, Adler et al. (2000), partly on the basis of their experience with the FENIX research programme run by the Chalmers University of Technology in Sweden, identify:

. . . the growth of a new class of applied research institutes that, together with consultancy operations, independent academic research institutes (think tanks), industrial research organisations, research-oriented non-governmental organisations etc., occupy a third research sector located between the academy and industry. (p. 128)

They set out five key characteristics for such institutes:

1. Sustained interaction between researchers and practitioners.

2. *An ability to create theoretically well founded solutions in real time that are designed to meet the specific needs and peculiarities of the client organisation.*
3. *A research programme that aims at knowledge production for partners as well as for a more general audience.*
4. *A continuous in-house metalogue [a process of reviewing, briefing and obtaining feedback on method] about research goals, methods, practices etc.*
5. *An ability to generate income that would cover the costs of retaining a core research and administrative staff.* (Adler et al 2000: 129)

They then go on to consider how academic researchers can retain their identities within these institutes.

The nature of the university

The discussion in the preceding sections suggests that changes in the ways in which knowledge is produced and used, and in the ways in which research and teaching relate to each other, are taking place. If this is so, we might also expect attention to be given to the nature of the university as a whole and its role within society. This is, indeed, the case, and adds to a long-standing literature (e.g. Smith and Langslow 1999; Smith and Webster 1997; Trow and Nybom 1991; Wyatt 1990). The book by Delanty (2001), discussed as Case Study 11.2 later in this chapter, is a major recent contribution to this literature. However, the most sustained contribution to research and writing on this topic over the last decade or so has been made by Barnett (1990, 1992, 1994, 1997, 2000, 2003; Barnett and Griffin 1997). Much of his writing is conceptual in nature, and firmly grounded within the philosophy of education.

Barnett began his project by attempting to provide a contemporary definition for 'the idea of higher education':

> . . . 'higher education' is essentially a matter of the development of the mind of the individual student. It is not just any kind of development that the idea points to. An educational process can be termed higher education when the student is carried on to levels of reasoning which make possible critical reflection on his or her experiences, whether consisting of propositional knowledge or of knowledge through action. These levels of reasoning and reflection are 'higher', because they enable the student to take a view (from above, as it were) of what has been learned. Simply, 'higher education' resides in the higher-order states of mind. (Barnett 1990: 202)

He went on to identify six 'minimal conditions for an educational process to justify the title "higher education" ':

1. *A deep understanding, by the student, of some knowledge claims.*
2. *A radical critique, by the same student, of those knowledge claims.*

3. *A developing competence to conduct that critique in the company of others.*
4. *The student's involvement in determining the shape and direction of that critique.*
5. *The student's self-reflection, with the student developing the capacity critically to evaluate his or her own achievements, knowledge claims and performance.*
6. *The opportunity for the student to engage in that inquiry in a process of open dialogue and cooperation.* (p. 203)

Clearly then, in Barnett's view, higher education is necessarily a very demanding process. Indeed, if these criteria were to be applied rigorously, it might be found that quite a few students and courses in our institutions of higher education could not meet them. In his later writing, Barnett moved on to associate higher education with the notion of becoming a 'critical being':

> *. . . a higher education for a genuinely learning society – a higher education for the critical life – imposes three conditions. First, students have to be exposed to multiple discourses . . . Secondly, and more controversially, the student will be exposed to wider understandings, questionings and potential impacts of her [sic] intellectual field . . . What is further required is a committed orientation on the part of the student to this form of life.* (Barnett 1997: 167–9)

His most recent writing has examined the challenges faced by the university 'in an age of supercomplexity' (Barnett 2000), and in countering ideologies of competition, quality, entrepreneurialism and managerialism (Barnett 2003: see also the discussion in Chapter 8 of this book). Throughout, his concern has been to stress the importance of the university as a key institution in society, and to address what it needs to do to continue to thrive in the future.

Case studies

The three case studies considered in this chapter comprise:

- a phenomenographic study of the conceptions of research held by senior researchers;
- a conceptual analysis of the contemporary position of the university within society; and
- a phenomenographic analysis of academics' different experiences of the relations between teaching and research.

Case Study 11.1

Angela Brew (2001a) Conceptions of Research: a phenomenographic study. *Studies in Higher Education*, 26, 3, 271–85.

Themes and Issues

Brew's focus in this article is on how research is experienced by established senior researchers. She argues that:

> There are a number of widely held assumptions about the nature of the research experience. One is that conceptions of research are determined by disciplinary differences. Another is that the methodology used or the kinds of research (i.e. strategic, applied or curiosity-driven) determine researchers' conceptions of research. Yet these assumptions tend to be based on researchers' personal experiences, not on empirical evidence... The changing context of higher education, however, provides an urgent reason for developing a systematic understanding of the nature of research as it is experienced... By identifying variation in experiences of research among senior academic researchers in different domains of inquiry and different types of university, the investigation reported here establishes a framework which can be used to explore the conceptions of research of other groups, for example, early career researchers, postgraduate students and their supervisors. (pp. 271–2)

Methods and Methodologies

Using the framework developed in Chapter 1, I would categorize this article as adopting a phenomenographical approach to researching knowledge. Phenomenographic research proceeds by focusing on a particular phenomenon of interest, collecting people's accounts of their experience of this phenomenon, 'bracketing out', in so far as possible, the researcher's own assumptions and experiences, and continuing the analysis until a full description of the phenomenon has been produced.

For this study, Brew interviewed 57 researchers in Australian universities, chosen so as to reflect three disciplinary groupings: sciences and technology, social sciences, and arts and humanities. The data collection had three stages, starting with a focus on one university, expanding this to cover four universities, and then discussing the initial findings in group meetings with some of the interviewees.

Level

I would categorize the level of this study as national, in that if focused on academics in Australian universities; though the initial stage, focusing on just one university, was institutional.

Analytical/Theoretical Framework

The article forms part of a more extensive study into the nature of research undertaken by the author (Brew 2001b). Noting the lack of an existing framework for the study, Brew has as her purpose the development of such a framework.

Related Literatures

While Brew argues that there is no necessary and direct relationship between the categories of research experience identified and particular disciplines, the connection between Brew's research and that focusing on different disciplinary experiences is clear (e.g. Becher and Trowler 2001; Neumann et al. 2002). There is also a link to another literature, that examining the relationship between the teaching and research functions in higher education (e.g. Drennan 2001; Robertson and Bond 2001).

Argument and Conclusions

Brew uses her data to identify four categories of research experience, organized along two dimensions – whether there was an external product or internal process orientation, and whether the researcher themselves was in the forefront of, or incidental to, awareness in the research. She describes these four categories as the domino (series of tasks), trading (a social phenomenon emphasizing products), layer (excavating reality) and journey (research transforms the researcher) conceptions. She then explores some of the implications of these variations for academic practices and exchange.

Case Study 11.2

Gerard Delanty (2001) *Challenging Knowledge: the university in the knowledge society*. Buckingham: Open University Press.

Themes and Issues

Delanty's key theme concerns the changing position of the university within society, as consequent upon the changing nature of knowledge and its use.

Methods and Methodologies

I have categorized this study as employing a conceptual approach. Delanty analyses a whole series of concepts – including knowledge, globalization, modernity, citizenship, capitalism, postmodernism and culture – to provide a theorized account of the contemporary position of the university within society.

Level

The book focuses at the system level. While the context is clearly a Western capitalist society, no particular society is focused on.

Analytical/Theoretical Framework

The framework for the argument presented in the book is taken from the literature on the sociology of knowledge and the social theory of modernity.

In creating this framework, Delanty reviews the work of a whole range of social theorists, including Bourdieu, Castells, Derrida, Foucault, Giddens, Habermas and Lyotard.

Related Literatures

In addition to the range of social theorists to whom Delanty refers, there is a significant literature on the nature of the university and its place in society (e.g. Barnett 1990, 2000; Barnett and Griffin 1997; Gibbons et al. 1994; Jacob and Hellstrom 2000; Nowotny et al. 2001; Scott 1998; Smith and Webster 1997).

Argument and Conclusions

Delanty argues that 'the university is no longer the crucial institution in society for the reproduction of instrumental/technical knowledge and is also no longer the codifier of a now fragmented national culture'. Rather, a 'new role and identity for the university is emerging around the democratization of knowledge' (p. 6). He reaches a positive, but challenging, conclusion:

> The university is the institution in society most capable of linking the require-ments of industry, technology and market forces with the demands of citizenship. Given the enormous dependence of these forces on university based experts, the university is in fact in a position of strength, not of weakness. While it is true that the new production of knowledge is dominated by an instrumentalization of knowledge and that as a result the traditional role of the university has been undermined, it is now in a position to serve social goals more fully than previously when other goals were more prominent. (p. 158)

Case Study 11.3

Jane Robertson and Carol Bond (2001) Experiences of the Relation Between Teaching and Research: what do academics value? *Higher Education Research and Development*, 20, 1, 5–19.

Themes and Issues

This article addresses an issue which has been of increasing interest, indeed concern, in recent years, namely the relationship between teaching and research and, in particular, how this is experienced by academics. The authors argue that:

> despite the increasing attention given this topic, there is virtually no research that addresses the actual nature of the relation between these two fundamental aspects of academic work. Furthermore, the continuing lack of such research may well contribute to the eventual loss of something that is of considerable value to the academy. (p. 6)

Methods and Methodologies

The article takes a phenomenographic approach. Seven academics were inter-viewed, and two others contributed information by email. In short, this was a small-scale study; indeed, the authors themselves refer to their sample as 'opportunistic'. The focus of attention in analysing this data was on the 'variation in experiences amongst and within the individuals' data' concerning 'the inter-relation of teaching and research'.

Level

The article may be characterized as focusing on the national level, as the data collected comes from academics working within the New Zealand higher education system.

Analytical/Theoretical Framework

The phenomenographic approach adopted to the analysis of the data leads to the creation of an analytical framework consisting of five 'qualitatively different experiences of the relation between research and teaching' (p. 10). These are:

A. research and teaching are mutually incompatible activities;
B. little or no connection exists between research and teaching at undergraduate level;
C. teaching is a means of transmitting new research knowledge;
D. teachers model and encourage a research/critical inquiry approach to learning;
E. teaching and research share a symbiotic relationship in a learning community.

Related Literatures

Robertson and Bond provide a useful review of the existing literature (e.g. Feldman 1987; Hattie and Marsh 1996; Hughes and Tight 1995; Neumann 1992) on the relationship between teaching and research in the first part of their article. Interestingly, the authors reveal that the starting point for their study was the reaction of a number of academics to reading a review of the Hattie and Marsh study in their university newsletter. The debate over the relation-ship between teaching and research shows little sign of abating (see, for example, Coate et al. 2001; Jenkins 2000), and is closely related to the literature on the nature of research (e.g. Brew 2001a – an article also considered in this chapter as a case study – 2001b).

Argument and Conclusions

Having identified 'five qualitatively different experiences of the relation between teaching and research', Robertson and Bond proceed to illustrate these through quotes from their data. They then consider the extent of variation in experiences, the relationships between the five categories, the affective dimension of academics' experiences, and the importance of their context. They conclude by arguing that:

> As with all research, this small study has generated many more questions than it answers, thus providing fertile ground for further exploration. (p. 16)

Ideas for further research

This review of contemporary research into knowledge suggests a number of issues for further research:

- more detailed studies of academics working within particular disciplines, sub-disciplines and inter-disciplinary fields;
- analyses of the processes of knowledge dissemination and use from within to beyond the university;
- research into the value(s) accorded to different kinds of knowledge, and different disciplines;
- studies of the relationships between research and other academic roles (as well as teaching);
- life history type research into how academics develop as researchers;
- research into the relations between academics' perceptions of research, disciplines and academic practices; and
- studies of the differential impact on parts of the university of changes in the ways knowledge is developed and used.

Part III

The process of researching higher education

As you will have realized long ago if you have read this far, the main section of this book – Part II – has been organized in terms of the key themes or issues which contemporary higher education researchers have been examining. While this was the primary mode of organization, however, attention was also given in the discussion in Chapters 4 to 11 to the methods and methodologies being employed by higher education researchers, and to the levels at which higher education research has been pitched.

In this, the last, section of the book, the focus will be placed on methods and methodologies (in Chapter 12) and levels of analysis (Chapter 13). A third and final chapter (Chapter 14) will then examine the process of researching. The intention in these three chapters is both to link the field of higher education research to social research more generally, and to offer practical guidance on researching higher education.

Method and methodology in researching higher education

Introduction

This chapter provides an overview of the methods and methodologies applied to researching higher education. In doing so, it makes links between higher education research and social research more generally, and offers a guide to the social research methods literature.

The chapter is organized in ten sections. First, the meanings of, and linkages between, methods and methodologies are discussed, and alternative categorizations are then reviewed. There then follow eight sections focusing on the eight key methods or methodologies identified in Chapter 1, and which have guided the discussion throughout this book:

- documentary analysis;
- comparative analysis;
- interviews;
- surveys and multivariate analyses;
- conceptual analysis;
- phenomenography;
- critical and feminist perspectives;
- auto/biographical and observational studies.

The final section then attempts to draw the discussion together and offer some conclusions.

Method and methodology

The distinction between method and methodology was briefly considered in Chapter 1, when the categorization used to organize the analysis presented in this book was introduced and justified. While these terms clearly share a common base, and are frequently used as synonyms or in overlapping ways, the distinction does have meaning. Thus, methods are essentially techniques for data collection and analysis, such as interviews or observations; whereas methodologies may be taken to refer to the underlying approaches or philosophies adopted by researchers.

The pragmatic eightfold categorization used in this book is something of a mixture of methods and methodologies. Documentary analysis, interviews, multivariate analysis, observational studies and surveys may be seen primarily as methods. Phenomenography, critical and feminist perspectives are essentially methodologies. The other categories referred to – auto/biographical studies, comparative analysis, conceptual analysis – could be interpreted as either method or methodology. Where they are employed consistently by a researcher over a period of time, these (and arguably other methods) probably represent a methodological standpoint; where they are used along with other methods, there are most likely simply viewed as just another method.

The literature on social research methods is vast – though relatively sparse on some topics – and there are numerous generic guides to their use. Some are pitched at the 'how to' audience (e.g. Blaxter et al. 2001; Burns 2000; Cohen et al. 2000; Denscombe 1998; Robson 1993), while others are presented in a more theorized fashion (e.g. Bechhofer and Paterson 2000; May 1997; Punch 1998; de Vaus 2001).

Classifications of social research methods vary, depending upon which authority is consulted, but share much in common. Blaxter et al. (2001), for example, offer a simple fourfold categorization, recognizing documents, interviews, observation and questionnaires as the fundamental methods for social data collection. Cohen et al. (2000) offer a more detailed categorization, though they use the term 'strategies for data collection and researching' rather than methods. They name three of the four methods recognized by Blaxter et al., not recognizing documents, adding to them accounts, multidimensional measurement (compare multivariate analysis), personal constructs, role playing and tests.

Methodologies are rather more contested, and a wide range of perspectives on them can be found in the literature. They may be seen as involving the adoption of a philosophical and value position on the part of the researcher. They also imply a concern with how data is to be analysed and presented as well as collected. The most fundamental and much argued methodological distinction, perhaps, is that between quantitative (e.g. Black 1999; Fielding and Gilbert 2000; Gorard 2001) and qualitative (e.g. Flick 2002; Mason 2002; Silverman 1997) forms of research.

Quantitative research may be characterized as being concerned with measuring key factors in as representative and valid a way as possible (e.g.

as in a large-scale survey), so that the results (for example after multivariate analysis) can be applied more generally. Qualitative research, by contrast, may be typified as being more concerned with exploring a particular phenomenon of interest in depth and in context, using the respondents' own words (for example through lengthy, unstructured interviews), and without making prior analytical assumptions (for example using grounded theory). But this is to dichotomize: both large-scale qualitative research and exploratory quantitative research are practised by social researchers, and the two approaches are often used in tandem within multi-method designs to provide confirmation or triangulation (Brannen 1992; Tashakkori and Teddlie 1998).

Three categorizations of social research are detailed in Table 12.1, alongside the eightfold schema used in this book. It can be seen that there are both overlaps and differences between Crotty's (1998) theoretical perspectives, de Vaus's (2001) research designs, Cohen et al.'s (2000) styles of educational research, and the classification of method/ologies used in this book. This variation is, in itself, supportive of the more pragmatic strategy adopted for this book.

Crotty, in a well thought out analysis, recognizes four hierarchical levels for thinking about the social research process, moving down from epistemology (e.g. objectivism) through theoretical perspective (see Table 12.1) and methodology to method. His list of methodologies includes experimental research, survey research, ethnography, phenomenological research, grounded theory, heuristic inquiry, action research, discourse analysis and feminist standpoint research (Crotty 1998: 5).

Clearly, then, there is no general agreement on what the key methods and methodologies for social research are. Much depends on the identity of the discipline, or sub-discipline, in which one is working, and on the methodological standpoint of the person making the categorization. There is also a wealth of specialized and detailed terminology in use, which can be confusing and off-putting to those approaching it for the first time. Those wishing to discover more about particular specialist methodologies that are not explored in detail here – typically because they have not been much applied to higher education research – will need to seek out more from the references given.

Four (at least) method/ologies that are applied to researching higher education have not been specifically identified in the categorization used in this book. In part, this is because to have identified all method/ologies would have over-complicated and fragmented the organization of the book. But there were also other reasons:

- *Case Studies* are widely employed as a method/ology for researching higher education, and there is a substantive literature on their use in social research generally (e.g. Bassey 1999; Stake 1995; Yin 2003a,

Table 12.1 Alternative Conceptions of Social Research: Styles, Designs, Theoretical Perspectives and Method/ologies

Styles of Educational Research (Cohen et al. 2000)	*Research Designs* (de Vaus 2001)
Naturalistic and ethnographic research	Experimental designs
Historical research	Longitudinal designs
Surveys, longitudinal, cross-sectional and trend studies	Cross-sectional designs
Case studies	Case study designs
Correlational research	
Ex post facto research	*Method/ologies* (this book)
	Documentary analysis
Theoretical Perspectives (Crotty 1998)	Comparative analysis
Positivism	Interviews
Constructionism	Surveys and multivariate analyses
Interpretivism	Conceptual analysis
Critical inquiry	Phenomenography
Feminism	Critical and feminist perspectives
Postmodernism	Auto/biographical and observational studies

2003b). Indeed, they are a classic approach to relatively small-scale research, and many of the studies that have been discussed in this book, which have examined practice or innovations in specific departments or institutions, could be described as case studies. And that is why the term has not been used in the organization of the book, as almost any piece of social research could be termed, in some sense, a case study. That is, the term is too generic, and too widely used in practice, to be useful for present purposes.

- *Evaluation* is another widely used term in educational research and practice, in part because it is seen as a standard stage in the course development/delivery/evaluation process. It can thus be seen as both an object for research and a research methodology (House and Howe 1999; Robson 2000; Rossi and Freeman 1993). That potential confusion is part of the reason why it has not been used as an organizational term here. My other reservation is that it is used, in practice, as loosely as case study is; indeed, the two terms are often seen almost synonymously.

- *Action Research* has been widely developed as a methodology for research within, for example, school education, social work and health care (e.g. Atweh et al. 1998; Greenwood and Levin 1998; Griffiths 1998; Hart and Bond 1995; McNiff et al. 1998; Morton-Cooper 2000). It has not, as yet, had much explicit use within higher education research, though the article by Kember (2000), examined in Chapter 4 as Case Study 4.1, does make use of this term. In essence, this could be seen as purely a matter of terminology. Many small-scale, evaluative case studies – which examine the application of innovative practice or policy within a course, department or institution – could be described as action research, though, in its pure sense, action research does imply a longer-term engagement to continuous improvement.

- *Ethnography* (Brewer 2000; Davies 1998; Fetterman 1998; Hammersley and Atkinson 1995; Hine 2000; van Maanen 1995), the study of people in their natural settings, has particular associations with research in social anthropology and sociology. Such an approach has also been applied to researching higher education, particularly in examining the lives of academics and students within universities, though the term is not commonly used. Here, what might be termed ethnographic studies are considered under other headings, notably interviews and auto/biographical and observational studies.

My aim in the remainder of this chapter is to review the use of what I have identified as the eight key method/ologies in higher education research.

Documentary analysis

Documents . . . do not simply reflect, but also construct social reality and versions of events. The search for documents' 'meaning' continues, but with researchers also exercising 'suspicion'. It is not then assumed that documents are neutral artefacts which independently report social reality (positivism), or that analysis must be rooted in that nebulous concept, practical reasoning. Documents are now viewed as media through which social power is expressed. They are approached in terms of the cultural context in which they were written and may be viewed 'as attempts at persuasion'. (May 1997: 164)

Given the fundamental importance of documents to social research, it is perhaps surprising that the literature on documentary analysis is both relatively limited in scale and fractured in focus. After all, it is difficult to imagine any one undertaking a meaningful piece of social research which did not involve some documentary analysis, even if this went no further than a limited reference to the existing research literature on the topic being studied. But this recognition may indicate the explanation for this apparent paradox. That is, documentary analysis, unless it is being carried out in some specialized manner, is so endemic to research (like writing – see the discussion of student and academic writing in Chapters 5 and 10) that it is easy to assume that little or no guidance is needed.

Amongst the available literature on this topic, we may recognize:

- some discussion in general research methods texts (e.g. May 1997);
- the occasional text focusing wholly on documentary analysis (e.g. Prior 2003);
- a small but growing literature on literature reviews (Bruce 1994; Fink 1998; Hart 1998, 2001);
- a related, again small but growing, literature on reading research and texts (e.g. Brown and Dowling 1997; Ekegren 1999);
- a literature focusing on historical research (e.g. McCulloch and Richardson 2000);
- a specialist literature on exploratory uses of text in research (e.g. Bauer and Gaskell 2000; Lee 2000).

Curiously, the policy analysis literature (e.g. Hammersley 1995; Ozga 2000) frequently gives little direct attention to documentary analysis.

The fracturing of this literature may be illustrated through two examples. First, Hart's (1998) book on 'doing a literature review' is directed, like much of this literature, at the postgraduate student audience. It covers the processes involved and skills needed to compile a literature review by practically examining issues such as purpose, planning, reading, analysing argument, organizing ideas and writing. While the book may be formally located within the 'how to' genre, it also has much to offer the more experienced researcher.

Second, McCulloch and Richardson (2000) provide an overview of historical research in education, giving attention to the use of published and unpublished sources of different kinds. They see research into the history of education as poorly regarded, falling between the disciplinary stools of education and history:

> Both in the educational research methods literature and in works of historiography, the treatment of historical research in education has often been shallow and cursory or problematic. Within the genre of educational research methods textbooks, historical study has usually been discussed in a perfunctory and superficial fashion, and recently this coverage has been marginalised further. Meanwhile, contemporary introductions to academic history and historiography most commonly ignore education. (p. 25)

Five of the 24 case studies of higher education research analysed in this book – Case Studies 7.1, 7.2, 8.1, 9.2 and 9.3 – were categorized as chiefly relying upon documentary analysis. Their concentration in research into the issues of quality (Chapter 7), system policy (Chapter 8) and institutional management (Chapter 9) is perhaps not surprising, as documents on institutional practices and national policies are widely available.

Of these five case studies, one (Case Study 8.1, Deem 2001) had the character of a review article or literature review, being based on a critique of two recently published books. Another (Case Study 9.3, Stensaker and Norgard 2001) was a piece of, relatively contemporary, historical research, based primarily on institutional and review documents. Interestingly, this is the only one of the five studies selected that contains a section specifically, if briefly, addressing the question of methods.

The other three case studies are analyses of particular kinds of documentary material on particular topics:

- Bowden (2000, Case Study 7.1) examines the validity and usefulness of the university league tables published in national newspapers in the United Kingdom.
- Harvey (2002, Case Study 7.2) examines the thinking on the monitoring of higher education, in terms of whether it is external or internal, focuses on quality or standards, and what use is made of self assessment, peer assessment and performance indicators.
- Ramsden (1998, Case Study 9.2) presents an overview of leadership and management in higher education through a summary and review of published research on these topics (including his own).

Comparative analysis

Comparative analysis, in its most general sense, is a term that can be attached to any form of research that is based on the making of comparisons. For example, a study that examined how two or more higher education institutions arranged for the induction of new students or staff could be termed a comparative study. More typically, however, the term is reserved for research that compares some element of experience in two or more different countries or systems. That, international, sense is the how the term is used in this book.

There is a distinct literature on comparative analysis and research: in the social sciences in general (e.g. Hantrais 1999; Hantrais and Mangen 1996), in education (e.g. Thomas 1998; Watson 2001) and in the specific field of higher education (Goedegebuure and van Vught 1994, 1996; Teichler 1996). There are also some educational journals that focus particularly on the application of the comparative method in educational research, including *Compare* and *Comparative Education*. While none of these journals focus specifically on higher education, they do publish comparative studies of higher education alongside articles focusing on other levels.

Watson (2001) succinctly sets out the reasoning behind many comparative studies:

> *One of the main purposes of comparative education has always been that of reform, learning from other situations with the express intention of borrowing ideas that might enable reform in one's own country context.* (p. 11)

May (1997, pp. 185–9) puts it rather differently and with more complexity, recognizing four related perspectives on comparative social research:

- *the import-mirror view, where one's own practices are examined in the context of others;*
- *the difference view, focusing on why societies develop in different ways;*
- *the theory development view, which sees comparative research as impacting beneficially on theory; and*
- *the prediction view, which believes that others' experiences can be useful in thinking about what might happen here.*

These perspectives are reflected in the substantial literature (e.g. Dolowitz et al. 2000; Kennett 2001; Marsh 1998) examining comparative social policies, including those on higher education, and, in particular, the transfer of policies and practices between countries.

Clearly, in making comparisons, and looking for potential transfers of policies or ideas, between different countries or systems, it is important to choose appropriate comparisons. This explains, of course, the focus of much comparative higher education research on European, particularly European Union countries. Such research is often to be found in journals such as the *European Journal of Education, Higher Education in Europe* and *Higher Education Policy*, and in books published by (formerly) Jessica Kingsley and Elsevier (see Chapters 2 and 3). It should be noted, though, that most of the contributions to these journals and books are national in focus, with the comparative element coming through in the editorial selection and contribution. The need for an appropriate comparison also explains the tendency, in both Australia and the United Kingdom, to look to the United States of America for inspiration. This does not, however, negate the usefulness of looking more widely, for example to East Asian countries, for comparative stimulus.

As Hantrais and Mangen (1996) point out, there are a number of ways in which comparative research may be carried out, ranging from the relatively straightforward and descriptive to the more complex and demanding:

> *The descriptive, or survey, method which will usually result in a state of the art review, is generally the first stage in any large-scale international comparative project . . . A juxtaposition approach is often adopted at this stage: data gathered by individuals or teams, according to agreed criteria, and derived either from existing materials or new empirical work, are presented side by side. Many projects never go far beyond data collection and collation since analysis and evaluation are so costly in terms of time and funding and tend to give rise to problems which may be avoided if the study is confined to description . . . Rather than each researcher or group of researchers investigating their own national context and then pooling information, a single researcher or team of researchers may formulate the problem and research hypotheses and carry out studies in more than one country, using replication of the experimental design, generally to collect and analyse new data. The method is often adopted when a smaller number of countries is involved and where researchers are required to have intimate knowledge of all the countries under study . . . it is generally described as the 'safari' approach. (p. 4)*

Their conclusions apply to higher education research as much as any other area of social research, with most studies adopting descriptive or juxtaposition approaches, and safari studies being relatively few and far between. This is hardly surprising, of course: it is difficult enough for one person to have expertise in policy and practice in one country. Extending this to two or more countries will often impose linguistic demands, as well as a need to be able to understand culturally different practices that may have familiar labels. Other typical problems with comparative research include:

> *. . . the management of research, availability of and access to comparable datasets and the definition of the research parameters and associated issues of equivalence of concepts.* (Hantrais and Mangen 1996: 5)

Yet, as Teichler argues, the effort to overcome such problems is surely worthwhile:

> *Information on other higher education systems is most fruitful in destroying conceptual thinking and reasoning based on narrow experience; comparative research is a goldmine for the early stages of conceptual restructuring. And comparisons are indispensable for understanding a reality shaped by common international trends, reforms frequently based on comparative observation, as well as growing trans-national activities and partial supra-national integration in higher education.* (Teichler 1996: 462–3)

Four of the case studies examined in this book – Case Studies 4.1, 6.3, 8.2 and 8.3 – have been categorized as adopting a comparative approach. Not surprisingly, two of these focus on aspects of system policy, the topic which has been most explored on a comparative basis in higher education.

One of these case studies, that by Teichler (2000b, Case Study 6.3) focuses on the kinds of problems identified by Hantrais and Mangen, in reviewing the difficulties in using and interpreting the available European data sets dealing with graduate employment. Another, by Jongbloed and Vossensteyn (2001, Case Study 8.2), makes use of information gathered from 11 OECD (Organisation for Economic Co-operation and Development) nations to explore the use of performance based funding within different higher education systems.

The other two comparative case studies referred to in this book are, in some ways, more challenging, in that they compare practice and experience across the north/south or developed/developing boundaries. Thus, Kember (2000, Case Study 4.1) uses his experience of working and researching within Hong Kong universities to challenge many of the stereotypes about Asian students' learning approaches, motivations and study practices deriving from the largely Western research literature. McBurnie and Ziguras (2001, Case Study 8.3) compare policies on the regulation of transnational higher education in Hong Kong and Malaysia with emerging policy in Australia.

Interviews

When we turn to discuss interviews and surveys (next section), we are in what might be called the heartland of social research. These method/ologies have been extensively applied to researching just about any social, and higher education, topic you can think of. They represent such obvious strategies to collecting data: you either ask people questions and listen to their responses, or you give them a set of questions with predetermined answers to tick or circle. Interviews and surveys may also be seen as representing what some would see as the qualitative/quantitative divide in social research, though I would argue that such a view is both simplistic and exaggerated.

The great majority of general texts on social research method/ologies give substantial attention, therefore, to different kinds of interviews – structured, semi-structured, unstructured, conversational, depth, individual, group or focus – and how they may be recorded and analysed. A growing literature is concerned with, in particular, the techniques – manual and computer-based – that may be used to analyse interviews and other forms of qualitative data (e.g. Coffey and Atkinson 1996; Dey 1993; Miles and Huberman 1994). While this could not be said to match the huge literature on quantitative data analysis, it is a step in the right direction. There is also a specialist literature focused exclusively on interviews (e.g. Arksey and Knight 1999; Keats 2000; Krueger and Casey 2000; Kvale 1996; Wengraf 2001).

While they may be highly popular, interviews, like all research method/ologies, are subject to a number of challenges and reservations:

> *Interviews are one method by which the human world may be explored, although it is the world of beliefs and meanings, not of actions, that is clarified by interview research. Since what people claim to think, feel or do does not necessarily align with their actions, it is important to be clear that interviews get at what people say, however sincerely, rather than at what they do. Is this still true if we interview people about what they have done? Probably. The longer ago, the less personally important or striking an event, the more discreditable or sensitive the behaviour, the less likely it is that the deed and the story will match up. But even a question about yesterday's actions might produce responses that differ from what observers might have noticed had they watched the action in question.* (Arksey and Knight 1999: 15–16)

Another key issue about interview-based research is the time and other resources required for their effective analysis. Questionnaire surveys employing multiple choice answers may be scanned directly into a computer, and then analysed in seconds using one or other of the well-established software systems. Even with the use of Atlas-TI, Ethnograph, NVivo, NUDIST or other software for textual analysis, however, the processes involved in analysing interview data and associated materials – transcription, coding, interpretation, theorizing and so on – typically take several times as long as the actual interviews. And, as with many research method/ologies, the great majority of the data collected ends up on the 'cutting room floor', and does not feature, or even appear to influence, the resulting book, article or report.

Only two of the case studies included in this book (Case Studies 6.1 and 10.3) were categorized as relying primarily on interviews. Many more could have been added, and some probably would have been had this not been such a well-used research method/ology. The first of these case studies was an example of research into the student experience, while the second focused on an aspect of academic work. Interviews have, however, been widely used to explore all of the eight key themes or issues identified.

Both of these studies are very explicit and up-front about the methods and methodologies they employed, and both are relatively large-scale examples of interview-based research. Thus, Ball et al. (2002, Case Study 6.1) base their analysis of the influence of students' social class in their choice of higher education course and institution on 120 interviews with students, 15 with teachers and 40 with parents at institutions in the London area. They also make use of questionnaire and observational data. The scale of Trowler and Knight's (2000, Case Study 10.3) study is slightly less, as it is based primarily on 74 interviews from two studies. But they also re-analysed data from a number of previous studies conducted by others, and their data comes from three different countries, so their study may be seen as international in scope. Most examples of the application of interviews to higher education research, by contrast, are based on much smaller samples, sometimes amounting to only a handful of interviews.

Surveys and multivariate analyses

As indicated in the previous section, surveys – typically seen as being quantitative in nature, and based on carefully designed questionnaires offering multiple choice answers – along with interviews, may be regarded as comprising the mainstays of social science, and higher education, research. Of course, in a more general sense, the term surveys can be used to cover interviews, observations, documentary and other analyses that involve selecting and studying a sample of people or things, but here we will focus on the questionnaire method, interpreting surveys in the following way:

> Survey research . . . *is the* method *of* collecting information *by asking a set of preformulated* questions *in a predetermined sequence in a structured* questionnaire *to a* sample *of individuals drawn so as to be* representative *of a defined* population. (Hutton 1990: 8)

As that quotation indicates, survey research both involves a specialist terminology and aspires to the ideas of objectivity and generalizability associated with the classic scientific method.

As with interviews, most general social research texts devote a good deal of attention to the design, administration and analysis of questionnaires (e.g. Ader and Mellenbergh 1999; Black 1999; Bryman and Cramer 2000; Fielding and Gilbert 2000; Wright 1997). Many specialized texts focus wholly on questionnaires and on different techniques for analysing the quantitative data they typically generate (e.g. Lavraka 1993; Moser and Kalton 1993; Oppenheim 1992; Sapsford 1999; de Vaus 1995). There is also another specialized literature that examines the use and analysis of secondary data sets, that is data collected by others, as in large-scale national surveys and official statistics (e.g. Levitas and Guy 1996).

Compared to interviews, questionnaire surveys are relatively easy to set up. Questionnaires can be pre-coded and, when completed, readily scanned straight into a computer. With the availability of quantitative analysis software, such as SPSS and Minitab, and even more widely of spreadsheet software like Lotus and Excel, results can be processed, analysed and presented very quickly. Indeed, this is one of the problems with quantitative analysis: it is so easy to do without really thinking about the nature or the appropriateness of the analysis being carried out.

For those using questionnaire surveys, then, key issues are the validity of the questions being asked, the appropriateness of the samples chosen, response rates, and the nature and levels of analysis carried out. The last of these may require only simple reportage of the frequencies of different responses to given questions, or the cross-tabulation of the answers to different questions (for example are the patterns of response different for men and women, or those following different degree courses?). Or it may mean the application of sophisticated multivariate analysis techniques, such as cluster, discriminant, factor and regression analysis.

Questionnaire surveys have been widely used to explore all of the key themes or issues for higher education research identified in this book. While, particularly for small-scale studies, the analyses carried out have usually been relatively simple, multivariate analyses have also been applied, most notably, but not exclusively, in teaching and learning research (see Chapter 4). Here, standardized instruments and questionnaires have been widely employed in medium- and large-scale surveys to produce the data to analyse, for example, students' approaches to study and learning styles.

Three of the case studies discussed in this book – Case Studies 4.3, 6.2 and 7.3 – have been categorized as being based upon surveys or multi-variate analyses. Prosser and Trigwell's study (1999, Case Study 4.3) is a good example of the use of multivariate analysis techniques to study student learning. They report on the administration of two established questionnaires – the Course Experience Questionnaire and the Study Process Questionnaire – to samples of 144, 274 and over 8000 students, and the subsequent analysis of the results using cluster and factor analysis to look for general patterns and groupings.

The other two case studies were smaller in scale and, at least in one case, made use of simpler forms of analysis. Thus, Norton et al. (2001) report on a study that administered three questionnaires to a sample of 267 students to explore the correlation between essay writing tactics, cheating behaviours and approaches to studying. Shevlin et al. (2000) administered a short questionnaire to 213 students, and then used factor analysis to assess whether there was a relationship between perceptions of academics' teaching effectiveness and their charisma.

Conceptual analysis

Conceptual analysis is one of the less common method/ological approaches to researching higher education (see Tables 2.2 and 3.3). As a research method in the social sciences, it is similar to documentary analysis in lacking a developed method/ological literature, though there are plenty of texts that have examined social concepts (e.g. Hughes 2002c; Tight 2002). There is also a connection with the specialist literatures, deriving in part from literary studies, on discourse (e.g. Gee 1996; Howarth 2000) and narrative (e.g. Josselson and Lieblich 1995, 1999).

The similarity between the method/ologies of documentary and conceptual analysis is arguably closer than that, such that conceptual analysis might be seen as a variant of documentary analysis, characterized by a greater degree of theorization and a more philosophical approach. Conceptual analysts also work to a large degree with documentary data, but their focus tends to be at the more idealized system level rather than, for example, at the national level (see Tables 2.6 and 3.7).

Conceptual analysis is concerned with ideas and their contested meanings, and with how this impacts on our understandings of the world. As Hughes argues:

> . . . researchers need to consider how the concepts they use relate to other conceptualisations . . . researchers need to be conceptually literate. Conceptual literacy is no more, and no less, than an act of sensitisation to the political implications of contestation over the diversity of conceptual meanings. In this it draws attention to the multiplicity of meanings that are invoked by the use of key terms; to the dualistic framing of language; to the art of deconstruction; and to the salience of focusing on language in use. (Hughes 2002c: 3)

All research, therefore, whether explicitly or only implicitly, involves some degree of conceptual usage and analysis.

Conceptual analysis has been applied to researching all of the key themes and issues identified in this book. The four case studies – Case Studies 4.2, 5.1, 10.2 and 11.2 – that have been categorized as using this approach confirm this, as each relates to a different key theme. Significantly, in at least three of these cases (the first three), the study considered forms part of a larger piece of research, making use of other method/ologies, and which, as a whole, would probably not have been characterized as conceptual analysis.

Thus, Barnett et al. (2001, Case Study 5.1) carried out an extensive interview-based study of United Kingdom universities, but the focus of the article considered in Chapter 5 was on our understanding of the higher education curriculum and of curriculum change. Barnett and his colleagues provide and analyse a model of the curriculum in terms of knowledge, action and self. Land's (2001, Case Study 10.2) work also involved interviews, in his case with academic developers working in United Kingdom institutions, but the focus of the article discussed is on identifying alternative models and theories of, and orientations to, academic development.

Laurillard (2002, Case Study 4.2) offers a conceptual analysis of learning technologies, with the intention of illuminating their application to student learning. She provides a 'conversational framework' to be used in considering which learning activities and technologies to use for different purposes. Finally, Delanty (2001, Case Study 11.2) focuses on the changing nature of knowledge and the position of the university in society, contributing to an area of debate to which Barnett (1990, 1994, 1997, 2000, 2003) has also made significant contributions.

Phenomenography

Phenomenography, as a methodology for researching higher education, is in a somewhat contradictory or paradoxical position. On the one hand, as the analysis presented in Chapters 2 and 3 makes clear, it is a relatively uncommon methodology in higher education research. Yet higher education is also one of the fields in which phenomenography has been most developed and applied.

Phenomenography is primarily an approach to data analysis, making use of data collected in a variety of ways, including through interviews and documents. It was developed in Sweden in the 1960s and 1970s, as an approach for studying student learning, by Marton and his colleagues, and may be related to phenomenology (Moustakas 1994) and other qualitative research methodologies. Marton defines phenomenography in the following fashion:

> . . . *the empirical study of the limited number of qualitatively different ways in which various phenomena in, and aspects of, the world around us are experienced, conceptualised, understood, perceived and apprehended.* (Marton 1994: 4424; see also Marton and Booth 1997)

Ashworth and Lucas (2000), in setting out practical guidance for the design, conduct and reporting of phenomenographic research, emphasize that:

... a paramount requirement for phenomenography [is] to be sensitive to the individuality of conceptions of the world – it must be grounded in the lived reality of its research participants. (p. 297)

This is achieved by 'bracketing' (Ashworth 1999), a process which 'refers to the need for the researcher to set aside his or her own assumptions, so far as is possible, in order to register the student's own point of view' (Ashworth and Lucas 2000: 297). A range of analytical techniques is suggested to help in this process. Analysis proceeds until the researchers feel that they have identified all the qualitatively different ways in which the phenomenon being studies is experienced or understood.

Phenomenography has been most widely applied within higher education to researching student learning, and, in particular, to understanding the different ways in which students understand learning and approach studying (Entwistle 1997; Marton et al. 1997; Prosser and Trigwell 1999). However, the two case studies examined in this book that have made use of it both relate to the theme of knowledge (Case Studies 11.1 and 11.3).

Brew's (2001a, Case Study 11.1) focus is on how researchers working within universities understand research. Her study is based on 57 interviews in four Australian universities, the phenomenographic analysis of which led her to identify four different categories of research experience. Robertson and Bond's (2001, Case Study 11.3) smaller scale study also made use of interviews, in their case with an opportunistic sample of only nine academics working in New Zealand. Their interest was in understanding how academics experienced the relation between the teaching and research roles, and their analysis identified five qualitatively different experiences of this.

Critical and feminist perspectives

Critical and feminist perspectives have been bracketed together here as they both take a critical stance to the status quo and our understandings of it, seeking to challenge these and advance alternative positions. Critical and feminist approaches to researching higher education are, like conceptual analysis and phenomenography, relatively uncommon. They also tend to appear outside the mainstream, or malestream, of writing on higher education; that is, within the feminist or critical, rather than higher education, literatures. They have a respectable pedigree, however, and are not to be ignored.

Smyth and Shacklock (1998) have defined critical research in the following terms:

Critical research is . . . centrally concerned with the simultaneous process of 'deconstruction' and 'reconstruction'. It works something like this. Within a piece of research, some core abstract concepts are located which are considered to be central; they are used repeatedly to interrogate situations of concrete lived reality in order to develop a new synthesis . . . The intent is to engage in a constant questioning and building up of theory and interpretations through repeated ongoing analysis until a coherent alternative reconstruction of the account is created. (pp. 3–4)

They advocate the adoption of reflexive strategies by critical researchers, to acknowledge the influence of 'the ideological and historical power dominant forms of inquiry' (p. 6: see also Alvesson and Skoldberg 2000; Hood et al. 1999), and enable the empowerment of the researcher and the research. Critical research has, to some extent, been overcome by the 'postmodern embrace' (Stronach and MacLure 1997: see also Scheurich 1997; Usher and Edwards 1994).

It may be seen as paralleled by the feminist research tradition (e.g. Hughes 2002c; Maynard and Purvis 1994; Ramazanoglu and Holland 2002; Reinharz 1992; Ribbens and Edwards 1998). Thus, Maynard (1994) has identified:

. . . three major and related concerns confronting feminists engaged in empirical social research. These are to do with the role of experience, the importance of 'race' and other forms of diversity, and the question of objectivity. (p. 23)

Within higher education, critical and feminist perspectives have perhaps been applied most commonly to understanding the experiences of academics and students (see the sections on 'the experience of different student groups' in Chapter 6, and on 'women academics' in Chapter 10). They have also, however, been employed in critiquing established practices in course design, institutional management and system policy.

As it happens, the two case studies discussed in this book that have been identified as adopting critical or feminist perspectives both relate to the theme of course design (Case Studies 5.2 and 5.3). Johnson et al. (2000, Case Study 5.2) provide an analysis of alternative practices in research student supervision, stressing the role of gender, basing their analysis on interviews with experienced and current supervisors. Scott (2000, Case Study 5.3), in a small-scale but tightly focused study, offers a critical perspective on understandings of critical thinking in student writing.

Auto/biographical and observational studies

The final method/ology for researching higher education identified, and to be considered in this chapter, is rather more popular than conceptual analysis, phenomenography and critical perspectives, though less popular than the key approaches of interviews, questionnaire surveys and documentary analysis. Auto/biographical and observational studies are essentially qualitative in nature, though observation, in particular, may be pursued from a quantitative perspective.

Observational approaches tend to have the advantage, particularly if the researcher is a participant (and therefore fairly unobtrusive) in the activities being observed (Lee 2000; Rodriguez and Ryave 2002; Webb et al. 2000), of being relatively easy to undertake. The researcher can simply take notes, during or after the events being observed, and make up their research strategy as they go along. However, such an approach frequently raises both access and ethical issues (see the discussion in Chapter 14). Yet, observational approaches appear to be relatively under-used, at least in an explicit sense, for researching higher education (though virtually all pieces of higher education research rely, to some extent, on personal observational experience).

Auto/biographical research (Chamberlayne et al. 2000; Roberts 2002), which may also be termed life history research (Goodson and Sikes 2001; Hatch and Wisniewski 1995; Josselson and Lieblich 1995, 1999; Plummer 2001), is much more popular as an explicit approach to higher education research. It has been particularly applied to exploring aspects of academic work and, to a lesser extent, the student experience. While it lacks the respect of those engaged in more quantitative, positivistic research, because of its individuality and lack of generalizability, it has the potential to illuminate the detail of experience, conveying what it was like to be there:

> *Biographical research is primarily interested in the 'life'. Methodologically we usually see the research procedure as involving the collection of the 'oral' account by an audio-tape interview or, rather less so, the requested written autobiography – both according to some evaluative criteria. However, there is increasing recognition that 'lesser' forms of material that appear to be even further from traditional standards of 'evidence', such as letters, diaries, logs and memoirs, among others, are to be included.* (Roberts 2002: 173)

Biographical or life history research, like any other method/ology is not, of course, without its challenges:

> *It may be . . . that life history, even more so than ethnography, forces the researcher to acknowledge the personal and emotional aspects of their work for themselves, for their informants, and for those who read or otherwise access their research and accounts or productions.* (Goodson and Sikes 2001: 105)

This raises, for Goodson and Sikes, a series of inter-related dilemmas for life history researchers to face. These are to do with the decision to adopt a life history approach, with the relationship between individual lives and their social settings, with informant/researcher power relations, with informants' involvement, and with the presentation of the research. However, the same, or parallel, dilemmas can be found in the use of all method/ologies.

Two of the case studies considered in this book (Case Studies 9.1 and 10.1) have been categorized as adopting auto/biographical methods. In one of these, Grant and Knowles (2000, Case Study 10.1) discuss the experience of parallel academic development interventions, designed to help facilitate the growth of women academics as writers. They make use of their own experiences and the reported experiences of the participants in their initiatives. In the other biographical case study, Jenkins and Ward (2001, Case Study 9.1) provide an oral history of the development of a geography department over a 30-year period. Their account consists chiefly of edited selections from interviews with current and former staff of the department.

Conclusions

I will close this chapter with three conclusions.

First, as the discussion in this chapter should have made clear, the eight key methods or methodologies identified in this book are not precise and clear-cut. Rather, they are more or less closely related, and frequently overlap. Though other analysts would have identified a different – perhaps more complex, perhaps simpler – typology, the analysis presented here should have at least indicated many of the issues involved in thinking about and applying method/ologies.

Second, and in the light of the analysis presented in Chapters 2 and 3, it is evident that some of the method/ologies discussed are more widely used than are others. Documentary analysis, interviews, surveys and multivariate analyses form the mainstay or the heartland for research into higher education, as they do for research into most areas of the social world.

Third, and here I have to try to set aside personal biases and preferences, it could be argued that it is the least popular method/ologies – comparative analysis, conceptual analysis, phenomenography, critical and feminist perspectives, auto/biographical and observational studies – that offer the most challenge and, potentially, the greatest rewards.

13

Researching higher education at different levels

Introduction

Part II (Chapters 4 to 11) of this book focused on the key themes or issues in researching higher education. The previous chapter (Chapter 12) examined the main methods or methodologies employed in this research. In this chapter, we will consider in more detail the third categorization of research applied in this book, that of the level at which research is pitched.

If you have read this far, it will have become apparent that there are relationships between themes or issues, methods and methodologies, and levels of research. Thus, some of the chapters in Part II of the book – for example Chapter 7 – can be read as being organized in terms of level as much as method/ology. These relationships will be drawn out further in this chapter.

Interestingly, level of research has rarely been an explicit issue in the social research method/ologies literature – except in the case of international and comparative research – but it clearly has particular relevance for higher education research.

The seven levels identified in Chapter 1 were:

- individual;
- course;
- department;
- institution;
- national;
- system;
- international;

Research into higher education at each of these levels will now be considered in turn.

Individual

The analysis in Chapters 2 and 3 revealed that higher education research pitched at the level of the individual – whether academic, student or other – was the least common in the samples examined. Indeed, only eight of 406 journal articles, and one of 284 books, were categorized in this way (see Tables 2.5 and 3.6).

This may not seem that surprising, as research focused on the individual may appear, at least to some, to lack credibility. What, for example, does the experience of a single student or academic have to tell us that is of more general interest? Yet, on the contrary, such experiences can be illuminating, exemplifying and adding detailed credibility to the relatively dry findings of large-scale surveys. We may also think of individuals such as senior institutional managers or policy-makers, whose involvement and experience over a number of years could yield valuable insights into the reasoning behind particular decisions.

This explains the existence of the *Innovation in Higher Education* series (e.g. Allan 1996; Richards 1997; Tolmie 1998), produced by Lancaster University, each volume of which contains several personal experiential accounts. The three volumes referred to, for example, focus on initial experiences of teaching at university, life as a professor, and achieving a first class degree. It also explains the publication of books, such as those edited by Slowey (1995) and Weil (1994), examining experiences of change management in universities.

There is a close linkage here between research focused at the individual level and the use of auto/biographical or life history techniques (see Chapter 12). Other method/ologies may be applied as well, however, including interviews and documentary analysis.

One other point to stress about individual level research, as well as the next two categories – course and department – is that, because it is small-scale, it is very feasible or do-able. But, by allowing the researcher to focus on perhaps just one individual, it can also be very in-depth and revealing.

Two of the case studies reviewed in Part II of this book (Case Studies 5.2 and 5.3) were classified as focusing at the individual level. Both relate to aspects of course design, though individual level research may also focus on themes such as academic work and the student experience.

Johnson et al. (2000, Case Study 5.2), while their research forms part of a larger project based on interviews with current and former academics, base their article directly on the experiences of just three individuals as research students. Scott (2000, Case Study 5.3) goes further in demonstrating how a worthwhile, and publishable, study can be based on a very small sample, as her article involves the analysis of one essay produced by one student. Clearly, what counts is the more general relevance of the issues being raised

– of supervisory practices in the former case, and understandings of critical thinking in the latter.

Course

Research at the level of the course is a much more common, and probably more respectable, undertaking than research focused at the individual level. The course, after all, forms a natural unit, both for higher education delivery and for relatively small-scale research. Many higher education research projects and publications consist of evaluations of innovations introduced at the course level. Not surprisingly, these appear far more frequently in the form of journal articles than books. Thus, as Table 3.6 shows, only one of the books examined was focused at the course level, while 55 of the journal articles categorized in Table 2.5 were. Many more such studies will never see the light of day as books or journal articles, but may still be influential within the departments or institutions where they are carried out.

Course level research tends to make use of the more popular method/ologies for higher education research, notably interviews and questionnaires. Given the smaller-scale nature of such research, it is not surprising, however, that auto/biographical methods are also quite popular.

The latter are evident in the single case study discussed in this book that was characterized as being pitched at the course level. In this, Grant and Knowles (2000, Case Study 10.1) explore – using their own reflections and the reported experiences of other participants – two interventions (a one week writing retreat and a peer mentoring group) designed to help facilitate the development of women academics as writers.

Again, as with research pitched at the level of the individual, the important considerations, if course level research is to make it into publication, are the more general interest and potential applicability of the ideas being examined. Yet, as with individual level research, course level research is very do-able, whether or not the researcher(s) involved are lecturers on or participants in the course(s) concerned.

Department

Research focused at the departmental level appears more popular than that focused on the individual, but rather less common than research focused on the course. This may seem a little surprising, as the department – or school, faculty, unit, centre or whatever other designation is used – like the course, seems an obvious entity for research, while still remaining relatively small-scale. Yet only 18 articles and, less surprisingly, just one book, in the samples analysed in Chapters 2 and 3 were pitched at the departmental level.

The department is not as small-scale as the course, however, with some departments being large and complex entities. Studying one's own department might also be a risky venture, raising all sorts of issues to do with power, privilege and access. While, therefore, the department might be seen as the institutional representation of the discipline or profession, it is easy to understand why researchers interested in subject-based issues might turn their attention to other institutions or levels.

For those researchers who have examined departmental working, interviews stand out as by far the most common research approach (see Table 2.6). Indeed, this was the method/ology adopted in the single example of this level of research examined as a case study in Chapter 9. In that article, Jenkins and Ward (2001, Case Study 9.1) present an innovative account of the history of one department over a 30-year period, focusing in particular on the development of its teaching identity. The article makes extensive use of oral history interviews conducted with current and former staff.

Of course, not all departments will be as conducive to the production of research of this kind, but the potential for more studies of this nature is clear. They might focus on any or all aspects of departmental life, including research profile, management practice, relations with other departments and the institution, and roles within the wider discipline or profession. Without such research, a critically important aspect of academic life is being overlooked.

Institution

The remaining four levels – institution, national, system and international – are the most popular for contemporary published research on higher education. As Tables 2.5 and 3.6 show, institutional level research is much more commonly published in the form of journal articles than in book form. Either the book form lends itself more to the larger scope apparently offered by research projects focusing at national, system or international levels, or publishers are less willing to take the risk of publishing books examining the experience of single institutions.

Institutional level studies tend to focus on the themes of institutional management (not surprisingly) or course design, and, to a lesser extent, academic work and the student experience. Like research into higher education as a whole, they make extensive use of documentary, survey and interview methods, but also auto/biographical techniques (see Table 2.6).

As indicated in Chapter 1, an intermediary level for research between institutional and national – regional – might have been recognized, to include studies looking at the experience of a group of institutions in one part of a country. In practice, however, few of the studies reviewed were of this nature.

Five of the case studies examined in Part II of this book (Case Studies 4.1, 6.1, 6.2, 7.3 and 9.3) are pitched at the institutional level. Two of these (4.1 and 6.1) might have been categorized as regional if that category had also been included. Kember's (2000, Case Study 4.1) might also have been described as national, however, in that it focuses on research into students' learning approaches carried out within universities in Hong Kong. Ball et al.'s (2002, Case Study 6.1) research sampled students in a group of London schools and colleges about their choice of higher education institutions and courses for study.

Case Studies 6.2 (Norton et al. 2001) and 7.3 (Shevlin et al. 2000) both made use of questionnaire surveys – in the former case in four higher education institutions spread across the United Kingdom, in the latter in a single university – to examine different aspects of student behaviours and perceptions. The final case study, 9.3 (Stensaker and Norgard 2001), is an interesting example of documentary analysis, assessing the development of one Norwegian university against its original aims over a 30-year period.

National

Research into higher education pitched at the national level is clearly the most popular category, as evidenced by recent book and journal publications (Tables 2.5 and 3.6). In essence, this is because everybody with an interest in higher education research has an opinion about current national policy and the state of higher education in their country, and many of them choose to express these opinions in print. Hence, the most popular theme for national level research is system policy, though with course design coming a fairly close second. Research at this level, however, covers all of the main themes or issues identified in this book.

With a major focus on system policy, it is not surprising that the most common method/ology for national level studies is documentary analysis. In other words, critiques of national policy rest to a large extent on national policy documents and other researchers' commentaries on them. Survey techniques are also a popular strategy, enabling a more or less representative national sample to be questioned, as are interviews.

Five of the case studies considered in this book – Case Studies 5.1, 7.1, 10.2, 11.1 and 11.3 – are pitched at the national level, indicating the spread of such studies across the themes identified. Interestingly, the selection did not include any questionnaire-based studies and only one documentary analysis. Four of the case studies chosen made use of interviews for data collection, in two cases leading to a phenomenographic analysis and in the other two to conceptual analysis.

Thus, Brew (2001a, Case Study 11.1) interviewed Australian academics to provide data for a phenomenographic analysis of conceptions of research, while Robertson and Bond (2001, Case Study 11.3) used a similar approach to analyse New Zealand academics' views of the relation between the teaching and research roles. Barnett et al. (2001, Case Study 5.1) carried out a national interview-based study of approaches to the higher education curriculum, but in the article considered focus on conceptual models of the curriculum and curriculum change. Land (2001, Case Study 10.2) took a similar strategy in surveying academic developers, and discusses conceptualizations of the academic development role.

In the fifth case study considered that focused at this level of analysis, Bowden (2000, Case Study 7.1) offers a critical review of the widespread publication of university league tables in national newspapers.

System

As set out in Chapter 1, the distinction between national and system level is a fine, but arguably significant, one. System level discussions, while they are undoubtedly informed by their authors' experience of one or more actual national systems of higher education, are couched in terms of some idealized or hoped for higher education system. Though system level research into higher education is less common than national and international level studies, they are more popular than any other level, particularly when published in book form.

The most popular themes for system level research are course design, teaching and learning, system policy and academic work, but examples can be found in all of the themes and issues identified. While the most common method/ology employed in system level research is, as it is for higher education research as a whole, documentary analysis, a strong relation with conceptual analysis is also apparent. Indeed, the great majority of conceptual analyses of higher education are pitched at the system level (Tables 2.6 and 3.7). Since both method/ology and level are idealized, this is, of course, not surprising.

Five of the case studies discussed in Part II of this book – Case Studies 4.2, 4.3, 7.2, 8.1 and 11.2 – were pitched at the system level. Two were categorized as using documentary analysis, with another two based on conceptual analysis and one using multivariate analysis.

Deem (2001, Case Study 8.1) provides a critical review of recent writing on the perceived development of entrepreneurialism and academic capitalism within globalized higher education systems. Harvey (2002, Case Study 7.2), in another documentary analysis, reviews the alternative approaches which have been adopted to quality monitoring of higher education institutions and activities.

Delanty (2001, Case Study 11.2) provides an extended conceptual analysis of the changing nature of knowledge and the position of the contemporary university within society. Laurillard (2002, Case Study 4.2), in part of a book, offers a conceptual analysis of learning technologies, and their relationship to learning activities and student learning.

In the fifth case study, Prosser and Trigwell (1999, Case Study 4.3) make use of multivariate analysis to explore how the learning and teaching experience may be improved.

International

The final level of analysis to be considered, international, was the second most common after national level studies, with a particular emphasis on publication in book form (see Tables 2.5 and 3.6). This is somewhat surprising, given the particular demands posed by carrying out research into two or more national systems. It may be explained, at least in part, by the productivity of a limited number of international researchers, and perhaps also by the popularity of books pitched at the international level (in terms of their potential sales) with publishers.

The analysis presented in Chapters 2 and 3 demonstrated a strong concentration of international level studies on system policy issues. Clearly, comparing national policies in two or more countries, and the possible implications of policies elsewhere for practice here, are key areas for research. However, international level studies could be found in all of the key themes and issues identified.

While large numbers of international level studies are based primarily on documentary analysis, there is a very strong relationship apparent with comparative analysis. After all, all comparative analyses, in the way the term has been used in this book, are by definition international in scope (see Tables 2.6 and 3.7). However, while comparative analysis may be the methodology, the methods used to make the comparison include such standard techniques as interviews and questionnaires.

Five of the case studies analysed in this book – Case Studies 6.3, 8.2, 8.3, 9.2 and 10.3 – adopted an international perspective to higher education research. Three of these (6.3, 8.2 and 8.3) were classified as adopting a comparative research perspective, one (9.2) as using documentary analysis, and the other one (10.3) as being interview-based.

The scale of these international level studies varies significantly, indicating the possibilities for relatively small-scale research of this kind. Thus, Trowler and Knight's (2000, Case Study 10.3) study of the socialization of new academics is based primarily on interviews within one United Kingdom university, supplemented by a smaller number of interviews in Canada and the re-analysis of available American data. Ramsden's (1998, Case Study 9.2) examination of management and leadership in higher education is based chiefly on published Australian and British research. And McBurnie and Ziguras's (2001, Case Study 8.3) analysis of transnational higher education restricts itself to comparing the policies in three selected Southeast Asian countries: Hong Kong, Malaysia and Australia.

The other two case studies reviewed are larger-scale in their geographic coverage, though both limit themselves to recognized groupings of countries. Teichler (2000b, Case Study 6.3) provides a critical review of the usefulness of available European Union databases for making reliable comparisons of graduate employment trends. Jongbloed and Vossensteyn (2001, Case Study 8.2) also focus on the developed world, in their case 11 countries in the Organisation for Economic Co-operation and Development (OECD). Their interest is in assessing the use made in different countries of performance-based funding of teaching and research.

Conclusions

I would draw three main conclusions from the analysis presented in this chapter:

- First, in thinking about research in higher education, there is clearly value in considering and reflecting upon the level at which such research is focused. This approach might be useful in thinking about some, but by no means all, other areas of social research.
- Second, it is apparent that most higher education research, at least most that makes it into publication, is pitched at course, institutional, national, system or international levels. Individual and departmental level research, by comparison, appears relatively under-developed and, therefore, in need of encouragement.
- Third, there are clearly relationships between levels of analysis, method/ologies applied and themes or issues for research. These suggest both contemporary strengths within higher education research and, conversely, aspects which need strengthening.

14

The process of researching

Introduction

This final chapter seeks to offer some practical guidance to those who are engaged in researching higher education, or who would like to be. It starts from the following assumptions:

- higher education is a growing activity;
- more and more people not only have an interest in it, but wish to research it, typically on a relatively small scale;
- many of them have little or no previous experience, either in researching higher education or in social research more generally;
- there is little available published guidance available specifically focused on researching higher education;
- much of the social research literature focuses on the mechanics of methods and methodologies; and
- hence there is a need for some more process-related guidance to researching higher education.

The remainder of the chapter is organized in seven sections. The first four of these aim to address the key questions about researching higher education; namely, why do it?, what to do?, how to do it?, and where to do it? Two further sections discuss how to progress research once it is under way, and what to do once you have finished it. The final section then attempts to draw the discussion in the chapter, and the book as a whole, to a conclusion.

Why research higher education?

There are many 'good' reasons, and doubtless some not so 'good', for researching higher education. Here I will identify four key, related reasons.

First, higher education needs researching. Higher education is now a mass activity, engaged in at some time in their lives, and increasingly more than once, by either the majority or a large minority of the population. It has numerous links with industrial and community activities, and absorbs major funding streams from governments, companies and individuals. As such, it matters a great deal to each of us and to our society as a whole. It is, therefore, a very worthy topic for research, through which we may hope to both understand this activity better and, hopefully, improve it in some ways.

Second, for interest. If you work within higher education, or study within it, or are concerned about it, it is quite likely that you will be intrigued by certain aspects of it. You might be asking yourself, for example, 'why do we do things like this?', 'are there other, perhaps better, ways of doing this?' or 'how do they do this in other departments, institutions or countries?'. Like me, you probably have loads of other things to do and little spare time, but – as some of the examples and case studies discussed in this book illustrate – it is quite feasible to turn this interest into small-scale and useful research.

Third, for credit. One aspect of the massification of higher education, to which attention has been drawn in different parts of this book, is the rapid expansion of initial and continuing training for academics in their various roles. If you are a new or probationary academic, you are increasingly likely to be required to undertake a professional induction programme, covering higher education in general and the teaching role in particular, for credit. Part of this programme will probably involve you in undertaking and writing up a small project; in other words, in doing a small-scale piece of higher education research.

Fourth, and finally, for publication. The increased attention being given to academics' training is linked to a concern with the quality of what academics do, and with assessing their performance in their different roles. Thus, for example, in the United Kingdom, as part of the research assessment exercise, academics are judged on the quality of their research as evidenced in their publication output. Similarly, when the quality of their teaching is being assessed, evidence of engagement in pedagogical research will be viewed favourably. While it may make most sense to focus your research and publications on your discipline or subject area, you might, therefore, also consider researching and publishing on some topic in higher education. Or, having transformed your interest in higher education into a research project, you may simply want to publish your results and conclusions, or just get your ideas out there as part of the debate.

What to research?

In each of the chapters in Part II of this book (Chapters 4 to 11), the concluding section has suggested several possible directions for further research into the theme or issue under discussion. Reading those chapters should also give you other ideas for research – perhaps extending or duplicating in another setting an existing research project – as well as a good overview of what is being researched in any area that engages you. But you may have your own ideas as well. Or you may have no choice, with, perhaps, your department or employer making it a condition of support that you research a particular topic of interest to them.

Leaving aside the subject or topic within higher education which you wish, or are going, to research, there are, I would suggest, two key factors to bear in mind before and as you go ahead. First, the research project should engage your interest, and, second, it should be feasible.

You are likely to have work, study and/or family demands on your time (if you haven't, and are still interested in researching higher education, that's fine too), alongside or within which you will have to fit the demands of undertaking small-scale research. So your research into higher education will probably be pushed into the margins of your time. Of necessity, therefore, you may need to progress your research in spare moments of time. These may occur in the morning before you go to work, in your lunch break, in the evening when the kids have gone to bed, at the weekend or during your vacation. These are, therefore, times when you might much rather be having a lie in, enjoying your lunch, loafing in front of the television, going down to the pub or just chilling out. If your research does not interest you sufficiently, it is unlikely to motivate you to seize what little spare time you have to progress it, rather than pursuing an easier path.

Bear in mind, though, that your interest might not be mainly, or only, in the topic you are researching. It could be – instead or as well – that your engagement lies in the method/ology you have chosen to adopt, perhaps because you've never employed it before but would like to become familiar with it.

Feasibility – or do-ability – is also a key issue. It is a characteristic of researchers, particularly those new to the field they are studying, to bite off rather more than they can chew. This is understandable, and to some extent desirable, as it is useful to leave yourself some scope to adjust your project as it progresses. And, unless you are very fortunate (or perhaps that should be unfortunate), it is likely that you will have to modify, perhaps radically change, your project while it is underway. But it is also important to start off with a project that is about the right size – neither too big nor too small – and is within your capabilities, to achieve in the time and with the resources you have available. Otherwise, you are likely to soon become disenchanted and de-motivated.

How will you know whether what you are proposing is more or less feasible? If you are unsure, get advice – from colleagues or friends, or from higher education researchers you know of or can get access to. Or read some of the published research studies referred to in this book, or that you have come across in other ways, and judge what their authors have managed to achieve.

How to research?

There are two aspects involved in this question, the method/ological and the financial. I will consider each of these in turn.

Chapter 12, which discusses the key methods and methodologies used for researching higher education, should provide a useful guide to how you might approach your research project. It also offers numerous references to the social research methods literature, where you can access more detailed information and guidance about the use of particular method/ologies for collecting and analysing data.

That chapter can be supplemented by a selective reading, or re-reading, of relevant passages in Chapters 4 to 11. You might want, for example, to review the discussion of research into particular themes or issues within higher education, and/or to seek out and study some of the published articles or books referred to. Bear in mind, though, that a surprising number of articles, and even books, that are based on research do not contain an account – or an adequate account – of how that research was carried out; so look at a number and focus on the most useful.

If you are relatively new to research, and to social research in particular, you might find it specially useful to look at one of a growing number of 'how to' research guides (e.g. Blaxter et al. 2001; Denscombe 1998; Robson 1993).

Another key aspect of research, even relatively small-scale research, is the potential costs involved. If you work within higher education, it may be that the major cost involved is your own time, and that any other costs – e.g. photocopying, postage, printing, travel – can be borne by your employer. If these costs are likely to mount up, however, you may need to get specific project funding. How to meet these costs?

In the first instance, most institutions of higher education, and many departments within them, have limited budgets available to support relevant small-scale research projects. If your project is relatively modest, and the costs involved amount to no more than a few thousand pounds, or their equivalent, this is an obvious funding strategy. If the research being undertaken is likely to benefit your department and/or institution in some way, and especially if it is being undertaken as part of a training programme required by your institution, you are likely to have a strong case for receiving financial support.

If your institution is unable or unwilling to support your project financially, or it cannot meet the costs involved, and you still wish to go ahead, you will, of course, need to look outside. There are at least four common sources for funding higher education research that you might explore:

- Relevant government departments, most obviously those dealing with education and training, typically fund a range of research projects. The topics and approach of many of these may, of course, be determined by the department concerned itself: that is, they will tend to be closely related to immediate policy concerns. A tendering process may be involved, with close oversight of the successful bidder during the research process itself. But your proposed project may fit in, or you may be able to interest those concerned with what you plan to do.
- National research councils, funded by government – such as the Economic and Social Research Council in the United Kingdom, or the Australian Research Council in Australia – also fund research focusing on higher education. Increasingly, this tends to be targeted on identified themes, but there is usually also scope for open project submissions.
- Some charitable organizations and private research foundations – such as the Leverhulme Trust and the Nuffield Foundation in the United Kingdom – also fund higher education research. In these cases, it is important, however, to check what the funder's priorities are at the time, as these may change. There are hundreds of smaller and local charities that might also help: ask around in your institution.
- Finally, private companies – particularly those that already have a connection with your institution, department or course, or have an interest in what you plan to research – may also be a possible source of funding.

Bear in mind, though, that the more funding you need, the longer the planning timescales involved and the lower your chances of success. So spend time carefully considering the possibilities before you decide to go ahead.

Where to research?

You may, of course, have little choice over where to research, if your employer, funder or sponsor has already predetermined this. But if you do have some choice, and you are working or studying in higher education, or have some connection with it, then you face a key decision. Should you research something to do with your own course, department, university or college, or should you look more widely?

There are advantages and disadvantages either way. If you do choose to research your own course, department or institution, access to people and documents should be relatively easy, and you start with the advantage of knowing a lot about the context. You may also be able to research something you are really committed to, and which may produce practical benefits for you and your colleagues.

Set against this, however, are issues to do with power, control and distance. While you may know a lot about the context for your study, you could be too close and too committed. You may think that you know the 'answer' already, and be determined to 'prove' it. If you are researching your own students, there are power relationships involved, and it may be that they tend to give you the responses they think you want or that will please you. If you are researching your colleagues or superiors, there are, again, power relationships involved, and you may feel unable to pursue particular issues or to say certain things (or you may be prevented from doing so).

Researching in another institution or setting, by contrast, has the advantage of giving you some distance. It will probably matter less if things don't go according to plan, or if you can't deliver what you set out to do. You can, literally, go away from the research setting at the end of the day, or when your project is finished. At the same time, researching away from your base can be refreshing, perhaps giving you insights into how things might be done somewhat differently. And you may make new, and helpful, contacts for the future.

The disadvantages of being an 'external' researcher are that you will be likely to know much less about the context for what you are exploring, and that you may find getting and maintaining access more difficult. To the staff and/or students of another college or university you may be little more than an added nuisance, someone to whom they feel that they owe nothing. Indeed, they may be concerned about co-operating with your research in case what they say is reported, or they are identifiable in your report or article. Here it helps if you can explain simply why what you are doing is relevant and should be of interest to them. Even if the head of department, course leader, manager or whoever agrees to your research, and grants you access, you will need to re-negotiate this repeatedly with everyone you are dealing with. You could get part way into your project and then find the door firmly shut in your face.

So if you do have the choice about whether to do some 'insider' research or not, you would be wise to spend a little time weighing up the pros and cons, and the options that you have. One other key issue implied by the discussion so far, and which is certainly worthy of consideration in deciding where (and what) to research, is that of ethics.

All research raises ethical issues, though in some cases these may be relatively minor. Library-based research, or research using pre-existing data sets, for example, is unlikely to raise serious questions of ethics. But if you are collecting your own empirical data, through a questionnaire survey, a series of interviews or participant observation, you should think through your ethical position and responsibilities. What effects might your research have on those you are researching? Will you be raising expectations you cannot satisfy? Is it possible that your enquiries will disturb some of those you are researching?

If you are working or studying in a department that deals with individuals' bodily or mental well being, such as psychology, nursing or social work, any research you propose will have to be approved in advance by an ethics committee. Sometimes these exist in other departments as well, and many professional bodies and disciplinary associations have established, and published, codes of ethics. If these apply to you, you will need to consult them and abide by their precepts. If such arrangements are not in place, you may find it useful to refer to one or more of the available texts that specifically deal with the ethical issues raised by social research (e.g. Hack 1997; Homan 1991; Lee 1993; Renzetti and Lee 1993; Rosnow and Rosenthal 1997; Walford 1994).

Progressing research

Having decided, more or less, why, what, how and where, it is time to get your research project underway. If you have experience of planning and delivering on complex activities – e.g. running a course or a family home – there may be little you need to know about progressing a small-scale research project. But if you would appreciate some guidance, let me suggest two, rather opposing, ways of thinking about progressing research.

First, and this may be most useful if you have a definite deadline for the completion of your work – and essential if you are seeking funding – there is the planned approach. Draw up a project outline and a schedule, breaking down what you have to do activity by activity, and assigning each of these to a particular time period in what seems the logical or appropriate order. Pilot your research plans – for example carry out and analyse a single interview, or send out a few draft questionnaires and process the completed ones – to check on how well they work, and how long the different stages in the process take. Leave yourself some spare capacity if you can, and don't forget to leave a substantial portion of time towards the end for thinking about what you have found and writing it up. Then follow your outline and schedule, adjusting it as and when necessary, when things don't quite work out as anticipated (they rarely do, so don't worry).

Second, an alternative strategy, perhaps most suited to those less burdened by commitments or pressured by the need to produce results. Just start anywhere, with something that engages you – an article, a quotation, a method, an interviewee – and follow your interests, changing directions as suits you. Research doesn't have to be a process that starts with an outline, moves through a literature review, a consideration of method/ologies, the collection and analysis of data, to the production of a report. It can be more creative and disorganized than that, and its only or chief purpose may be to stimulate your thinking and keep it fresh. But, be warned, if you take this strategy you may never know when you've finished.

Publishing and disseminating research

Research can be an end in itself, or you may feel that what you are discovering is only of interest to you. Most higher education researchers, however, probably feel some need to share their experiences and findings, and would benefit from so doing. While you are unlikely to have come up with any truly radical new thinking – which of us can really claim ever to have done that? – that does not mean that your conclusions will not be of interest to others.

You may choose to limit the dissemination of your findings to those for whom they have, or appear to have, the most immediate relevance. That may be those on your course, in your department or institution, within your professional body or disciplinary association. You might issue an internal report or deliver a seminar. Or you could choose to go beyond this, and engage with other higher education researchers through their journals and/or at their conferences.

Table 14.1 gives further details on the 17 specialist academic journals that focus on higher education, the contents of which were analysed in Chapter 2. Table 14.2 lists details on four major associations devoted to studying higher education, each of which organizes regular conferences for the presentation and discussion of research findings.

In using these tables, please bear in mind a number of points:

- Only the specialist, English language, higher education journals and associations operating outside of North America have been listed. There are many other journals – some academic, some professional – that accept articles on higher education. These tend to focus either on education as a whole or on other disciplines. In the United Kingdom, for example, a whole series of disciplinary based journals focusing on higher education are in the process of development. Much the same applies to associations and conferences. So there are many more opportunities than are listed here.

Table 14.1 Academic Journals Focusing on Higher Education

You are advised to check on these details before considering or sending an article to one of these journals. Editorial details change from time to time, and online submission is becoming more common.

Active Learning in Higher Education

Publisher	Paul Chapman
Website	www.sagepub.co.uk
Number of Issues per Year	3
Editor	Lynne Baldwin
Address for Correspondence	Institute for Learning and Teaching
	Genesis 3
	Innovation Way
	York Science Park
	Heslington
	York YO10 5DQ
	United Kingdom

Assessment and Evaluation in Higher Education

Publisher	Taylor and Francis
Website	www.tandf.co.uk
Number of Issues per Year	6
Editor	William Scott
Address for Correspondence	Department of Education
	University of Bath
	Bath BA2 7AY
	United Kingdom

European Journal of Education

Publisher	Blackwells
Website	www.blackwellpublishing.com
Number of Issues per Year	4
Editors	Jean-Pierre Jallade and Jose-Gines Mora
Address for Correspondence	European Institute of Education and Social Policy
	Universite de Paris IX-Dauphine
	1 Place du Marechal de Lattre de Tassigny
	F-75116 Paris
	France

Higher Education

Publisher	Kluwer
Website	www.wkap.nl
Number of Issues per Year	8

| Editors | Grant Harman, Gary Rhoades, Ulrich Teichler and Dai Hounsell |
| Address for Correspondence | Kluwer Academic Publishers PO Box 17 3300 AA Dordrecht The Netherlands |

Higher Education in Europe

Publisher	Taylor and Francis
Website	www.tandf.co.uk
Number of Issues per Year	4
Editor	Leland Barrows
Address for Correspondence	European Centre for Higher Education 39 Stirbel Voda Street R-70732 Bucharest Romania

Higher Education Management

Publisher	Organisation for Economic Co-operation and Development
Website	www.sourceoecd.org
Number of Issues per Year	4
Editor	Michael Shattock
Address for Correspondence	OECD/IMHE 2 rue Andre-Pascal 75775 Paris Cedex 16 France

Higher Education Policy

Publisher	Palgrave
Website	www.palgrave-journals.com
Number of Issues per Year	4
Editor	Guy Neave
Address for Correspondence	International Association of Universities Unesco House 1 rue Miollis 75732 Paris Cedex 15 France

Higher Education Quarterly

Publisher	Blackwells
Website	www.blackwellpublishing.com
Number of Issues per Year	4
Editor	Oliver Fulton

Address for Correspondence

Department of Educational Research
Cartmel College
Lancaster University
Lancaster LA1 4YL
United Kingdom

Higher Education Research and Development

Publisher	Taylor and Francis
Website	www.tandf.co.uk
Number of Issues per Year	3
Editors	Margot Pearson, Linda Hort
Address for Correspondence	The HERDSA Office
	PO Box 516
	Jamison Centre
	ACT 2614
	Australia

Higher Education Review

Publisher	Tyrell Burgess
Website	
Number of Issues per Year	3
Editor	John Pratt
Address for Correspondence	3 Albert Mansions
	Crouch Hill
	London N8 9RE
	United Kingdom

International Journal for Academic Development

Publisher	Taylor and Francis
Website	www.tandf.co.uk
Number of Issues per Year	2
Editors	David Baume, Christopher Knapper
	and Angela Brew
Address for Correspondence	by email (details on website)

Journal of Geography in Higher Education

Publisher	Taylor and Francis
Website	www.tandf.co.uk
Number of Issues per Year	3
Editors	Martin Haigh and David Higgitt
Address for Correspondence	Hugh Matthews
	Division of Geographical Studies
	Park Campus
	University College Northampton
	Northampton NN2 7AL
	United Kingdom

Journal of Higher Education Policy and Management

Publisher	Taylor and Francis
Website	www.tandf.co.uk
Number of Issues per Year	2
Editors	Ian Dobson and Angel Calderon
Address for Correspondence	PO Box 8001
	Monash University
	Victoria 3168
	Australia

Quality in Higher Education

Publisher	Taylor and Francis
Website	www.tandf.co.uk
Number of Issues per Year	3
Editor	Lee Harvey
Address for Correspondence	Surrey Building
	Sheffield Hallam University
	City Campus
	Howard Street
	Sheffield S1 1WB
	United Kingdom

Studies in Higher Education

Publisher	Taylor and Francis
Website	www.tandf.co.uk
Number of Issues per Year	4
Editor	Malcolm Tight
Address for Correspondence	Institute of Education
	University of Warwick
	Coventry CV4 7AL
	United Kingdom

Teaching in Higher Education

Publisher	Taylor and Francis
Website	www.tandf.co.uk
Number of Issues per Year	4
Editor	Jon Nixon
Address for Correspondence	School of Education
	University of Sheffield
	388 Glossop Road
	Sheffield S10 2JA
	United Kingdom

Tertiary Education and Management

Publisher	Kluwer
Website	
Number of Issues per Year	4
Editor	Roddy Begg
Address for Correspondence	Director of Alumni Relations
	University of Aberdeen
	Regent Walk
	Aberdeen AB24 3FX
	United Kingdom

Table 14.2 Higher Education Associations

Consortium of Higher Education Researchers

Website	www.cher@hochschulforschung.uni-kassel.de
Address	CHER
	Wissenschaftliches Zentrum fur Berufs- und
	Hochschulforschung
	Universitat Gesamthochschule Kassel
	D-34109 Kassel
	Germany

European Association for Institutional Research

Website	www.eair.uva.nl
Address	EAIR
	Herengracht 487
	1017 BT Amsterdam
	The Netherlands

Higher Education Research and Development Society of Australia

Website	www.herdsa.org.au
Address	The HERDSA Office
	PO Box 516
	Jamison Centre
	ACT 2614
	Australia

Society for Research into Higher Education

Website	www.srhe.ac.uk
Address	76 Portland Place
	London W1B 1NT
	United Kingdom

- The details given were correct, or as correct as I could make them, at the time I completed this book (Easter 2003). They will change over time, so please check on the current situation before you get in touch.
- If you intend to send off an article, or a conference paper proposal, to one of these journals or associations, it makes sense to do some home-work in advance. As the analysis in Chapter 2 suggests, different journals have different emphases, so it helps to pick the most appropriate one for your work. Similarly, conferences usually have themes, though they also often have open sessions where any recent research can be presented.
- It also has to be said that the popularity of journals and conferences varies – at any one time and over time – so you will find it easier to get published or presented in less demanding settings. You could, for example, ask the editor of a journal you are interested in how long it takes to review an article, how long they might have to wait until publica-tion if their article was accepted, and what proportion of the articles submitted are accepted.
- Don't interpret rejection as the end of the world, but make use of any advice you are given to do further work on your article or presentation, or to look elsewhere for publication.

Happy disseminating! You may be surprised by what you learn.

Conclusions

I'd like to close this chapter, and the book as a whole, by offering one final piece of advice and a little personal reflection.

First, the last piece of advice. One of the things I hope I have achieved in putting together this book is to demonstrate that small-scale research into higher education is not only feasible, but also potentially very rewarding, both to the researcher and to those who read or hear of their work. If you're doubtful, look again at some of the examples that have been used in the book. So don't be put off by thinking that you have nothing to contribute.

Second, the reflection. Writing this book has been both enjoyable and extremely demanding. In fact, I think I would have to say that it has been the most demanding project I have ever undertaken. There was a long period when I just couldn't seem to make sense of what I was trying to do. The structure I've ended up with makes a lot of sense to me now, and I have a good deal of commitment to it, so I hope that it is useful to you as well. But I wouldn't want to claim that it was perfect.

References

Acker, S., Black, E. and Hill, T. (1994) Research Students and their Supervisors in Education and Psychology, in R. Burgess (ed.) *Postgraduate Education and Training in the Social Sciences: processes and products.* London: Jessica Kingsley.

Ader, H. and Mellenbergh, G. (eds) (1999) *Research Methodology in the Life, Behavioural and Social Sciences.* London: Sage.

Adler, N., Hellstrom, T., Jacob, M. and Norrgren, F. (2000) A Model for the Institutionalisation of University-Industry Partnerships: the FENIX research programme, in M. Jacob and T. Hellstrom (eds) *The Future of Knowledge Production in the Academy.* Buckingham: Open University Press.

Ahola, S. and Kokko, A. (2001) Finding the Best Possible Students: student selection and its problems in the field of business, *Journal of Higher Education Policy and Management,* 23(2): 191–203.

Albrighton, F. and Thomas, J. (eds) (2001) *Managing External Relations.* Buckingham: Open University Press.

Aldrich, R. (2002) *The Institute of Education 1902–2002: a centenary history.* London: Institute of Education.

Allan, D. (ed.) (1996) *In At The Deep End: first experiences of university teaching.* Lancaster: Unit for Innovation in Higher Education.

Allen, R. and Layer, G. (1995) *Credit-based Systems as Vehicles for Change in Universities.* London: Kogan Page.

Altbach, P. (ed.) (1996) *The International Academic Profession: portraits of fourteen countries.* Princeton, NJ: Carnegie Foundation for the Advancement of Learning.

Altbach, P. (1997) Research on Higher Education: global perspectives, in J. Sadlak and P. Altbach (eds) *Higher Education Research at the Turn of the New Century: structures, issues and trends.* New York: Garland.

Altbach, P. and Engberg, D. (2001) *Higher Education: a worldwide inventory of centers and programs.* Phoenix: Oryx Press.

Altbach, P. and Lewis, L. (1996) The Academic Profession in International Perspective, in P. Altbach (ed.) *The International Academic Profession: portraits of fourteen countries.* Princeton, NJ: Carnegie Foundation for the Advancement of Learning.

Alvesson, M. and Skoldberg, K. (2000) *Reflexive Methodology: new vistas for qualitative research*. London: Sage.

Archer, L., Hutchings, M. and Ross, A. (eds) (2003) *Higher Education and Social Class*. London: RoutledgeFalmer.

Arksey, H. and Knight, P. (1999) *Interviewing for Social Scientists*. London: Sage.

Arksey, H., Marchant, I. and Simmill, C. (1994) *Juggling for a Degree: mature students' experience of university life*. Lancaster: Lancaster University Unit for Innovation in Higher Education.

Armitage, A., Bryant, R., Dunnill, R., Hammersley, M., Hayes, D., Hudson, A. and Lawes, S. (1999) *Teaching and Learning in Post-compulsory Education*. Buckingham: Open University Press.

Ashcroft, K. (1996) Series Introduction, in K. Ashcroft and D. Palacio *Researching into Assessment and Evaluation in Colleges and Universities*. London: Kogan Page.

Ashcroft, K. and Foreman-Peck, L. (1995) *The Lecturer's Guide to Quality and Standards in Colleges and Universities*. London: Falmer Press.

Ashworth, A. and Harvey, R. (1994) *Assessing Quality in Further and Higher Education*. London: Jessica Kingsley.

Ashworth, J. (1998) A Waste of Resources? Social rates of return to higher education in the 1990s, *Education Economics*, 6(1): 27–44.

Ashworth, P. (1999) 'Bracketing' in Phenomenology: renouncing assumptions in hearing about student cheating, *International Journal of Qualitative Studies in Education*, 12: 707–22.

Ashworth, P., Bannister, P. and Thorne, P. (1997) Guilty in Whose Eyes? University students' perceptions of cheating and plagiarism in academic work and assessment, *Studies in Higher Education*, 22(2): 187–203.

Ashworth, P. and Lucas, U. (2000) Achieving Empathy and Engagement: a practical approach to the design, conduct and reporting of phenomenographic research, *Studies in Higher Education*, 25(3): 295–308.

Askling, B. (2001) Higher Education and Academic Staff in a period of Policy and System Change, *Higher Education*, 41: 157–81.

Askling, B., Henkel, M. and Kehm, B. (2001) Concepts of Knowledge and their Organisation in Universities, *European Journal of Education*, 36(3): 341–50.

Asmar, C. (1999) Is there a Gendered Agenda in Academia? The research experience of female and male PhD graduates in Australian universities, *Higher Education*, 38: 255–73.

Assiter, A. (1995) *Transferable Skills in Higher Education*. London: Kogan Page.

Assiter, A. and Shaw, E. (eds) (1993) *Using Records of Achievement in Higher Education*. London: Kogan Page.

Atweh, B., Kemmis, S. and Weeks, P. (1998) *Action Research in Practice: partnerships for social justice in education*. London: Sage.

Aylett, R. and Gregory, K. (eds) (1996) *Evaluating Teacher Quality in Higher Education*. London: Falmer.

Bagilhole, B. (2002) Challenging Equal Opportunities: changing and adapting male hegemony in academia, *British Journal of Sociology of Education*, 23(1): 19–33.

Ball, S., Davies, J., David, M. and Reay, D. (2002) 'Classification' and 'Judgement': social class and the 'cognitive structures' of choice in higher education, *British Journal of Sociology of Education*, 23(1): 51–72.

Ball, S., Maguire, M. and Macrae, S. (2000) *Choice, Pathways and Transitions Post-16: new youth, new economies in the global city*. London: RoutledgeFalmer.

Banks, M., Bates, I., Breakwell, G., Bynner, J., Euler, N., Jamieson, L. and Roberts, K. (1992) *Careers and Identities*. Buckingham: Open University Press.

Bargh, C., Bocock, J., Scott, P. and Smith, D. (2000) *University Leadership: the role of the chief executive*. Buckingham: Open University Press.

Bargh, C., Scott, P. and Smith, D. (1996) *Governing Universities: changing the culture?* Buckingham: Open University Press.

Barnes-Powell, T. and Letherby, G. (1998) 'All in a Day's Work': gendered care work in higher education, in D. Malina and S. Maslin-Prothero (eds) *Surviving the Academy: feminist perspectives*. London: Falmer Press.

Barnett, R. (1990) *The Idea of Higher Education*. Buckingham: Open University Press.

Barnett, R. (1992) *Improving Higher Education: total quality care*. Buckingham: Open University Press.

Barnett, R. (1994) *The Limits of Competence: knowledge, higher education and society*. Buckingham: Open University Press.

Barnett, R. (1997) *Higher Education: a critical business*. Buckingham: Open University Press.

Barnett, R. (2000) *Realizing the University in an Age of Supercomplexity*. Buckingham: Open University Press.

Barnett, R. (2003) *Beyond All Reason: living with ideology in the university*. Buckingham: Open University Press.

Barnett, R. and Griffin, A. (eds) (1997) *The End of Knowledge in Higher Education*. London: Cassell.

Barnett, R., Parry, G. and Coate, K. (2001) Conceptualising Curriculum Change, *Teaching in Higher Education*, 6(4): 435–49.

Bartlett, A. and Mercer, G. (2000) Reconceptualising Discourses of Power in Postgraduate Pedagogies, *Teaching in Higher Education*, 5(2): 195–204.

Bassey, M. (1999) *Case Study Research in Educational Settings*. Buckingham: Open University Press.

Bauer, M. and Gaskell, G. (eds) (2000) *Qualitative Researching with Text, Image and Sound*. London: Sage.

Baxter, A. and Britton, C. (2001) Risk, Identity and Change: becoming a mature student, *International Studies in Sociology of Education*, 11(1): 87–102.

Baxter Magolda, M. (1992) *Knowing and Reasoning in College: gender-related patterns in students' intellectual development*. San Francisco: Jossey-Bass.

Becher, T. (1989) *Academic Tribes and Territories: intellectual enquiry and the cultures of disciplines*. Buckingham: Open University Press.

Becher, T. (1999) *Professional Practices: commitment and capability in a changing environment*. New Brunswick, NJ: Transaction.

Becher, T., Henkel, M. and Kogan, M. (1994) *Graduate Education in Britain*. London: Jessica Kingsley.

Becher, T. and Kogan, M. (1992) *Process and Structure in Higher Education*, 2nd edn. London: Routledge.

Becher, T. and Trowler, P. (2001) *Academic Tribes and Territories: intellectual enquiry and the culture of disciplines*, 2nd edn. Buckingham: Open University Press.

Bechhofer, F. and Paterson, L. (2000) *Principles of Research Design in the Social Sciences*. London: Routledge.

Bell, R. and Tight, M. (1993) *Open Universities: a British tradition?* Buckingham: Open University Press.

Bennett, N., Dunne, E. and Carre, C. (2000) *Skills Development in Higher Education and Employment*. Buckingham: Open University Press.

Berry, C. (1999) University League Tables: artefacts and inconsistencies in individual rankings, *Higher Education Review*, 21(2): 3–10.

Bessant, J. (2002) Dawkins' Higher Education Reforms and how Metaphors work in Policy Making, *Journal of Higher Education Policy and Management*, 24(1): 87–99.

Betts, M. and Smith, R. (1998) *Developing the Credit-based Modular Curriculum in Higher Education: challenge, choice and change*. London: Falmer Press.

Biggs, J. (1999) *Teaching for Quality Learning at University: what the student does*. Buckingham: Open University Press.

Biggs, J. (2003) *Teaching for Quality Learning at University: what the student does*, 2nd edn. Buckingham: Open University Press.

Bird, J. (1996) *Black Students and Higher Education: rhetorics and realities*. Buckingham: Open University Press.

Black, T. (1999) *Doing Quantitative Research in the Social Sciences: an integrated approach to research design, measurement and statistics*. London: Sage.

Blair, D. and Hitchens, D. (1998) *Campus Companies – UK and Ireland*. Aldershot: Ashgate.

Blaxter, L., Hughes, C. and Tight, M. (1998a) Telling it how it is: accounts of academic life, *Higher Education Quarterly*, 52(3): 300–15.

Blaxter, L., Hughes, C. and Tight, M. (1998b) Writing on Academic Careers, *Studies in Higher Education*, 23(3): 281–95.

Blaxter, L., Hughes, C. and Tight, M. (1998c) *The Academic Career Handbook*. Buckingham: Open University Press.

Blaxter, L., Hughes, C. and Tight, M. (2001) *How to Research*, 2nd edn. Buckingham: Open University Press.

Blumenthal, P. (ed.) (1995) *Academic Mobility in a Changing World*. London: Jessica Kingsley.

Bocock, J. and Watson, D. (eds) (1994) *Managing the University Curriculum: making common cause*. Buckingham: Open University Press.

Bolton, A. (2000) *Managing the Academic Unit*. Buckingham: Open University Press.

Boud, D., Cohen, R. and Walker, D. (eds) (1993) *Using Experience for Learning*. Buckingham: Open University Press.

Boud, D. and Feletti, G. (eds) (1997) *The Challenge of Problem-based Learning*, 2nd edn. London: Kogan Page.

Boud, D. and Miller, N. (eds) (1996) *Working with Experience: animating learning*. London: Routledge.

Boud, D. and Solomon, N. (eds) (2001) *Work-based Learning: a new higher education?* Buckingham: Open University Press.

Boud, D. and Walker, D. (1998) Promoting Reflection in Professional Courses: the challenge of context, *Studies in Higher Education*, 23(2): 191–206.

Bourner, T., Bowden, R. and Laing, S. (2001) Professional Doctorates in England, *Studies in Higher Education*, 26(1): 65–83.

Bourner, T., Katz, T. and Watson, D. (eds) (2000) *New Directions in Professional Higher Education*. Buckingham: Open University Press.

Bowden, R. (2000) Fantasy Higher Education: university and college league tables, *Quality in Higher Education*, 6(1): 41–60.

Brannen, J. (1992) *Mixing Methods: qualitative and quantitative research*. Aldershot: Avebury.

Braun, D. and Merrien, F-X. (eds) (1999) *Towards a New Model of Governance for Universities? A comparative view*. London: Jessica Kingsley.

Braxton, J. and Hargens, L. (1996) Variations Among Academic Disciplines: analytical frameworks and research, in J. Smart (ed.) *Higher Education: handbook of theory and research*, Vol. XI. New York: Agathon.

Brennan, J., Fedrowitz, J., Huber, M. and Shah, T. (eds) (1999) *What Kind of University? International perspectives on knowledge, participation and governance*. Buckingham: Open University Press.

Brennan, J., Lyon, E., McGeevor, P. and Murray, K. (1993) *Students, Courses and Jobs*. London: Jessica Kingsley.

Brennan, J., Kogan, M. and Teichler, U. (1995) *Higher Education and Work*. London: Jessica Kingsley.

Brennan, J. and Shah, T. (2000) Quality Assessment and Institutional Change: experiences from 14 countries, *Higher Education*, 40: 331–49.

Brennan, J., de Vries, P. and Williams, R. (1997) *Standards and Quality in Higher Education*. London: Jessica Kingsley.

Brew, A. (ed.) (1995) *Directions in Staff Development*. Buckingham: Open University Press.

Brew, A. (2001a) Conceptions of Research: a phenomenographic study, *Studies in Higher Education*, 26(3): 271–85.

Brew, A. (2001b) *The Nature of Research: inquiry in academic contexts*. London: RoutledgeFalmer.

Brew, A. (2003) The Future of Research and Scholarship in Academic Development, in H. Eggins and R. Macdonald (eds) *The Scholarship of Academic Development*. Buckingham: Open University Press.

Brewer, J. (2000) *Ethnography*. Buckingham: Open University Press.

Bridges, P., Cooper, A., Evanson, P., et al. (2002) Coursework Marks High, Examination Marks Low: discuss. *Assessment and Evaluation in Higher Education*, 27(1): 35–48.

Brock, M. and Curthoys, M. (eds) (2000) *The History of the University of Oxford: Volume VII, Nineteenth-Century Oxford: Part 2*. Oxford: Oxford University Press.

Brockbank, A. and McGill, I. (1998) *Facilitating Reflective Learning in Higher Education*. Buckingham: Open University Press.

Brookfield, S. and Preskill, S. (1999) *Discussion as a Way of Teaching: tools and techniques for university teachers*. Buckingham: Open University Press.

Brooks, A. (1997) *Academic Women*. Buckingham: Open University Press.

Brooks, A. and Mackinnon, A. (eds) (2001) *Gender and the Restructured University*. Buckingham: Open University Press.

Brown, A. and Dowling, P. (1997) *Doing Research/Reading Research: a mode of interrogation for education*. London: Routledge.

Brown, G. and Atkins, M. (2002) *Effective Teaching in Higher Education*. London: Routledge.

Brown, G., Bull, J. and Pendlebury, M. (1997) *Assessing Student Learning in Higher Education*. London: Routledge.

Brown, S. and Glasner, A. (eds) (1999) *Assessment Matters in Higher Education: choosing and using diverse approaches.* Buckingham: Open University Press.

Brown, S. and Knight, P. (1994) *Assessing Learners in Higher Education.* London: Kogan Page.

Bruce, C. (1994) Research Students' Early Experiences of the Dissertation Literature Review, *Studies in Higher Education,* 19(2): 217–29.

Bryman, A. and Cramer, D. (2000) *Quantitative Data Analysis with SPSS Release 10 for Windows,* 2nd edn. London: Routledge.

Bullard, J. and McLean, M. (2000) Jumping Through Hoops? Philosophy and practice expressed in geographers' teaching portfolios, *Journal of Geography in Higher Education,* 24(1): 37–52.

Burgess, R. (ed.) (1994) *Postgraduate Education and Training in the Social Sciences: processes and products.* London: Jessica Kingsley.

Burgess, R. (ed.) (1997) *Beyond the First Degree: graduate education, lifelong learning and careers.* Buckingham: Open University Press.

Burgess, R., Pole, C. and Hockey, J. (1994) Strategies for Managing and Supervising the Social Science PhD, in R. Burgess (ed.) *Postgraduate Education and Training in the Social Sciences: processes and products.* London: Jessica Kingsley.

Burgess, R. et al. (1998) Postgraduate Education in Europe, *European Journal of Education,* 33(2) (special issue).

Burgess, T., Locke, M., Pratt, J. and Richards, N. (1995) *Degrees East: the making of the University of East London: 1892–1992.* London: Athlone Press.

Burke, P. (2002) *Accessing Education: effectively widening participation.* Stoke-on-Trent: Trentham Books.

Burn, B., Cerych, L. and Smith, A. (eds) (1990) *Study Abroad Programmes.* London: Jessica Kingsley.

Burns, R. (2000) *Introduction to Research Methods,* 4th edn. London: Sage.

Butler, A. and Landells, M. (1995) Taking Offence: research as resistance to sexual harassment in academia, in L. Morley and V. Walsh (eds) *Feminist Academics: creative agents for change.* London: Taylor and Francis.

Callender, C. (2003) Student Financial Support in Higher Education: access and exclusion, in M. Tight (ed.) *Access and Exclusion.* Oxford: Elsevier Science.

Campbell, A. (2000) Cultural Diversity: practising what we preach in higher education, *Teaching in Higher Education,* 5(3): 373–84.

Campbell, J., Smith, D. and Brooker, R. (1998) From Conception to Performance: how undergraduate students conceptualise and construct essays, *Higher Education,* 36: 449–69.

Cannon, R. and Newble, D. (2000) *A Handbook for Teachers in Universities and Colleges: a guide to improving teaching methods,* 4th edn. London: Kogan Page.

Cantwell, R., Archer, J. and Bourke, S. (2001) A Comparison of the Academic Experiences and Achievement of University Students entering by Traditional and Non-traditional Means, *Assessment and Evaluation in Higher Education,* 26(3): 221–34.

Carson, L. (2001) Gender Relations in Higher Education: exploring lecturers' perceptions of student evaluations of teaching, *Research Papers in Education,* 16(4): 337–58.

Cave, M., Hanney, S., Henkel, M. and Kogan, M. (1997) *The Use of Performance Indicators in Higher Education: the challenge of the quality movement,* 3rd edn. London: Jessica Kingsley.

Chalmers, D. and Fuller, R. (1996) *Teaching for Learning at University*. London: Kogan Page.

Chamberlayne, P., Bornat, J. and Wengraf, T. (2000) *The Turn to Biographical Methods in Social Science*. London: Routledge.

Chatterton, P. and Goddard, J. (2000) The Response of Higher Education Institutions to Regional Needs, *European Journal of Education*, 35(4): 475–96.

Christie, H., Munro, M. and Rettig, H. (2001) Making Ends Meet: student incomes and debt, *Studies in Higher Education*, 26(3): 363–83.

Clark, B. (ed.) (1984) *Perspectives on Higher Education: eight disciplinary and comparative views*. Berkeley: University of California Press.

Clark, B. (1998) *Creating Entrepreneurial Universities: organisational pathways of transformation*. New York: Elsevier.

Coate, K., Barnett, R. and Williams, G. (2001) Relationships Between Teaching and Research in Higher Education in England, *Higher Education Quarterly*, 55(2): 158–74.

Coats, M. (1994) *Women's Education*. Buckingham: Open University Press.

Coffey, A. and Atkinson, P. (1996) *Making Sense of Qualitative Data*. Thousand Oaks, CA: Sage.

Coffield, F. and Williamson, B. (eds) (1997) *Repositioning Higher Education*. Buckingham: Open University Press.

Cohen, L., Manion, L. and Morrison, K. (2000) *Research Methods in Education*, 5th edn. London: RoutledgeFalmer.

Colebatch, H. (2002) Through a Glass Darkly: policy development on higher degree completions in Australia, *Journal of Higher Education Policy and Management*, 24(1): 27–35.

Cook, A. (2001) Assessing the Use of Flexible Assessment, *Assessment and Evaluation in Higher Education*, 26(6): 539–49.

Cook, I. (2000) 'Nothing can ever be the case of "us" and "them" again': exploring the politics of difference through border pedagogy and student journal writing, *Journal of Geography in Higher Education*, 24(1): 13–27.

Cornford, J. and Pollock, N. (2003) *Putting the University Online: information, technology and organizational change*. Buckingham: Open University Press.

Cowan, J. (1998) *On Becoming an Innovative University Teacher: reflection in action*. Buckingham: Open University Press.

Cowen, R. (ed.) (1996) *The Evaluation of Higher Education Systems*. London: Kogan Page.

Cox, B. (1994) *Practical Pointers for University Teachers*. London: Kogan Page.

Cox, R., Miller, A. and Imrie, B. (1998) *Student Assessment in Higher Education*. London: Kogan Page.

Cox, S. and Heames, R. (1999) *Managing the Pressures in Teaching*. London: Routledge.

Craft, A. (ed.) (1992) *Quality Assurance in Higher Education*. London: Falmer Press.

Crawford, K., Gordon, S., Nicholas, J. and Prosser, M. (1998) Qualitatively Different Experiences of Learning Mathematics at University, *Learning and Instruction*, 8: 455–68.

Cree, V. and Macaulay, C. (eds) (2000) *Transfer of Learning in Professional and Vocational Education*. London: RoutledgeFalmer.

Croot, D. and Chalkley, B. (1999) Student Recruitment and the Geography of Undergraduate Geographers in England and Wales, *Journal of Geography in Higher Education*, 23(1): 21–47.

Crotty, M. (1998) *The Foundations of Social Research: meaning and perspective in the research process*. London: Sage.

Cryer, P. (1996) *The Research Student's Guide to Success*. Buckingham: Open University Press.

Cuthbert, R. (ed.) (1996) *Working in Higher Education*. Buckingham: Open University Press.

Daniel, J. (1996) *Mega Universities and the Knowledge Media: technology strategies for higher education*. London: Kogan Page.

David, M. and Woodward, D. (eds) (1998) *Negotiating the Glass Ceiling: careers of senior women in the academic world*. London: Falmer Press.

Davies, C. (1998) *Reflexive Ethnography*. London: Routledge.

Davies, P. (ed.) (1995) *Adults in Higher Education: international perspectives in access and participation*. London: Jessica Kingsley.

Dawn, T., Harkin, J. and Turner, G. (2000) *Teaching Young Adults*. London: Routledge.

Day, A. (1996) *How to Get Research Published in Journals*. Aldershot: Gower.

Dearlove, J. (1997) The Academic Labour Process: from collegiality and professionalism to managerialism and proletarianisation?, *Higher Education Review*, 30(1):56–75.

Deem, R. (1998) 'New Managerialism' and Higher Education: the management of performances and cultures in universities in the United Kingdom, *International Studies in Sociology of Education*, 8(1): 47–70.

Deem, R. (1999) Power and Resistance in the Academy: the case of women academic managers, in S. Whitehead and R. Moodley (eds) *Transforming Managers: gendering change in the public sector*. London: UCL Press.

Deem, R. (2001) Globalisation, New Managerialism, Academic Capitalism and Entrepreneurialism in Universities: is the local dimension still important?, *Comparative Education*, 37(1): 7–20.

Deem, R. (2003) Managing to Exclude? Manager-academic and staff communities in contemporary UK universities, in M. Tight (ed.) *Access and Exclusion*. Oxford: Elsevier Science.

Deem, R. and Brehony, K. (2000) Doctoral Students' Access to Research Cultures: are some more unequal than others?, *Studies in Higher Education*, 25(2): 149–65.

Deem, R. and Johnson, R. (2000) Managerialism and University Managers: building new academic communities or disrupting old ones?, in I. McNay (ed.) *Higher Education and its Communities*. Buckingham: Open University Press.

Delamont, S., Atkinson, P. and Parry, O. (1997) *Supervising the PhD: a guide to success*. Buckingham: Open University Press.

Delamont, S., Atkinson, P. and Parry, O. (2000) *The Doctoral Experience: success and failure in Graduate School*. London: Falmer.

Delanty, G. (2001) *Challenging Knowledge: the university in the knowledge society*. Buckingham: Open University Press.

Denscombe, M. (1998) *The Good Research Guide for Small-scale Social Research Projects*. Buckingham: Open University Press.

Devlin, M. (2002) Taking Responsibility for Learning Isn't Everything: a case for developing tertiary students' conceptions of learning, *Teaching in Higher Education*, 7(2): 125–38.

Dey, I. (1993) *Qualitative Data Analysis: a user-friendly guide for social scientists*. London: Routledge.

Dixon, C. (1986) *The Institute: a history of the University of London Institute of Education, 1932–1972*. London: University of London Institute of Education.

Dobson, I. (2003) Access to University in Australia: who misses out?, in M. Tight (ed.) *Access and Exclusion*. Oxford: Elsevier Science.

Dolowitz, D., Hulme, R., Nellis, M. and O'Neill, F. (2000) *Policy Transfer and British Social Policy: learning from the USA?* Buckingham: Open University Press.

Drennan, L. (2001) Quality Assessment and the Tension between Teaching and Research, *Quality in Higher Education*, 7(3): 167–78.

Dukes, P. (ed.) (1995) *The Universities of Aberdeen and Europe: the first three centuries*. Aberdeen: Aberdeen University Press.

Dunne, E. (1999) *The Learning Society: international perspectives*. London: Kogan Page.

Dysthe, O. (2002) The Learning Potential of a Web-mediated Discussion in a University Course, *Studies in Higher Education*, 27(3): 339–52.

Earwaker, J. (1992) *Helping and Supporting Students*. Buckingham: Open University Press.

Edwards, A. and Knight, P. (eds) (1995) *Assessing Competence in Higher Education*. London: Kogan Page.

Edwards, R. (1993) *Mature Women Students: separating or connecting family and education*. London: Taylor and Francis.

Edworthy, A. (2000) *Managing Stress*. Buckingham: Open University Press.

Egerton, M. (2001a) Mature Graduates I: occupational attainment and the effects of labour market duration, *Oxford Review of Education*, 27(1): 135–50.

Egerton, M. (2001b) Mature Graduates II: occupational attainment and the effects of social class, *Oxford Review of Education*, 27(2): 271–86.

Eggins, H. (ed.) (1997) *Women as Leaders and Managers in Higher Education*. Buckingham: Open University Press.

Eggins, H. and Macdonald, R. (eds) (2003) *The Scholarship of Academic Development*. Buckingham: Open University Press.

Ekegren, P. (1999) *The Reading of Theoretical Texts*. London: Routledge.

Elkin, J. and Law, D. (eds) (2000) *Managing Information*. Buckingham: Open University Press.

Ellis, R. (ed.) (1993) *Quality Assurance for University Teaching*. Buckingham: Open University Press.

Enders, J. (2000) Academic Staff in Europe: changing employment and working conditions, in M. Tight (ed.) *Academic Work and Life: what it is to be an academic, and how this is changing*. Oxford: Elsevier Science.

Enders, J. (ed.) (2001) *Academic Staff in Europe: changing contexts and conditions*. Westport, CT: Greenwood.

Engestrom, Y. (1987) *Learning by Expanding: an activity theoretical approach to developmental research*. Helsinki: Orienta-Konsultit.

Entwistle, N. (1997) Introduction: phenomenography in higher education, *Higher Education Research and Development*, 16: 127–34.

Entwistle, N., Hanley, M. and Hounsell, D. (1979) Identifying Distinctive Approaches to Studying, *Higher Education*, 8: 365–80.

van Ernst, B., Paterson, H., Langworthy, A., Costello, B. and Jones, M. (2001) Of Boxes and Bridges: a quality experience in the interface of higher education and the workplace, *Assessment and Evaluation in Higher Education*, 26(5): 437–48.

Evans, L. and Abbott, I. (1998) *Teaching and Learning in Higher Education*. London: Cassell.

Evans, N. (2000) *Experiential Learning Around the World: employability and the global economy*. London: Jessica Kingsley.

Fairbairn, G. and Winch, C. (1996) *Reading, Writing and Reasoning: a guide for students*. Buckingham: Open University Press.

Falchikov, N. (2001) *Learning Together: peer tutoring in higher education*. London: RoutledgeFalmer.

Fallows, S. and Steven, C. (2000) *Integrating Key Skills in Higher Education: employability, transferable skills and learning for life*. London: Kogan Page.

Farnham, D. (ed.) (1999) *Managing Academic Staff in Changing University Systems: international trends and comparison*. Buckingham: Open University Press.

Farrington, D. (1994) *The Law of Higher Education*. London: Butterworths.

Feldman, K. (1987) Research Productivity and Scholarly Accomplishment of College Teachers as Related to their Instructional Effectiveness, *Research in Higher Education*, 26: 227–91.

Fenwick, T. (2002) Problem-based Learning, Group Process and the Mid-career Professional: implications for graduate education, *Higher Education Research and Development*, 21(1): 5–21.

Fetterman, D. (1998) *Ethnography: step by step*, 2nd edn. Thousand Oaks, CA: Sage.

Fielding, J. and Gilbert, G. (2000) *Understanding Social Statistics*. London: Sage.

Fink, A. (1998) *Conducting Research Literature Reviews: from paper to the Internet*. Thousand Oaks, CA: Sage.

Fisher, S. (1994) *Stress in Academic Life: the mental assembly line*. Buckingham: Open University Press.

Flick, U. (2002) *An Introduction to Qualitative Research*, 2nd edn. London: Sage.

Florax, R. (1992) *The University: a regional booster*. Aldershot: Ashgate.

Frackmann, E. (1997) Research on Higher Education in Western Europe: from policy advice to self-reflection, in J. Sadlak and P. Altbach (eds) *Higher Education Research at the Turn of the New Century: structures, issues and trends*. New York: Garland.

Fraser, K. (2001) Australasian Academic Developers' Conceptions of the Profession, *International Journal of Academic Development*, 6(1): 54–64.

Freeman, H., Patel, D., Ryan, S. and Scott, B. (2000) *The Virtual University: the Internet and resource-based learning*. London: Kogan Page.

Freeman, R. and Lewis, R. (1998) *Planning and Implementing Assessment*. London: Kogan Page.

Frost, P. and Taylor, S. (eds) (1996) *Rhythms of Academic Life: personal accounts of careers in academia*. Thousand Oaks, CA: Sage.

Fry, H., Ketteridge, S. and Marshall, S. (1999) *A Handbook for Teaching and Learning in Higher Education*. London: Kogan Page.

Fuller, S. (2000) *The Governance of Science*. Buckingham: Open University Press.

Fulton, O. (1996a) Which Academic Profession are you in?, in R. Cuthbert (ed.) *Working in Higher Education*. Buckingham: Open University Press.

Fulton, O. (1996b) The Academic Profession in England on the Eve of Structural

Reform, in P. Altbach, *The International Academic Profession: portraits of fourteen countries*. Princeton, NJ: Carnegie Foundation for the Advancement of Teaching.

Gayle, V., Berridge, D. and Davies, R. (2002) Young People's Entry into Higher Education: quantifying influential factors, *Oxford Review of Education*, 28(1): 5–20.

Gee, J. (1996) *Social Linguistics and Literacies: ideology in discourses*, 2nd edn. London: Taylor and Francis.

Gellert, C. (ed.) (1998) *Innovation and Adaptation in European Higher Education: the changing conditions of advanced teaching and learning in Europe*. London: Jessica Kingsley.

Gewirtz, S., Ball, S. and Bowe, R. (1995) *Markets, Choice and Equity in Education*. Buckingham: Open University Press.

Gibbons, M., Limoges, C., Nowotny, H. et al. (1994) *The New Production of Knowledge: the dynamics of science and research in contemporary societies*. London: Sage.

Gibbs, G. (1995) The Relationship Between Quality in Research and Quality in Teaching, *Quality in Higher Education*, 1(2): 145–57.

Gibbs, G., Habeshaw, T. and Yorke, M. (2000) Institutional Learning and Teaching Strategies in English Higher Education, *Higher Education*, 40: 351–72.

Gledhill, J. (1999) *Managing Students*. Buckingham: Open University Press.

Goedegebuure, L., Kaiser, F., Maassen, P. et al. (1994) *Higher Education Policy: an international comparative perspective*. Oxford: Pergamon.

Goedegebuure, L. and van Vught, F. (eds) (1994) *Comparative Policy Studies in Higher Education*. Twente, the Netherlands: Centre for Higher Education Policy Studies.

Goedegebuure, L. and van Vught, F. (1996) Comparative Higher Education Studies: the perspective from the policy sciences, *Higher Education*, 32: 371–96.

Goodlad, S. (1995) *The Quest for Quality: sixteen forms of heresy in higher education*. Buckingham: Open University Press.

Goodlad, S. (ed.) (1998) *Mentoring and Tutoring by Students*. London: Kogan Page.

Goodson, I. and Sikes, P. (2001) *Life History Research in Educational Settings: learning from lives*. Buckingham: Open University Press.

Gorard, S. (2001) *Quantitative Methods in Educational Research: the role of numbers made easy*. London: Continuum.

Gosling, D. (2001) Educational Development Units in the UK: what are they doing five years on?, *International Journal for Academic Development*, 6(1): 74–90.

Graham, B. (2000) *Moving on in Your Career*. London: RoutledgeFalmer.

Grant, B. and Knowles, S. (2000) Flights of Imagination: academic women be(com)ing writers, *The International Journal for Academic Development*, 5(1): 6–19.

Gray, H. (ed.) (1999) *Universities and the Creation of Wealth*. Buckingham: Open University Press.

Green, B., Maxwell, T. and Shanahan, P. (eds) (2001) *Doctoral Education and Professional Practice: the next generation?* Armidale, NSW: Kardoorair Press.

Green, D. (ed) (1994) *What is Quality in Higher Education?* Buckingham: Open University Press.

Greenwood, D. and Levin, M. (1998) *Introduction to Action Research: social research for social change*. Thousand Oaks, CA: Sage.

Greer, L. (2001) Does Changing the Method of Assessment of a Module Improve the Performance of a Student?, *Assessment and Evaluation in Higher Education*, 26(2): 127–38.

Grey, M. (2002) Drawing with Difference: challenges faced by international students in an undergraduate business degree, *Teaching in Higher Education*, 7(2): 153–66.

Griffin, G. (1998) Uneven Developments: women's studies in higher education in the 1990s, in D. Malina and S. Maslin-Prothero (eds) *Surviving the Academy: feminist perspectives*. London: Falmer Press.

Griffiths, M. (1998) *Educational Research for Social Justice: getting off the fence*. Buckingham: Open University Press.

Griffiths, S. (ed.) (1996) *Beyond the Glass Ceiling: forty women whose ideas shape the modern world*. Manchester: Manchester University Press.

Gurr, G. (2001) Negotiating the 'Rackety Bridge': a dynamic model for aligning supervisory style with research student development, *Higher Education Research and Development*, 20(1): 81–92.

Hack, V. (1997) *Targeting the Powerful: international prospect research*. London: Association for Information Management.

Halvorsen, E. (2002) Gender Audit, in G. Howie and A. Tauchert (eds) *Gender, Teaching and Research in Higher Education: challenges for the 21st century*. Aldershot: Ashgate.

Hammersley, M. (1995) *The Politics of Social Research*. London: Sage.

Hammersley, M. and Atkinson, P. (1995) *Ethnography: principles in practice*, 2nd edn. London: Routledge.

Hannan, A. and Silver, H. (2000) *Innovating in Higher Education: teaching, learning and institutional cultures*. Buckingham: Open University Press.

Hantrais, L. (1999) Contextualisation in Cross-national Comparative Research, *International Journal of Social Research Methodology*, 2(2): 93–108.

Hantrais, L. and Mangen, S. (1996) Method and Management of Cross-national Social Research, in L. Hantrais and S. Mangen (eds) *Cross-national Research Methods in the Social Sciences*. London: Pinter.

Hare, P. (ed.) (1997) *Structure and Financing of Higher Education in Russia, Ukraine and the EU*. London: Jessica Kingsley.

Harman, G. (2000a) Allocating Research Infrastructure Grants in Post-binary Higher Education Systems: British and Australian approaches, *Journal of Higher Education Policy and Management*, 22(2): 111–26.

Harman, G. (2000b) Academic Work and Values in Australian Higher Education, 1977 to 1997, in M. Tight (ed.) *Academic Work and Life: what it is to be an academic, and how this is changing*. Oxford: Elsevier Science.

Harman, G. (2000c) Institutional Mergers in Australian Higher Education since 1960, *Higher Education Quarterly*, 54(4): 343–66.

Harman, G. (2001) University-Industry Research Partnerships in Australia: extents, benefits and risks, *Higher Education Research and Development*, 20(3): 245–64.

Harman, K. (2002) Merging Diverse Campus Cultures into Coherent Educational Communities: challenges for higher education leaders, *Higher Education*, 44: 91–114.

Harry, K. (ed.) (1999) *Higher Education Through Open and Distance Learning*. London: Routledge.

Hart, C. (1998) *Doing a Literature Review: releasing the social science research imagination.* London: Sage.

Hart, C. (2001) *Doing a Literature Review: a comprehensive guide for the social sciences.* London: Sage.

Hart, E. and Bond, M. (1995) *Action Research for Health and Social Care: a guide to practice.* Buckingham: Open University Press.

Harvey, L. (2000) New Realities: the relationship between higher education and employment, *Tertiary Education and Management,* 6(1): 3–17.

Harvey, L. (2002) Evaluation for What?, *Teaching in Higher Education,* 7(3): 245–63.

Harvey, L. and Associates (1997) *The Student Satisfaction Manual.* Buckingham: Open University Press.

Harvey, L. and Knight, P. (1996) *Transforming Higher Education.* Buckingham: Open University Press.

Haselgrove, S. (ed.) (1994) *The Student Experience.* Buckingham: Open University Press.

Hatch, J. and Wisniewski, R. (eds) (1995) *Life History and Narrative.* London: Falmer.

Hatt, S., Kent, J. and Britton, C. (eds) (1999) *Women, Research and Careers.* Basingstoke: Macmillan Press.

Hattie, J. and Marsh, H. (1996) The Relationship Between Research and Teaching: a meta-analysis, *Review of Educational Research,* 66:507–42.

Hawkridge, D. (1993) *Challenging Educational Technology.* London: Athlone Press.

Hayden, M. and Parry, S. (1997) Research on Higher Education in Australia and New Zealand, in J. Sadlak and P. Altbach (eds) *Higher Education Research at the Turn of the New Century: structures, issues and trends.* New York: Garland.

Hayes, D. and Wynyard, R. (eds) (2002) *The McDonaldization of Higher Education.* Westport, CT: Bergin and Garvey.

Hayton, A. and Paczuska, A. (eds) (2002) *Access, Participation and Higher Education: policy and practice.* London: Kogan Page.

Heath, T. (2002) A Quantitative Analysis of PhD Students' Views of Supervision, *Higher Education Research and Development,* 21(1): 41–53.

Henkel, M. (2000) *Academic Identities and Policy Change in Higher Education.* London: Jessica Kingsley.

Henkel, M. and Little, B. (1999) *Changing Relationships Between Higher Education and the State.* London: Jessica Kingsley.

Heywood, J. (2000) *Assessment in Higher Education: of student learning, teaching, programmes and institutions.* London: Jessica Kingsley.

Hill, F. (1995) Managing Service Quality in Higher Education: the role of the student as primary consumer, *Quality Assurance in Education,* 3(3): 10–21.

Hine, C. (2000) *Virtual Ethnography.* London: Sage.

Hodkinson, P. and Sparkes, A. (1997) Careership: a sociological theory of career decision making, *British Journal of Sociology of Education,* 18(1): 29–44.

Holroyd, C. (2000) Are Assessors Professional? Student assessment and the professionalism of academics, *Active Learning in Higher Education,* 1(1): 28–44.

Homan, R. (1991) *The Ethics of Social Research.* Harlow: Longman.

Hood, S., Mayall, B. and Oliver, S. (eds) (1999) *Critical Issues in Social Research: power and prejudice.* Buckingham: Open University Press.

House, E. and Howe, K. (1999) *Values in Evaluation and Social Research.* Thousand Oaks, CA: Sage.

Houston, D. and Studman, C. (2001) Quality Management and the University: a deafening clash of metaphors?, *Assessment and Evaluation in Higher Education*, 26(5): 475–87.

Howarth, D. (2000) *Discourse*. Buckingham: Open University Press.

Howie, G. and Tauchert, A. (eds) (2002) *Gender, Teaching and Research in Higher Education: challenges for the 21st century*. Aldershot: Ashgate.

Hudson, R., Maslin-Prothero, S. and Oates, L. (eds) (1997) *Flexible Learning in Action: case studies in higher education*. London: Kogan Page.

Huff, A. (1999) *Writing for Scholarly Publication*. London: Sage.

Hughes, C. (1999) The Dire in Self-Directed Learning, *Adults Learning*, 11(2): 7–9.

Hughes, C. (2002a) Pedagogies of, and for, Resistance, in G. Howie and A. Tauchert (eds) *Gender, Teaching and Research in Higher Education: challenges for the 21st century*. Aldershot: Ashgate.

Hughes, C. (2002b) *Women's Contemporary Lives: within and beyond the mirror*. London: Routledge.

Hughes, C. (2002c) *Key Concepts in Feminist Theory and Research*. London: Sage.

Hughes, C. and Tight, M. (1995) Linking University Teaching and Research, *Higher Education Review*, 28: 51–65.

Huisman, J. (1995) *Differentiation, Diversity and Dependency in Higher Education: a theoretical and empirical analysis*. Utrecht: Lemma.

Humfrey, C. (1999) *Managing International Students: recruitment to graduation*. Buckingham: Open University Press.

Hunt, C. (2001) Climbing out of the Void: moving from chaos to concepts in the presentation of a thesis, *Teaching in Higher Education*, 6(3): 351–67.

Hutton, P. (1990) *Survey Research for Managers: how to use surveys in management decision-making*, 2nd edn. Basingstoke, Macmillan.

Ives, E., Drummond, D. and Schwarz, L. (2000) *The First Civic University: Birmingham 1880–1980 – an introductory history*. Birmingham: University of Birmingham Press.

Jackson, C. and Tinkler, P. (2001) Back to Basics: a consideration of the purposes of the PhD viva, *Assessment and Evaluation in Higher Education*, 26(4): 355–66.

Jacob, M. and Hellstrom, T. (eds) (2000) *The Future of Knowledge Production in the Academy*. Buckingham: Open University Press.

James, R. (2000) Non-traditional Students in Australian Higher Education: persistent inequities and the new ideology of 'student choice', *Tertiary Education and Management*, 6: 105–18.

James, R. (2001) Participation Disadvantage in Australian Higher Education: an analysis of some effects of geographical location and socioeconomic status, *Higher Education*, 42: 455–72.

Jarvis, P. (2001) *Universities and Corporate Universities: the higher learning industry in global society*. London: Kogan Page.

Jenkins, A. (2000) The Relationship Between Teaching and Research: where does geography stand and deliver?, *Journal of Geography in Higher Education*, 24(3): 325–52.

Jenkins, A., Breen, R., Lindsay, R. and Brew, A. (2003) *Reshaping Teaching in Higher Education: linking teaching with research*. London: Kogan Page.

Jenkins, A., Jones, L. and Ward, A. (2001) The Long-term Effect of a Degree on Graduate Lives, *Studies in Higher Education*, 26(2): 147–61.

Jenkins, A. and Walker, L. (eds) (1994) *Developing Student Capability Through Modular Courses.* London: Kogan Page.

Jenkins, A. and Ward, A. (2001) Moving with the Times: an oral history of a geography department, *Journal of Geography in Higher Education,* 25(2): 191–208.

Johnes, J. and Taylor, J. (1991) *Performance Indicators in Higher Education.* Buckingham: Open University Press.

Johnson, L., Lee, A. and Green, B. (2000) The PhD and the Autonomous Self: gender, rationality and postgraduate pedagogy, *Studies in Higher Education,* 25(2): 135–47.

Johnson, R. (2000) The Authority of the Student Evaluation Questionnaire, *Teaching in Higher Education,* 5(4): 419–34.

Jongbloed, B. and Vossensteyn, H. (2001) Keeping up Performances: an international survey of performance-based funding in higher education, *Journal of Higher Education Policy and Management,* 23(2): 127–45.

Josselson, R. and Lieblich, A. (eds) (1995) *Interpreting Experience: the narrative study of lives.* Thousand Oaks, CA: Sage.

Josselson, R. and Lieblich, A. (eds) (1999) *Making Meaning of Narratives.* Thousand Oaks, CA: Sage.

Kaiser, F., Florax, R., Koelman, J. and van Vught, F. (1992) *Public Expenditure on Higher Education: a comparative study in the member states of the European Community.* London: Jessica Kingsley.

Keats, D. (2000) *Interviewing: a practical guide for students and professionals.* Buckingham: Open University Press.

Kehm, B., Maiworm, F., Over, A. et al. (1997) *Integrating Europe Through Cooperation Among Universities: the experiences of the TEMPUS programme.* London: Jessica Kingsley.

Kekale, J. (2002) Conceptions of Quality in Four Different Disciplines, *Tertiary Education and Management,* 8(1): 65–80.

Kells, H. (1992) *Self-Regulation in Higher Education: a multi-national perspective on collaborative systems of quality assurance and control.* London: Jessica Kingsley.

Kember, D. (2000) Misconceptions about the Learning Approaches, Motivation and Study Practices of Asian Students, *Higher Education,* 40: 99–121.

Kennett, P. (2001) *Comparative Social Policy.* Buckingham: Open University Press.

Kinnell, M. (ed.) (1990) *The Learning Experiences of Overseas Students.* Buckingham: Open University Press.

Kivinen, O. and Ahola, S. (1999) Higher Education as Human Risk Capital: reflections on changing labour markets, *Higher Education,* 38: 191–208.

Klenowski, V. (2002) *Developing Portfolios for Learning and Assessment.* London: RoutledgeFalmer.

Knapper, C., and Cropley, A. (2000) *Lifelong Learning in Higher Education,* 3rd edn. London: Kogan Page.

Knight, J. and de Wit, H. (eds) (1997) *Internationalisation of Higher Education in Asia Pacific Countries.* Amsterdam: European Association for International Education.

Knight, P. (1997) *Masterclass: learning, teaching and curriculum in taught master's degrees.* London: Cassell.

Knight, P. (ed.) (1999) *Assessment for Learning in Higher Education.* London: Kogan Page.

Knight, P. (2002a) *Being a Teacher in Higher Education*. Buckingham: Open University Press.

Knight, P. (2002b) Learning from Schools. *Higher Education*, 44: 283–98.

Knight, P. (2002c) Summative Assessment in Higher Education: practices in disarray, *Studies in Higher Education*, 27(3): 275–86.

Knight, P. and Trowler, P. (1999) It Takes a Village to Raise a Child: mentoring and the socialisation of new entrants to the academic professions, *Mentoring and Tutoring*, 7(1): 23–34.

Knight, P. and Trowler, P. (2001) *Departmental Leadership in Higher Education*. Buckingham: Open University Press.

Kogan, M. and Hanney, S. (2000) *Reforming Higher Education*. London: Jessica Kingsley.

Kogan, M., Moses, I. and El-Khawas, E. (1994) *Staffing Higher Education: meeting new challenges*. London: Jessica Kingsley.

Kolbert, J. (2000) *Keele, the First Fifty Years: a portrait of the university, 1950–2000*. Keele: Melandrium Books.

Krueger, R. and Casey, M. (2000) *Focus Groups: a practical guide for applied research*, 3rd edn. Thousand Oaks, CA: Sage.

Kvale, S. (1996) *Inter Views: an introduction to qualitative research interviewing*. Thousand Oaks, CA: Sage.

Kwiek, M. (2001) Globalization and Higher Education, *Higher Education in Europe*, 26(1): 27–38.

Kyvik, S. (2000) Academic Work in Norwegian Higher Education, in M. Tight (ed.) *Academic Work and Life: what it is to be an academic, and how this is changing*. Oxford: Elsevier Science.

Lafferty, G. and Fleming, J. (2000) The Restructuring of Academic Work in Australia: power, management and gender, *British Journal of Sociology of Education*, 21(2): 257–67.

Land, R. (2001) Agency, Context and Change in Academic Development, *The International Journal for Academic Development*, 6(1): 4–20.

Laurillard, D. (2002) *Rethinking University Teaching: a conversational framework for the effective use of learning technologies*. London: RoutledgeFalmer.

Lave, J. and Wenger, E. (1991) *Situated Learning: legitimate peripheral participation*. Cambridge: Cambridge University Press.

Lavraka, P. (1993) *Telephone Survey Methods: sampling, selection and supervision*, 2nd edn. London: Sage.

Lawless, C. and Richardson, J. (2002) Approaches to Studying and Perceptions of Academic Quality in Distance Education, *Higher Education*, 44: 257–82.

Lea, M. and Nicoll, K. (eds) (2002) *Distributed Learning: social and cultural approaches to practice*. London: RoutledgeFalmer.

Lea, M. and Stierer, B. (eds) (2000) *Student Writing in Higher Education: new contexts*. Buckingham: Open University Press.

Lea, M. and Street, B. (1998) Student Writing in Higher Education: an academic literacies approach, *Studies in Higher Education*, 23(2): 157–72.

Leach, L., Neutze, G. and Zepke, N. (2001) Assessment and Empowerment: some critical questions, *Assessment and Evaluation in Higher Education*, 26(4): 293–305.

Lee, R. (1993) *Doing Research on Sensitive Topics*. London: Sage.

Lee, R. (2000) *Unobtrusive Methods in Social Research*. Buckingham: Open University Press.

Levitas, R. and Guy, W. (eds) (1996) *Interpreting Official Statistics*. London: Routledge.

Lillis, T. (2001) *Student Writing: access, regulation, desire*. London: Routledge.

Lillis, T. and Turner, J. (2001) Student Writing in Higher Education: contemporary confusion, traditional concerns, *Teaching in Higher Education*, 6(1): 57–68.

Liston, C. (1999) *Managing Quality and Standards*. Buckingham: Open University Press.

Littlemore, J. (2001) The Use of Metaphor in University Lectures and the Problems that it causes for Overseas Students, *Teaching in Higher Education*, 6(3): 333–49.

Lockwood, F. (ed.) (1994) *Materials Production in Open and Distance Learning*. London: Paul Chapman.

Lockwood, F. and Gooley, A. (eds) (2001) *Innovation in Open and Distance Learning: successful development of online and web-based learning*. London: Kogan Page.

Luey, B. (1995) *Handbook for Academic Authors*, 3rd edn. New York: Cambridge University Press.

Lum, G. (1999) Where's the Competence in Competence-based Education and Training?, *Journal of Philosophy of Education*, 33(3): 403–18.

Lunneborg, P. (1994) *OU Women: undoing educational obstacles*. London: Cassell.

McBurnie, G. (2001) Globalization: a new paradigm for higher education policy, *Higher Education in Europe*, 26(1): 11–26.

McBurnie, G. and Ziguras, C. (2001) The Regulation of Transnational Higher Education in Southeast Asia: case studies of Hong Kong, Malaysia and Australia, *Higher Education*, 42: 85–105.

McCulloch, G. and Richardson, W. (2000) *Historical Research in Educational Settings*. Buckingham: Open University Press.

McInnis, C. (2000a) Changing Academic Work Roles: the everyday realities challenging quality in teaching, *Quality in Higher Education*, 6(2): 143–52.

McInnis, C. (2000b) Towards New Balance or New Divides? The changing work roles of academics in Australia, in M. Tight (ed.) *Academic Work and Life: what it is to be an academic, and how this is changing*. Oxford: Elsevier Science.

McInnis, C. (2001) Researching the First Year Experience: where to from here?, *Higher Education Research and Development*, 20(2): 105–14.

McKenzie, K. and Schweitzer, R. (2001) Who Succeeds at University? Factors predicting academic performance in first year Australian university students, *Higher Education Research and Development*, 20(1): 21–33.

McLean, M. (2001) Can we Relate Conceptions of Learning to Student Academic Achievement?, *Teaching in Higher Education*, 6(3): 399–413.

McNamara, D. and Harris, R. (eds) (1997) *Overseas Students in Higher Education: issues in teaching and learning*. London: Routledge.

McNay, I. (1995) From the Collegial Academy to Corporate Enterprise: the changing cultures of universities, in T. Schuller (ed.) *The Changing University?* Buckingham: Open University Press.

McNiff, J., Whitehead, J. and Lomax, P. (1998) *You and Your Action Research Project*. London: Routledge.

McWilliam, E., Hatcher, C. and Meadmore, D. (1999) Developing Professional Identities: remaking the academic for corporate times, *Pedagogy, Culture and Society*, 7(1): 55–72.

McWilliam, E., Singh, P. and Taylor, P. (2002) Doctoral Education, Danger and Risk Management, *Higher Education Research and Development*, 21(2): 119–29.

Maanen, J. van (ed.) (1995) *Representation in Ethnography*. London: Sage.

Maassen, P. (1996) *Governmental Steering and the Academic Culture: the intangibility of the human factor in Dutch and German universities*. Utrecht, De Tijdstroom.

Maassen, P. (2000) Higher Education Research: the hourglass structure and its implications, in U. Teichler and J. Sadlak (eds) *Higher Education Research: its relationship to policy and practice*. Oxford: Pergamon.

Macdonald, I. (2001) The Teaching Community: recreating university teaching, *Teaching in Higher Education*, 6(2): 153–67.

Macfarlane, B. (2000) Inside the Corporate Classroom, *Teaching in Higher Education*, 5(1): 51–60.

Maclellan, E. (2001) Assessment for Learning: the differing perceptions of tutors and students, *Assessment and Evaluation in Higher Education*, 26(4): 307–18.

Macpherson, K. (2002) Problem-solving Ability and Cognitive Maturity in Undergraduate Students, *Assessment and Evaluation in Higher Education*, 27(1): 5–22.

Maiworm, F., Steube, W. and Teichler, U. (1991) *Learning in Europe. The ERASMUS Experience: a survey of the 1988–89 ERASMUS students*. London: Jessica Kingsley.

Maiworm, F. and Teichler, U. (1996) *Study Abroad and Early Career: experiences of former ERASMUS students*. London: Jessica Kingsley.

Malina, D. and Maslin-Prothero, S. (eds) (1998) *Surviving the Academy: feminist perspectives*. London: Falmer Press.

Marginson, S. (2000) Rethinking Academic Work in the Global Era, *Journal of Higher Education Policy and Management*, 22(1): 23–35.

Marginson, S. (2002) Nation-building Universities in a Global Environment: the case of Australia, *Higher Education*, 43: 409–28.

Marginson, S. and Considine, M. (2000) *The Enterprise University: power, governance and reinvention in Australia*. Cambridge: Cambridge University Press.

Marsh, D. (ed.) (1998) *Comparing Policy Networks*. Buckingham: Open University Press.

Martin, E. (1999) *Changing Academic Work: developing the learning university*. Buckingham: Open University Press.

Marton, F. (1994) Phenomenography, in T. Husen and T. Postlethwaite (eds) *International Encyclopedia of Education*, Vol. 8, 2nd edn. Oxford: Pergamon.

Marton, F. and Booth, S. (1997) *Learning and Awareness*. Mahwah, NJ: Lawrence Erlbaum.

Marton, F., Dall'Alba, G. and Beaty, E. (1993) Conceptions of Learning, *International Journal of Educational Research*, 19(3): 277–300.

Marton, F., Hounsell, D. and Entwistle, N. (eds) (1997) *The Experience of Learning*. 2nd edn. Edinburgh: Scottish Academic Press.

Mason, J. (2002) *Qualitative Researching*, 2nd edn. London: Sage.

Mason, R. (1994) *Using Communications Media in Open and Flexible Learning*. London: Kogan Page.

Mavin, S. and Bryans, P. (2002) Academic Women in the UK: mainstreaming our experiences and networking for action, *Gender and Education*, 14(3): 235–50.

May, T. (1997) *Social Research: issues, method and process*, 2nd edn. Buckingham: Open University Press.

Maynard, M. (1994) Methods, Practice and Epistemology: the debate about feminism and research, in M. Maynard and J. Purvis (eds) *Researching Women's Lives From a Feminist Perspective*. London: Taylor and Francis.

Maynard, M. and Purvis, J. (eds) (1994) *Researching Women's Lives From a Feminist Perspective*. London: Taylor and Francis.

Meehan, D. (1999) The Under-representation of Women Managers in Higher Education: are there issues other than style?, in S. Whitehead and R. Moodley (eds) *Transforming Managers: gendering change in the public sector*. London: UCL Press.

Meek, L. (2000) Diversity and Marketisation of Higher Education: incompatible concepts?, *Higher Education Policy*, 13: 23–39.

Meek, L., Goedegebuure, L., Kivinen, O. and Rinne, R. (eds) (1996) *The Mockers and Mocked: comparative perspectives on differentiation, convergence and diversity in higher education*. Oxford: Pergamon.

Merrill, B. (1999) *Gender, Change and Identity: mature women students*. Aldershot: Ashgate.

Meyer, J. and Boulton-Lewis, G. (eds) (2003) Variation in Dissonance in Learning Patterns: towards an emerging theory?, *Studies in Higher Education*, 28(1) (special issue).

Meyer, J. and Vermunt, J. (eds) (2000) Dissonant Study Orchestration in Higher Education: manifestation and effects, *European Journal of Psychology of Education*, 15 (special issue).

Middlehurst, R. (1993) *Leading Academics*. Buckingham: Open University Press.

Middleton, C. (2000) Models of State and Market in the 'Modernisation' of Higher Education, *British Journal of Sociology of Education*, 21(4): 537–54.

Miles, M. and Huberman, A. (1994) *Qualitative Data Analysis: an expanded sourcebook*. London: Sage.

Miller, H. (1995) *The Management of Change in Universities: universities, state and economy in Australia, Canada and the United Kingdom*. Buckingham: Open University Press.

Mirza, H. (1995) Black Women in Higher Education: defining a space/finding a place, in L. Morley and V. Walsh (eds) *Feminist Academics: creative agents for change*. London: Taylor and Francis.

Montgomery, F. and Collette, C. (2001) Students Speaking, *Teaching in Higher Education*, 6(3): 299–308.

Moogan, Y., Baron, S. and Harris, K. (1999) Decision-making Behaviour of Potential Higher Education Students, *Higher Education Quarterly*, 53(3): 211–28.

Moon, J. (1999a) *Learning Journals: a handbook for academics, students and professional development*. London: Kogan Page.

Moon, J. (1999b) *Reflection in Learning and Professional Development: theory and practice*. London: Kogan Page.

Moore, E. (2000) The Changing Patterns of University Studies: towards lifelong learning in Finnish universities, *Higher Education Management*, 12(3): 113–27.

Morgan, C. and O'Reilly, M. (1999) *Assessing Open and Distance Learners*. London: Kogan Page.

Morley, L. and Walsh, V. (eds) (1995) *Feminist Academics: creative agents for change*. London: Taylor and Francis.

Morley, L. and Walsh, V. (eds) (1996) *Breaking Boundaries: women in higher education*. London: Taylor and Francis.

Morris, H. (2000) The Origins, Forms and Effects of Modularisation and Semesterisation in Ten UK-based Business Schools, *Higher Education Quarterly*, 54(3): 239–58.

Morss, K. and Murray, R. (2001) Researching Academic Writing within a Structured Programme: insights and outcomes, *Studies in Higher Education*, 26(1): 35–52.

Morton-Cooper, A. (2000) *Action Research in Health Care*. Oxford: Blackwell.

Moser, C. and Kalton, G. (1993) *Survey Methods in Social Investigation*. Aldershot: Dartmouth.

Moustakas, C. (1994) *Phenomenological Research Methods*. Thousand Oaks, CA: Sage.

Mouwen, K. (2000) Strategy, Structure and Culture of the Hybrid University: towards the university of the 21st century, *Tertiary Education and Management*, 6: 47–56.

Moxley, D., Najor-Durack, A. and Dumbrigue, C. (2001) *Keeping Students in Higher Education: successful practices and strategies for retention*. London: Kogan Page.

Murray, R. (2002) *How to Write a Thesis*. Buckingham: Open University Press.

Mutch, A. (2002) Thinking Strategically About Assessment, *Assessment and Evaluation in Higher Education*, 27(2): 163–74.

National Committee of Inquiry into Higher Education (1997) *Higher Education in the Learning Society*. Norwich: HMSO.

Neave, G. and van Vught, F. (eds) (1994) *Government and Higher Education Relationships Across Three Continents: the winds of change*. Oxford: Pergamon.

Neumann, R. (1992) Perceptions of the Teaching-Research Network: a framework for analysis, *Higher Education*, 23: 159–71.

Neumann, R., Parry, S. and Becher, T. (2002) Teaching and Learning in their Disciplinary Contexts: a conceptual analysis, *Studies in Higher Education*, 27(4): 405–17.

Newstead, S., Franklyn-Stokes, A. and Armstead, P. (1996) Individual Differences in Student Cheating, *Journal of Educational Psychology*, 88(2): 229–41.

Nicoll, K. (1997) 'Flexible Learning': unsettling practices, *Studies in Continuing Education*, 19(2): 100–11.

Nicholls, G. (2000) *Professional Development in Higher Education*. London: Kogan Page.

Nicholls, G. (2002) *Developing Teaching and Learning in Higher Education*. London: RoutledgeFalmer.

Nord, D. and Weller, G. (eds) (2002) *Higher Education Across the Circumpolar North: a circle of learning*. Basingstoke: Palgrave.

Norton, L., Dickins, T. and McLaughlin Cook, N. (1996) Rules of the Game in Essay Writing, *Psychology Teaching Review*, 5(1): 1–14.

Norton, L., Tilley, A., Newstead, S. and Franklyn-Stokes, A. (2001) The Pressures of

Assessment in Undergraduate Courses and their Effect on Student Behaviours, *Assessment and Evaluation in Higher Education*, 26(3): 269–84.

Nowotny, H., Scott, P. and Gibbons, M. (2001) *Re-thinking Science: knowledge and the public in an age of uncertainty.* Cambridge: Polity Press.

Oppenheim, A. (1992) *Questionnaire Design, Interviewing and Attitude Measurement*, 2nd edn. London: Pinter.

Opper, S., Teichler, U. and Carlson, J. (1990) *Impacts of Study Abroad Programmes on Students and Graduates.* London: Jessica Kingsley.

Osborne, R. (1996) *Higher Education in Ireland: north and south.* London: Jessica Kingsley.

Ozga, J. (2000) *Policy Research in Educational Settings: contested terrain.* Buckingham: Open University Press.

Palfreyman, D. and Warner, D. (eds) (1998) *Higher Education and the Law: a guide for managers.* Buckingham: Open University Press.

Parker, M. and Jary, D. (1995) The McUniversity: organisations, management and academic subjectivity, *Organization*, 2(2): 319–38.

Parry, S. (1998) Disciplinary Discourse in Doctoral Theses, *Higher Education*, 36: 273–99.

Pascall, G. and Cox, R. (1993) *Women Returning to Higher Education.* Buckingham: Open University Press.

Patterson, G. (2000) Findings of Economies of Scale in Higher Education: implications for strategies of merger and alliance, *Tertiary Education and Management*, 6: 259–69.

Peelo, M. (1994) *Helping Students With Study Problems.* Buckingham: Open University Press.

Penrose, J. (1999) Using Personal Research to Teach the Significance of Socially Constructed Categories, *Journal of Geography in Higher Education*, 23(2): 227–39.

Phillips, E. and Pugh, D. (2000) *How to Get a PhD: a handbook for students and their supervisors*, 3rd edn. Buckingham: Open University Press.

Piper, D. (1994) *Are Professors Professional? The organisation of university examinations.* London: Jessica Kingsley.

Plummer, K. (2001) *Documents of Life 2: an invitation to critical humanism*, 2nd edn. London: Sage.

Pope, N. (2001) An Examination of the Use of Peer Rating for Formative Assessment in the Context of the Theory of Consumption Values, *Assessment and Evaluation in Higher Education*, 26(3): 235–46.

Potter, S. (ed.) (2002) *Doing Postgraduate Research.* London: Sage.

Potts, A. (1997) *College Academics.* Charlestown, NSW: William Michael.

Pratt, J. (1997) *The Polytechnic Experiment 1965–1992.* Buckingham: Open University Press.

Price, L. and Priest, J. (1996) Activists as Change Agents: achievements and limitations, in L. Morley and V. Walsh (eds) *Breaking Boundaries: women in higher education.* London: Taylor and Francis.

Prichard, C. (2000) *Making Managers in Universities and Colleges.* Buckingham: Open University Press.

Prichard, C. and Willmott, H. (1997) Just How Managed is the McUniversity?, *Organization Studies*, 18(2): 287–316.

Prior, L. (2003) *Using Documents in Social Research*. London: Sage.

Prosser, M., Hazel, E., Trigwell, K. and Lyons, F. (1996) Qualitative and Quantitative Indicators of Students' Understanding of Physics Concepts, *Research and Development in Higher Education*, 19: 670–5.

Prosser, M., Hazel, E., Trigwell, K. and Lyons, F. (1997) Students' Experiences of Studying Physics Concepts: the effects of disintegrated perceptions and approaches. Paper presented at the 7th European Conference for Research on Learning and Instruction, Athens.

Prosser, M. and Trigwell, K (1999) *Understanding Learning and Teaching: the experience in higher education*. Buckingham: Open University Press.

Prosser, M., Trigwell, K. and Taylor, P. (1994) A Phenomenographic Study of Academics' Conceptions of Science Learning and Teaching, *Learning and Instruction*, 4: 217–31.

Punch, K. (1998) *Introduction to Social Research: quantitative and qualitative approaches*. London: Sage.

Race, P. (1998) *The Lecturer's Toolkit*. London: Kogan Page.

Race, P. (1999) *2000 Tips for Lecturers*. London: Kogan Page.

Radford, J., Raaheim, K., de Vries, P. and Williams, R. (1997) *Quantity and Quality in Higher Education*. London: Jessica Kingsley.

Raffe, D., Brannen, K., Fairgrieve, J. and Martin, C. (2001) Participation, Inclusiveness, Academic Drift and Parity of Esteem: a comparison of post-compulsory education and training in England, Scotland, Wales and Northern Ireland, *Oxford Review of Education*, 27(2): 173–203.

Ramazanoglu, C. and Holland, J. (2002) *Feminist Methodology: challenges and choices*. London: Sage.

Ramburuth, P. and McCormick, J. (2001) Learning Diversity in Higher Education: a comparative study of Asian international and Australian students, *Higher Education*, 42: 333–50.

Ramsden, P. (1992) *Learning to Teach in Higher Education*. London: Routledge.

Ramsden, P. (1998) *Learning to Lead in Higher Education*. London: Routledge.

Ramsden, P., Prosser, M., Trigwell, K. and Martin, E. (1997) Perceptions of Academic Leadership and the Effectiveness of University Teaching. Paper presented at the Annual Conference of the Australian Association for Research in Education, Brisbane.

Rana, R. (2000) *Counselling Students: a psychodynamic perspective*. Basingstoke: Macmillan.

Raschke, C. (2003) *The Digital Revolution and the Coming of the Postmodern University*. London: RoutledgeFalmer.

Read, B., Francis, B. and Robson, J. (2001) 'Playing Safe': undergraduate essay writing and the presentation of the student 'voice', *British Journal of Sociology of Education*, 22(3): 387–99.

Reay, D., Ball, S. and David, M. (2002) 'It's taking me a long time but I'll get there in the end': mature students on access courses and higher education choice, *British Educational Research Journal*, 28(1): 5–19.

Reed, M. and Deem, R. (2002) New Managerialism: the manager-academic and technologies of management in universities: looking forward to virtuality?, in K. Robins and F. Webster (eds) *The Virtual University: knowledge, markets and management*. Oxford: Oxford University Press.

Reinharz, S. (1992) *Feminist Methods in Social Research*. New York: Oxford University Press.

Renzetti, C. and Lee, R. (eds) (1993) *Researching Sensitive Topics*. London: Sage.

Ribbens, J. and Edwards, R. (eds) (1998) *Feminist Dilemmas in Qualitative Research: public knowledge and private lives*. London: Sage.

Richards, J. (ed.) (1997) *Uneasy Chairs: life as a professor*. Lancaster: Unit for Innovation in Higher Education.

Richardson, J. (1990) Reliability and Replicability of the Approaches to Studying Questionnaire, *Studies in Higher Education*, 15: 155–68.

Richardson, J. (1994) Cultural Specificity of Approaches to Studying in Higher Education: a literature review, *Higher Education*, 27: 449–68.

Richardson, J. (2000) *Researching Student Learning: approaches to studying in campus-based and distance education*. Buckingham: Open University Press.

de Ridder-Symoens, H. (ed.) (1992) *A History of the University in Europe. Volume I: Universities in the Middle Ages*. Cambridge: Cambridge University Press.

de Ridder-Symoens, H. (ed.) (1996) *A History of the University in Europe. Volume II: Universities in Early Modern Europe (1500–1800)*. Cambridge: Cambridge University Press.

Ritzer, G. (1998) *The McDonaldization Thesis: explorations and extensions*. Thousand Oaks, CA: Pine Forge Press.

Ritzer, G. (2000) *The McDonaldization of Society: new century edition*. Thousand Oaks: Sage, Pine Forge Press.

Ritzer, G, (2002) Enchanting McUniversity: towards a spectacularly irrational university quotidian, in D. Hayes and R. Wynyard (eds) *The McDonaldization of Higher Education*. Westport, CT: Bergin and Garvey.

Roberts, B. (2002) *Biographical Research*. Buckingham: Open University Press.

Robertson, J. and Bond, C. (2001) Experiences of the Relation between Teaching and Research: what do academics value?, *Higher Education Research and Development*, 20(1): 5–19.

Robins, K. and Webster, F. (eds) (2002) *The Virtual University: knowledge, markets and management*. Oxford: Oxford University Press.

Robson, C. (1993) *Real World Research: a resource for social scientists and practitioner researchers*. Oxford: Blackwell.

Robson, C. (2000) *Small-scale Evaluation: principles and practice*. London: Sage.

Rodriguez, N. and Ryave, A. (2002) *Systematic Self-Observation*. London: Sage.

Rosnow, R. and Rosenthal, R. (1997) *People Studying People: artifacts and ethics in behavioural research*. New York: W. H. Freeman.

Rossi, P. and Freeman, H. (1993) *Evaluation: a systematic approach*, 5th edn. Newbury Park, CA: Sage.

Rowland, S. (2000) *The Enquiring University Teacher*. Buckingham: Open University Press.

Rowley, G. (1997) Mergers in Higher Education: a strategic analysis, *Higher Education Quarterly*, 51(3): 251–63.

Ruegg, W. (1992) Foreword, in H. de Ridder-Symoens (ed.) *A History of the University in Europe. Volume I: Universities in the Middle Ages*. Cambridge: Cambridge University Press.

Rumble, G. (2001) Re-inventing Distance Education, *International Journal of Lifelong Education*, 20(1–2): 31–43.

Salmi, J. and Verspoor, A. (eds) (1994) *Revitalizing Higher Education*. Oxford: Pergamon.

Sapsford, R. (1999) *Survey Research*. London: Sage.

Savin-Baden, M. (2000) *Problem-based Learning in Higher Education: untold stories*. Buckingham: Open University Press.

Scheurich, J. (1997) *Research Method in the Postmodern*. London: Falmer.

Schuetze, H. and Slowey, M. (eds) (2000) *Higher Education and Lifelong Learners: international perspectives on change*. London: RoutledgeFalmer.

Schuller, T. (ed.) (1995) *The Changing University?* Buckingham: Open University Press.

Schuller, T., Raffe, D., Morgan-Klein, B. and Clark, I. (1999) *Part-time Higher Education: policy, practice and experience*. London: Jessica Kingsley.

Schwartz, P., Mennin, S. and Webb, G. (2000) *Problem-based Learning: case studies, experience, practice*. London: Kogan Page.

Scott, M. (2000) Student, Critic and Literary Text: a discussion of 'critical thinking' in a student essay, *Teaching in Higher Education*, 5(3): 277–88.

Scott, P. (1995) *The Meanings of Mass Higher Education*. Buckingham: Open University Press.

Scott, P. (ed.) (1998) *The Globalisation of Higher Education*. Buckingham: Open University Press.

Scott, P. (ed.) (2000) *Higher Education Re-formed*. London: Falmer Press.

Severiens, S. and Ten Dam, G. (1998) Gender and Learning: comparing two theories, *Higher Education*, 35: 329–50.

Severiens, S., Ten Dam, G. and van Hout Walters, B. (2001) Stability of Processing and Regulation Strategies: two longitudinal studies on student learning, *Higher Education*, 42: 437–53.

Shattock, M. (1994) *The UGC and the Management of British Universities*. Buckingham: Open University Press.

Shattock, M. (ed.) (1996) *The Creation of a University System*. Oxford: Blackwell.

Shattock, M. (2002) Re-balancing Modern Concepts of University Governance, *Higher Education Quarterly*, 56(3): 235–44.

Shear, M. (1996) *Wits: a university in the apartheid era*. Johannesburg: Witwatersrand University Press.

Shevlin, M., Banyard, P., Davies, M. and Griffiths, M. (2000) The Validity of Student Evaluation of Teaching in Higher Education: love me, love my lectures?, *Assessment and Evaluation in Higher Education*, 25(4): 397–405.

Silver, H., and Silver, P. (1997) *Students: changing roles, changing lives*. Buckingham: Open University Press.

Silverman, D. (ed.) (1997) *Qualitative Research: theory, method and practice*. London: Sage.

Skelton, A. (2000) 'Camping it up to make them laugh?' Gay men teaching in higher education, *Teaching in Higher Education*, 5(2): 181–93.

Slaughter, S. and Leslie, G. (1997) *Academic Capitalism*. Baltimore, MD: Johns Hopkins University Press.

Slowey, M. (ed.) (1995) *Implementing Change From Within Universities and Colleges: 10 personal accounts*. London: Kogan Page.

Smart, R. (1994) *On Others' Shoulders: an illustrated history of the Polhill and Lansdowne Colleges, now De Montfort University Bedford*. Bedford: De Montfort University Bedford.

Smeby, J-C. (2002) Consequences of Project Organisation in Graduate Education, *Teaching in Higher Education*, 7(2): 139–51.

Smeby, J-C. and Stensaker, B. (1999) National Quality Assessment Systems in the Nordic Countries: developing a balance between external and internal needs?, *Higher Education Policy*, 12: 3–14.

Smith, A. and Webster, F. (eds) (1997) *The Postmodern University? Contested visions of higher education in society*. Buckingham: Open University Press.

Smith, D. and Langslow, A. (eds) (1999) *The Idea of a University*. London: Jessica Kingsley.

Smith, H., Armstrong, M. and Brown, S. (1999) *Benchmarking and Threshold Standards in Higher Education*. London: Kogan Page.

Smith, J. and Naylor, R. (2001) Determinants of Degree Performance in UK Universities: a statistical analysis of the 1993 student cohort, *Oxford Bulletin of Economics and Statistics*, 63(1): 29–60.

Smyth, J. (ed.) (1995) *Academic Work: the changing labour process in higher education*. Buckingham: Open University Press.

Smyth, J. and Shacklock, G. (1998) Behind the 'Cleansing' of Socially Critical Research Accounts, in G. Shacklock and J. Smyth (eds) *Being Reflexive in Critical Educational and Social Research*. London: Falmer.

Spencer-Matthews, S. (2001) Enforced Cultural Change in Academe. A practical case study: implementing quality management systems in higher education, *Assessment and Evaluation in Higher Education*, 26(1): 51–9.

Sporn, B. (1999) *Adaptive University Structures*. London: Jessica Kingsley.

Squires, G. (1987) *The Curriculum Beyond School*. London: Hodder and Stoughton.

Squires, G. (1990) *First Degree: the undergraduate curriculum*. Buckingham: Open University Press.

Stake, R. (1995) *The Art of Case Study Research*. Thousand Oaks, CA: Sage.

Stensaker, B. and Norgard, J. D. (2001) Innovation and Isomorphism: a case-study of university identity struggle 1969–1999, *Higher Education*, 42: 473–92.

Stephenson, J. and Laycock, M. (eds) (1993) *Using Learning Contracts in Higher Education*. London: Kogan Page.

Stewart, S. and Richardson, B. (2000) Reflection and its Place in the Curriculum on an Undergraduate Course: should it be assessed?, *Assessment and Evaluation in Higher Education*, 25(4): 369–80.

Stronach, I. and MacLure, M. (1997) *Educational Research Undone: the postmodern embrace*. Buckingham: Open University Press.

Styles, I. and Radloff, A. (2001) The Synergistic Thesis: student and supervisor perspectives, *Journal of Further and Higher Education*, 25(2): 97–106.

Sullivan, K. (2002) Credit and Grade Transfer within the European Union's SOC-RATES Programme: unity in diversity or head in the sand?, *Assessment and Evaluation in Higher Education*, 27(1): 65–74.

Sunderland, J. (2002) New Communication Practices, Identity and the Psychological Gap: the affective function of email on a distance doctoral programme, *Studies in Higher Education*, 27(2): 233–46.

Tait, J. and Knight, P. (eds) (1996) *The Management of Independent Learning*. London: Kogan Page.

Tam, M. (2001) Measuring Quality and Performance in Higher Education, *Quality in Higher Education*, 7(1): 47–54.

Tashakkori, A. and Teddlie, C. (1998) *Mixed Methodology: combining qualitative and quantitative approaches*. Thousand Oaks, CA: Sage.

Taylor, I. (1997) *Developing Learning in Professional Education: partnerships for practice*. Buckingham: Open University Press.

Taylor, J. (2002) Changes in Teaching and Learning in the period to 2005: the case of postgraduate higher education in the UK, *Journal of Higher Education Policy and Management*, 24(1): 53–73.

Taylor, P. (1999) *Making Sense of Academic Life: academics, universities and change*. Buckingham: Open University Press.

Teichler, U. (1996) Comparative Higher Education: potentials and limits, *Higher Education*, 32: 431–65.

Teichler, U. (1999a) Higher Education Policy and the World of Work: changing conditions and challenges, *Higher Education Policy*, 12: 285–312.

Teichler, U. (1999b) Research on the Relationships between Higher Education and the World of work: past achievements, problems and new challenges, *Higher Education*, 38: 169–90.

Teichler, U. (2000a) New Perspectives of the Relationship between Higher Education and Employment, *Tertiary Education and Management*, 6:76–92.

Teichler, U. (2000b) Graduate Employment and Work in Selected European Countries, *European Journal of Education*, 35(2): 141–56.

Teichler, U. and Maiworm, F. (1994) *Transition to Work: the experiences of former ERASMUS students*. London: Jessica Kingsley.

Thomas, D. (ed.) (1995) *Flexible Learning Strategies in Higher and Further Education*. London: Cassell.

Thomas, H. (2001) *Managing Financial Resources*. Buckingham: Open University Press.

Thomas, R. (1998) *Conducting Educational Research: a comparative view*. Westport, CT: Bergin and Garvey.

Thomson, A. (1996) *Critical Reasoning: a practical introduction*. London: Routledge.

Thorpe, M. (2002) Rethinking Learner Support: the challenge of collaborative online learning, *Open Learning*, 17(2): 105–19.

Tight, M. (1994) Crisis, What Crisis? Rhetoric and reality in higher education, *British Journal of Educational Studies*, 42(4): 363–74.

Tight, M. (1996) University Typologies Re-examined, *Higher Education Review*, 29(1): 57–77.

Tight, M. (1999) Writing in British Higher Education Journals 1993–98: concerns and omissions, *Higher Education Review*, 31(3): 3–20.

Tight, M. (2000a) Reporting on Academic Work and Life: a year of *The Times Higher Education Supplement*, in M. Tight (ed.), *Academic Work and Life: what it is to be an academic, and how this is changing*. Oxford: Elsevier Science.

Tight, M. (ed.) (2000b) *Academic Work and Life: what it is to be an academic, and how this is changing*. Oxford: Elsevier Science.

Tight, M. (2000c) Do League Tables Contribute to the Development of a Quality Culture? Football and higher education compared, *Higher Education Quarterly*, 54(1): 22–42.

Tight, M. (2002) *Key Concepts in Adult Education and Training*, 2nd edn. London: RoutledgeFalmer.

Tight, M. (ed.) (2003a) *The RoutledgeFalmer Reader in Higher Education*. London: RoutledgeFalmer.

Tight, M. (2003b) The Organisation of Academic Knowledge: a comparative perspective. *Higher Education* (forthcoming).

Tinkler, P. and Jackson, C. (2000) Examining the Doctorate: institutional policy and the PhD examination process in Britain, *Studies in Higher Education*, 25(2): 167–80.

Tolmie, P. (ed.) (1998) *How I Got my First Class Degree*, 2nd edn. Lancaster: Lancaster University Unit for Innovation in Higher Education.

Tomlin, R. (1998) Research League Tables: is there a better way?, *Higher Education Quarterly*, 52(2): 204–20.

Toohey, S. (1999) *Designing Courses for Higher Education*. Buckingham: Open University Press.

Torrance, M., Thomas, G. and Robinson, E. (2000) Individual Differences in Undergraduate Essay-writing Strategies: a longitudinal study, *Higher Education*, 39: 181–200.

Tovey, P. (1994) *Quality Assurance in Continuing Professional Education: an analysis*. London: Routledge.

Tricker, T., Rangecroft, M., Long, P. and Gilroy, P. (2001) Evaluating Distance Education Courses: the student perception, *Assessment and Evaluation in Higher Education*, 26(2): 165–77.

Trow, M. and Nybom, T. (eds) (1991) *University and Society: essays on the social role of research and higher education*. London: Jessica Kingsley.

Trowler, P. (1998) *Academics Responding to Change: new higher education frameworks and academic cultures*. Buckingham: Open University Press.

Trowler, P. (2001) Captured by the Discourse? The socially constitutive power of the new higher education discourse in the UK, *Organization*, 8(2): 183–201.

Trowler, P. and Knight, P. (2000) Coming to Know in Higher Education: theorising faculty entry to new work contexts, *Higher Education Research and Development*, 19(1): 27–42.

Tuire, P. and Erno, L. (2001) Exploring Invisible Scientific Communities: studying networking relations within an educational research community – a Finnish case, *Higher Education*, 42: 493–513.

Tynjala, P. (1997) Developing Education Students' Conceptions of the Learning Process in Different Learning Environments, *Learning and Instruction*, 7(3): 277–92.

Usher, R. and Edwards, R. (1994) *Postmodernism and Education*. London: Routledge.

Valimaa, J. (1998) Culture and Identity in Higher Education Research, *Higher Education*, 36: 119–38.

de Vaus, D. (1995) *Surveys in Social Research*, 4th edn. Sydney, Allen and Unwin.

de Vaus, D. (2001) *Research Design in Social Research*. London: Sage.

Vermunt, J. (1996) Metacognitive, Cognitive and Affective Aspects of Learning Styles and Strategies: a phenomenographic analysis, *Higher Education*, 31: 25–50.

Vroeijenstijn, T. (1994) *Improvement and Accountability: navigating between Scylla and Charybdis*. London: Jessica Kingsley.

Wade, W., Hodgkinson, K., Smith, A. and Arfield, J. (eds) (1994) *Flexible Learning in Higher Education*. London: Kogan Page.

Walford, G. (ed.) (1994) *Researching the Powerful in Education.* London: UCL Press.

Walker, M. (ed.) (2001) *Reconstructing Professionalism in University Teaching: teachers and learners in action.* Buckingham: Open University Press.

Warner, D, and Crosthwaite, E. (eds) (1995) *Human Resource Management in Higher and Further Education.* Buckingham: Open University Press.

Warner, D. and Kelly, G. (eds) (1994) *Managing Educational Property: a handbook for schools, colleges and universities.* Buckingham: Open University Press.

Warner, D. and Leonard, C. (1997) *The Income Generation Handbook.* Buckingham: Open University Press.

Warner, D. and Palfreyman, D. (eds) (1996) *Higher Education Management: the key elements.* Buckingham: Open University Press.

Warner, D. and Palfreyman, D. (eds) (2001) *The State of UK Higher Education: managing change and diversity.* Buckingham: Open University Press.

Watson, D. (2000) *Managing Strategy.* Buckingham: Open University Press.

Watson, D., Brooks, J., Coghill, C., Lindsay, R. and Scurry, D. (1989) *Managing the Modular Course: perspectives from Oxford Polytechnic.* Milton Keynes: Open University Press.

Watson, D. and Taylor, R. (1998) *Lifelong Learning and the University: a post-Dearing agenda.* London: Falmer Press.

Watson, K. (ed.) (2001) *Doing Comparative Education Research: issues and problems.* Oxford: Symposium.

Webb, E., Campbell, D., Schwartz, R. and Sechrest, L. (2000) *Unobtrusive Measures,* revised edn. Thousand Oaks, CA: Sage.

Webb, G. (1994) *Making the Most of Appraisal: career and professional development planning for lecturers.* London: Kogan Page.

Webb, G. (1996) *Understanding Staff Development.* Buckingham: Open University Press.

Weil, S. (ed.) (1994) *Introducing Change From the Top in Universities and Colleges: 10 personal accounts.* London: Kogan Page.

Wengraf, T. (2001) *Qualitative Research Interviewing.* London: Sage.

Whiston, T. and Geiger, R. (eds) (1992) *Research and Higher Education: the United Kingdom and the United States.* Buckingham: Open University Press.

White, T. (2001) *Investing in People: higher education in Ireland from 1960 to 2000.* Dublin, Institute of Public Administration.

Williams, C. (2002) Learning On-line: a review of recent literature in a rapidly expanding field, *Journal of Further and Higher Education,* 26(3): 263–72.

Williams, J. (ed.) (1997) *Negotiating Access to Higher Education: the discourse of selectivity and equity.* Buckingham: Open University Press.

Williams, R. (1997) The UK's External Examiner System: its rise or demise?, in J. Radford, K. Raaheim, P. de Vries and R. Williams, *Quantity and Quality in Higher Education.* London: Jessica Kingsley.

Willmott, H. (1995) Managing the Academics: commodification and control in the development of university education in the UK, *Human Relations,* 48(9): 993–1027.

Winter, R. and Maisch, M. (1996) *Professional Competence and Higher Education: the ASSET programme.* London: Falmer Press.

Wolfendale, S. and Corbett, J. (eds) (1996) *Opening Doors: learning support in higher education.* London: Cassell.

Wood, F. and Meek, L. (2002) Over-reviewed and Underfunded? The evolving policy context of Australian higher education research and development, *Journal of Higher Education Policy and Management*, 24(1): 7–25.

Wright, C. and O'Neill, M. (2002) Service Quality Evaluation in the Higher Education Sector: an empirical investigation of students' perceptions, *Higher Education Research and Development*, 21(1): 23–39.

Wright, D. (1997) *Understanding Statistics: an introduction for the social sciences*. London: Sage.

Wyatt, J. (1990) *Commitment to Higher Education: seven West European thinkers on the essence of the university*. Buckingham: Open University Press.

Yee, A. (ed.) (1995) *East Asian Higher Education: traditions and transformations*. Oxford: Pergamon.

Yin, R. (2003a) *Case Study Research: design and methods*, 2nd edn. Newbury Park, CA: Sage.

Yin, R. (2003b) *Applications of Case Study Research*, 2nd edn. Newbury Park, CA: Sage.

Yorke, M. (1997) A Good League Guide?, *Quality Assurance in Education*, 5(2): 61–72.

Yorke, M. (1999) *Leaving Early: undergraduate non-completion in higher education*. London: Falmer Press.

Yorke, M. (2000) The Quality of the Student Experience: what can institutions learn from data relating to non-completion?, *Quality in Higher Education*, 6(1): 61–75.

Yorke, M. (2002) Degree Classifications in English, Welsh and Northern Irish Universities: trends, 1994–95 to 1998–99, *Higher Education Quarterly*, 56(1): 92–108.

Yorke, M. (2003) The Prejudicial Papers? Press Treatment of UK higher education performance indicators, 1999–2001, in M. Tight (ed.) *Access and Exclusion*. Oxford: Elsevier Science.

Yorke, M., Barnett, G., Bridges, P. et al. (2002) Does Grading Method Influence Honours Degree Classification?, *Assessment and Evaluation in Higher Education*, 27(3): 269–79.

Zepke, N. and Leach, L. (2002) Appropriate Pedagogy and Technology in a Cross-cultural Distance Education Context, *Teaching in Higher Education*, 7(3): 309–21.

Zuber-Skerritt, O. and Ryan, Y. (eds) (1994) *Quality in Postgraduate Education*. London: Kogan Page.

Index

The Society for Research into Higher Education

The Society for Research into Higher Education (SRHE), an international body, exists to stimulate and coordinate research into all aspects of higher education. It aims to improve the quality of higher education through the encouragement of debate and publication on issues of policy, on the organization and management of higher education institutions, and on the curriculum, teaching and learning methods.

The Society is entirely independent and receives no subsidies, although individual events often receive sponsorship from business or industry. The Society is financed through corporate and individual subscriptions and has members from many parts of the world. It is an NGO of UNESCO.

Under the imprint *SRHE & Open University Press*, the Society is a specialist publisher of research, having over 80 titles in print. In addition to *SRHE News*, the Society's newsletter, the Society publishes three journals: *Studies in Higher Education* (three issues a year), *Higher Education Quarterly* and *Research into Higher Education Abstracts* (three issues a year).

The Society runs frequent conferences, consultations, seminars and other events. The annual conference in December is organized at and with a higher education institution. There are a growing number of networks which focus on particular areas of interest, including:

Access	Learning Environment
Assessment	Legal Education
Consultants	Managing Innovation
Curriculum Development	New Technology for Learning
Eastern European	Postgraduate Issues
Educational Development Research	Quantitative Studies
FE/HE	Student Development
Funding	Vocational Qualifications
Graduate Employment	

Benefits to members

Individual

- The opportunity to participate in the Society's networks
- Reduced rates for the annual conferences
- Free copies of *Research into Higher Education Abstracts*

- Reduced rates for *Studies in Higher Education*
- Reduced rates for *Higher Education Quarterly*
- Free copy of *Register of Members' Research Interests* – includes valuable reference material on research being pursued by the Society's members
- Free copy of occasional in-house publications, e.g. *The Thirtieth Anniversary Seminars Presented by the Vice-Presidents*
- Free copies of *SRHE News* which informs members of the Society's activities and provides a calendar of events, with additional material provided in regular mailings
- A 35 per cent discount on all SRHE/Open University Press books
- The opportunity for you to apply for the annual research grants
  - Inclusion of your research in the *Register of Members' Research Interests*

Corporate

- Reduced rates for the annual conference
- The opportunity for members of the Institution to attend SRHE's network events at reduced rates
  - Free copies of *Research into Higher Education Abstracts*
- Free copies of *Studies in Higher Education*
- Free copies of *Register of Members' Research Interests* – includes valuable reference material on research being pursued by the Society's members
- Free copy of occasional in-house publications
- Free copies of *SRHE News*
- A 35 per cent discount on all SRHE/Open University Press books
- The opportunity for members of the Institution to submit applications for the Society's research grants
- The opportunity to work with the Society and co-host conferences
- The opportunity to include in the *Register of Members' Research Interests* your Institution's research into aspects of higher education

Membership details: SRHE, 76 Portland Place, London
W1B 1NT, UK Tel: 020 7637 2766. Fax: 020 7637 2781.
email: srhe@mailbox.ulcc.ac.uk
world wide web: http://www.srhe.ac.uk./srhe/
Catalogue: SRHE & Open University Press, McGraw-Hill
Education, McGraw-Hill House, Shoppenhangers Road,
Maidenhead,
Berkshire SL6 2QL. Tel: 01628 502500. Fax: 01628 770224.
email: enquiries@openup.co.uk – web: www.openup.co.uk

CHALLENGING KNOWLEDGE

Gerard Delanty

For far too long, we have waited for a book that recorded the ideas of the modern university. Now, in Gerard Delanty's new book, we have it. Delanty has faithfully set out the views of the key thinkers and, in the process, has emerged with an idea of the university that is his. We are in his debt.

Professor Ronald Barnett, University of London

Gerard Delanty is one of the most productive and thought-provoking social theorists currently writing in the UK. He brings to his work a sophisticated and impressively cosmopolitan vision. Here he turns his attention to higher education, bringing incisive analysis and a surprising optimism as regards the future of the university. This is a book which will stimulate all thinking people – especially those trying to come to terms with mass higher education and its tribulations.

Professor Frank Webster, University of Birmingham

For too long social theory, the sociology of knowledge and studies in higher education have mutually ignored each other. Gerard Delanty, founding editor of the *European Journal of Social Theory*, was just the right person to bring them into dialogue. Indeed 'dialogue' and 'communication' are his watchwords for revamping the institutional mission of the university.

Professor Steve Fuller, University of Warwick

Drawing from current debates in social theory about the changing nature of knowledge, this book offers the most comprehensive sociological theory of the university that has yet appeared. Delanty views the university as a key institution of modernity and as the site where knowledge, culture and society interconnect. He assesses the question of the crisis of the university with respect to issues such as globalization, the information age, the nation state, academic capitalism, cultural politics and changing relationships between research and teaching. Arguing against the notion of the demise of the university, his argument is that in the knowledge society of today a new identity for the university is emerging based on communication and new conceptions of citizenship. It will be essential reading for those interested in changing relationships between modernity, knowledge, higher education and the future of the university.

Contents

192pp   0 335 20578 X (Paperback)   0 335 20579 8 (Hardback)

BEYOND ALL REASON
LIVING WITH IDEOLOGY IN THE UNIVERSITY

Ronald Barnett

A major work . . . provocative, unsettling and profoundly challenging. I think it should be prescribed reading for all vice-chancellors.
Colin Bundy, Director of the School of Oriental and African Studies,
University of London

Ron Barnett's latest book lives up to, and possibly exceeds, the high standards he has set himself in his previous books – which are now established as the premier series of reflective books on higher education.
Peter Scott, Vice-Chancellor, Kingston University

Beyond All Reason argues that ideologies are now multiplying on campus and that, consequently, the university as a place of open debate and reason is in jeopardy. The book examines, as case studies, the ideologies of competition, quality, entrepreneurialism and managerialism. All of these movements have a positive potential but, in being pressed forward unduly, have become pernicious ideologies that are threatening to undermine the university.

Ronald Barnett argues that it is possible to realize the university by addressing the ideals present in the idea of the university, and so developing positive projects for the university. These 'utopian ideologies' may never be fully realized but, pursued seriously, they can counter the pernicious ideologies that beset the university. In this way, it is possible for the idea of the university to live on and be practised in the twenty-first century.

Beyond All Reason offers a bold optimistic statement about the future of universities and offers ideas for enabling universities to be 'universities' in the contemporary age. It will be of interest and value not just to students of higher education but also to vice-chancellors, administrators, academics generally and those who care about the future of universities.

Contents

192pp   0 335 20893 2 (Paperback)   0 335 20894 0 (Hardback)

FOR A RADICAL HIGHER EDUCATION
AFTER POSTMODERNISM

Richard Taylor, Jean Barr and Tom Steele

This is a timely and a challenging work. The contemporary debate about the purposes of higher education needs to be refocused: on the transmission of values as well as the utility of skills; on its emancipatory as well as its instrumental roles in modern society. This book should be read by students and their teachers, as well as by policy-makers and their pay-masters.

David Watson, Director, University of Brighton

This is a forceful restatement of the classic 'Left' analysis of both the short-comings, and radical potential, of higher education. In an age of soft-focus sound-bite New Labour politics such a restatement is badly needed. The authors take no prisoners in their critique of postmodernism as an empty and conformist discourse that inhibits radical action. Not everyone will agree with this book, but everyone should read it.

Peter Scott, Vice-Chancellor, Kingston University

Higher education is being transformed, not least because of its rapid expansion. What should be the priorities, objectives and purposes of this new higher education? Much current policy development for universities and colleges is implicitly based on postmodernist ideas. *For a Radical Higher Education* explores these postmodernist approaches through social and political theory, philosophy, cultural studies and feminism, and proposes radical alternatives. It argues that, although postmodernism has provided useful insights and corrections to other frames of reference, it leads often to a reactionary and conformist position. Its emphases on relativism, consensus and apolitical cynicism in relation to all progressive perspectives, effectively gives support to those who see higher education increasingly incorporated into technicism and free market cultures. In contrast, this book argues for a revitalized and radical university, characterized by critical, sceptical enquiry, tolerance, and a commitment to humanistic, egalitarian politics.

Contents

192pp   0 335 20868 1 (Paperback)   0 335 20869 X (Hardback)